HOLLYWOOD FAITH

HOLLYWOOD FAITH

Holiness, Prosperity, and Ambition in a Los Angeles Church

GERARDO MARTI

RUTGERS UNIVERSITY PRESS
New Brunswick, New Jersey, and London

Library of Congress Cataloging-in-Publication Data

Marti, Gerardo, 1965–
　Hollywood faith : holiness, prosperity, and ambition in a Los Angeles church / Gerardo Marti.
　　　　p. cm.
　Includes bibliographical references and index.
　ISBN 978-0-8135-4348-2 (hardcover : alk. paper)—ISBN 978-0-8135-4349-9 (pbk. : alk. paper)
　 1. Christianity and culture—California—Los Angeles.　 2. Hollywood (Los Angeles, Calif.)—Religion.　 3. Church work.　 4. Ethnicity—Religious aspects—Christianity. I. Title.
　BR115.C8M2399 2008
　277.94′94083—dc22　　　　　　　　　　　　　　　　　　　　　　2007044908

A British Cataloging-in-Publication record for this book is available from the British Library.

Visit our Web site: http://rutgerspress.rutgers.edu

Manufactured in the United States of America

With love to my wife, Laura, and our children,
Miranda, Zachary, Nathan, and Genevieve

The believer who has communed with his god is not simply a man who sees new truths that the unbeliever knows not; he is a man who is stronger. Within himself, he feels more strength to endure the trials of existence or to overcome them.

—Emile Durkheim,
Elementary Forms of Religious Life

Through these doors walk champions of life.

—Sign over sanctuary doors
at Oasis Christian Center

Contents

Preface and Acknowledgments

Situated on a busy street in metropolitan Los Angeles, and with most of its congregation participants in the film business, the Oasis Christian Center strategically interacts with the Hollywood entertainment industry and negotiates social change by providing a religious identity as overcomer and champion that anchors its members' difficult career choices and failed opportunities. By focusing on outreach to the entertainment community, Oasis creates spaces of community for ambitious people who find their personal goals frustrated, systems overwhelming, and relationships fractured. Here, they can achieve great confidence in a God who wants to use their talents to fulfill cosmic purposes. In the end, Oasis emerges as a way to resolve tensions of modern, urban life when ambition outpaces the ability to accomplish. To deal with their desire to succeed, individuals subsume themselves to a moral system that sanctions ambition and provides handles on how to work through failure, cope with challenges from overwhelming social structures, and manage exploitation and injustice. This new religious option fits a life context increasingly common among workers in the United States and allows for the continued strength of religion in the modern world.

Hollywood Faith falls squarely into the emerging scholarly tradition labeled by R. Stephen Warner (1993, 2004, 2005) the new paradigm approach to American religion, which encompasses the work of such notable scholars of religion as Donald Miller, Nancy Ammerman, Rodney Stark, Roger Finke, Daniel Olson, Lynn Davidman, Andrew Greeley, James Davidson Hunter, Wade Clark Roof, Meredith McGuire, and Mary Jo Neitz. The term "new paradigm" embraces the unexpected, entrepreneurial forms churches can take and is now the dominant approach taken by scholars of American religion. Congregations, it turns out, are excellent vehicles for capturing and expressing social change. This perspective recognizes that congregations are free to adapt their operation to local cultures, and a growing number of scholars are taking notice.[1]

The intense interaction among the people of Oasis Christian Center contributed immeasurably to my own growing understanding of religion in our contemporary world. With warmth and hospitality, Pastors Philip and Holly Wagner, staff, and members generously shared their life experiences and insights into the church. I thank them for welcoming this stranger into their family.

At Davidson College, special thanks to my Sociology of Hollywood seminar students for our interactions in 2005. I especially thank Justin Hartanov, Ellen Oplinger, and Kristen Shields for their permission to work with some of the arguments from their final papers. Also, thanks to Jane Reid for transcription assistance and Joel Blanford for formatting assistance.

Kristi Long, past editor of social sciences and religion at Rutgers University Press, first expressed interest in this project in 2003, and Adi Hovav, the current editor, graciously carried it through to completion. I appreciate Brad Christerson (Biola University), Elaine Howard Ecklund (SUNY Buffalo), and, most especially, Lynn Schofield Clark (University of Denver) for helpful comments on an early draft. Fred Kniss (Loyola University Chicago) provided excellent feedback on the full manuscript. Also, Professors Don Miller and Jon Miller received me as a visiting research associate in the Center for Religion and Civic Culture at the University of Southern California during the summers of 2005 and 2006 to think and write. Michael Emerson (Rice University), H. Edward Ransford (University of Southern California), and Jon Johnston (Pepperdine University) continue to provide unfailing support.

Finally, this book is dedicated to my wife, Laura, for her support of my scholarly pursuits. I also dedicate this book to our beautiful children, Genevieve, Nathan, Zachary, and Miranda.

HOLLYWOOD FAITH

1   Introduction

> DONNA: We were standing outside looking at the
> star of Jesus Christ that we have out front. And you
> know me, being the actress, pointed and said, "I'm
> going to have one of these one day."

Grauman's Chinese Theater is the symbolic center of Hollywood, but less than two miles south on Wilshire Boulevard sits Destiny Theater, the art deco–style home of the Oasis Christian Center. The theater is several blocks from the famous Walk of Fame, sidewalks dotted with more than two thousand star-shaped plaques bearing the bronze-engraved names of celluloid celebrities, radio personalities, and entertainment idols. But on this boulevard in front of Destiny Theater sits a single, specially crafted bronze star. On the field where an official Walk of Fame star contains a symbol such as a microphone or a movie camera to indicate the honoree's area of expertise, this one depicts a cross-shaped sword laid diagonally over an open Bible. The honoree is "Jesus Christ—The Son of God." This emblem represents a bold attempt to establish a spiritual center for the Hollywood entertainment industry, one that affirms ambitions for wealth and fame for all believers.

On a Saturday night, I walk past Jesus' Hollywood star to find the celebration service in full swing. A pulsing wave of music hits me as I enter the lobby. The sloped floor leads into the auditorium, and a small sign over the entrance reads, "Through these doors walk champions of life." The auditorium is packed, and everyone is on their feet, black and white, singing and swaying, many with hands raised, most with big smiles. An usher points to an open seat several rows down. I am immediately surrounded by worshipers. Sitting is out of the question, but, after a moment, standing feels all right. The music is an engaging blend of funk, gospel, and R&B and seductively invites even a church novice to stand, clap, move, and groove as the songs continue.

> 'Cause I love you, Lord, and your amazing grace,
> You comfort me, through everything.
> I fall on my knees, with a childlike faith,

I will lift my voice to you and sing,
I'm a child of the king.

Everyone is deeply engaged, following lyrics printed on big, wide, colorful screens, and it's safe to sway to the music because all eyes are focused on the activity up front. The six-piece band includes drums, bass, electric guitar, synthesizer, congas, and a saxophone with musicians impressively in sync in a blast of composed sound. The group of five black and white worship leaders and an even more diverse choir of eight enthusiastically guide the crowd through song transitions. The music is new to me, and I found out later that members of the congregation write more than 80 percent of the songs.

The music picks up the pace amid whoops and cheers.

Lord of Lords, King of Kings, holy, mighty,
Perfect in every way, giver of amazing grace.

Musical changes are smooth, and another transition shifts the rhythm into a deep, syncopated drumming.

Overcomers, wanna hear you,
Who of them that love the Lord, me wanna see you,
If you're not one of them, my God will fill you,
With his joy and his love, Jesus will free you. Oooaahh-ugh!

Many are now jumping up and down. Hands are raised in the air. I notice a few Hispanics and Asians now, both on and off the platform.

From conversations and pastoral messages in previous services, I know many people here are in the entertainment industry. The metaphor of worshiping in a converted movie house near the center of Hollywood is hard to ignore. The auditorium has been modernized, yet the platform and seating maintain the theatre ambience. The worship space seems to represent the sacralizing desire embraced by believers here to see their pursuit of success in Hollywood as a holy endeavor that energetically glorifies God.

The musical devotion continues without weakening until the last song comes to a passionate finish.

When I need you all that I do is call you, Lord, and you come through for me,
Every time, you never let me down,
You promised me if I believe, all that I need I will receive it all,
Every time, you never let me down.

The music ends, and people are laughing and hugging each other. Two young women in front of me turn to each other brimming with excitement and camaraderie as they give each other high fives before taking their seats. Worship is a time of bonding with God and each other, but here worship also is an accomplishment, a victory, and a spiritual triumph. What happens in this building is part corporate adoration and part shared participation in an invigorating spiritual rally. By the time I sit down I should be tired, but instead I feel slightly euphoric, and I'm smiling too.

The Champions of Oasis

In my narrative, I rely on information gathered through twelve months of ethnographic fieldwork and fifty in-depth interviews, staying close to the lived experiences of participants in this multiracial church, who, like the believers sharing this worship rally with me, are the champions of the Oasis Christian Center (see the appendix). I explore Oasis's twenty-year history via the memories of long-term participants as they correlated with each other and with the few print resources available. And although the actions and beliefs of congregational leaders are vital to understanding this congregation, the focus of attention is rank-and-file members and attenders. I wanted to see how the racially diverse people of Oasis interact and how they shape and are shaped by their lives in and around Hollywood in relation to their involvement in this congregation. I looked at other salient aspects of the church, including its theology and its geographic location, in order to understand how this congregation emerged and how it continually reproduces itself. In the process, I explored sociohistorical dynamics affecting the development of Oasis, including the rapid urbanization of Los Angeles, the expansion of the Hollywood film industry, the spread of Pentecostalism, and the increased mainstream merging of commercial culture and religious culture in the twentieth century. This large, multiracial church that would not have been possible a century ago is a fascinating combination of theology, economics, race relations, and urban community.

Pastored by a husband-and-wife team, Philip and Holly Wagner, Oasis is a nondenominational charismatic church distinguished by a particular blend of Holiness/Word of Faith theology that mixes a charismatic emphasis on the Holy Spirit with a practical emphasis on relational and financial well-being (see chapter 6). The church began in 1983 as a small group of entertainment industry believers who met for Bible study in Beverly Hills at an Academy Award winner's home, and the church's implicit focus on reaching out to those in the Hollywood entertainment industry remains. While Christian churches still dominantly express protest and hostility against the evils of Hollywood, the Oasis Christian Center is a large, racially diverse church that creatively accommodates itself to the entertainment industry and successfully attracts many who strive to succeed in this frequently harsh and often irreverent business.

In view of the historic friction between Christianity and Hollywood, the core question guiding the writing of this book is, How do Hollywood-focused attenders resolve the tensions between holiness and the pursuit of fame and profit? I was initially puzzled about how a spirit-filled church could aggressively promote ambition and send the faithful into the world to succeed in a materialistic, exploitative, and profit-driven industry. I mistakenly expected Oasis leaders to domesticate ambition as a way to protect their people from a dangerous world. Since Oasis intentionally strives for relevance to those in the entertainment industry where success is measured in fame and profit, this book explores how the congregation negotiates the pursuit of these goals and its successful approach to dealing with uncertainty and failure amidst ongoing disappointment and heartache.

I found that Oasis boldly sends godly people into a godless, temptation-filled world because the church has confidence that the inspiration to succeed is disciplined by morally binding, community-honoring action. To articulate my understanding of how Oasis accomplishes this, I initially drew on a theoretical framework particularly influenced by Emile Durkheim (especially from his work *The Elementary Forms of Religious Life*) and current scholarship using Durkheim's most recently discovered writings. Since religious identities are reflections of moral communities, this book contributes to our understanding of how congregations shape, negotiate, and reshape moral imperatives that provide day-to-day meaning and also guide everyday behavior through duty-bound religious identities.

In the end, the thoughts and feelings of Oasis members reveal them to be ambitious, upwardly mobile people working in difficult, risky careers at the turn of the twenty-first century. These believers are neither strange nor unusual; rather, the message and ministry of the congregation is shaped in response to the extraordinary life conditions of people attempting to manage their economic selves in the midst of inherently unmanageable careers and overarching socio-historic changes. While I cannot say who would be predisposed to become a member of the Oasis Christian Center, what I can say is that the congregation is made up of people who have a particular orientation toward themselves and their world and that there is a profound affinity between the religious resources made available to them at Oasis and the economic circumstances that structure their lives as a whole. Oasis not only acknowledges but innovatively manages and negotiates the conditions of their life, especially the economic conditions of a changing urban labor market—conditions facing millions who belong to the emerging creative class in capitalist-driven, metropolitan regions throughout America (Florida 2002).

Broadly speaking, Oasis is a congregation focused on resolving the ongoing tensions of modern, urban life that result when ambition outpaces the ability to accomplish. In appealing to these ambitions while theologically accommodating the frustrations, Oasis creates an attractive, welcoming place for people of diverse racial groups who face these experiences, regardless of their specific career path. In dealing with the desire to succeed, individuals subsume themselves to a religious system that sanctions ambition and provides handles on how to work through failure, cope with challenges from overwhelming social structures, and manage exploitation and injustice.

In short, by helping entertainment industry workers negotiate their desires for fame through religious devotion, Oasis pioneers a new religious identity for an emerging generation of workers within the creative class who actively brand themselves, seek celebrity for their creative skills, and manage the uncertainties of career trajectories apart from established job roles. Examining Oasis and the corporate identity forged among its members within its broad historical context allows for a sustained reflection on the impact of social change on congregational life in the United States and its implications for the future of American religion.

Observing the Oasis Christian Center

I came to Oasis shortly after conducting an extensive case study of Mosaic, another large, diverse Los Angeles church (Marti 2005). As scholars learned more about this innovative church, some suggested that the circumstances that led to the development of Mosaic were so unique that they were essentially unrepeatable. But over the course of my interviews, I discovered Oasis, which resembled Mosaic in several important ways. By conducting a study at Oasis, I intended to embark on a comparative study to assess the uniqueness of Mosaic, particularly how similarities and differences between these churches account for their racial composition.

Once I began visiting Oasis, I found several characteristics that make this church especially interesting. First, its more than two thousand attenders make it one of the largest multiracial congregations in the country. According to church records, Oasis grew from around five hundred to over two thousand weekly attenders between 2000 and 2003, remarkable growth for any church but especially rare for a multiracial church. Only 5 percent of Protestant churches have at least 20 percent of attenders of a different race or ethnicity than the majority. Moreover, evangelicals are overwhelmingly white, so the cultivation of a diverse evangelical church is particularly notable.[1] Oasis is a dominantly black/white congregation (African Americans comprise 45 percent of the membership) with a growing number of Asians and Hispanics. Despite challenges and obstacles that reinforce segregation among churches, Oasis actualizes the dream of a growing number of church leaders who desire to see vibrant, self-funding, racially integrated communities. And as Oasis continues to grow, it continues to diversify.

Without intentionally trying to recreate the past, Oasis resurrects the early interracial heritage of Pentecostalism characterized by a sacred enthusiasm expressed through passionate, stand-on-your-feet worship. Mixed into this holy excitement, Oasis is hip, young, and media rich, making it a place that feels familiar to anyone who frequents newly constructed malls, lavish movie theatres, and trendy restaurants. At peak times before and after worship services, the atmosphere of Oasis is rich with service-with-a-smile servers, hustle-and-bustle crowds, electronic images, and distraction-friendly places to hang out. Oasis is not a traditional church; rather, its style is consistent with that of worship communities recently labeled new paradigm churches (Miller 1997). Among other things, these churches are characterized by contemporary cultural forms in music, visual arts, graphic arts, and dance.

In terms of overall style, Oasis combines a savvy connection to commercialized entertainment culture with a set of theological streams developed in the past century. The most important influence is the charismatic surge that began in U.S. churches in the 1960s and spread rapidly across the globe. A byproduct of the Pentecostal movement from the turn of the twentieth century, this neo-Pentecostalism "puts less emphasis on the baptism of the Holy Spirit and speaking in tongues, and more in the power of the Holy Spirit for healing, prophetic utterances, vibrant worship in music, and prosperity for believers" (Lee 2005, 34). According to Donald Miller and Tetsunao Yamamori: "As Pentecostals have become upwardly mobile, better educated, and more affluent, they have begun viewing the world differently. Pentecostals no longer see the world as a place from which to escape—the sectarian view—but instead as a place they want to make better" (2007, 30).

Not only are neo-Pentecostals overall better off economically than their religious ancestors, they avoid denominational affiliations, incorporate rather than exclude professional classes, show greater accommodation to material prosperity, and practice energetic and technologically sophisticated worship. Miller and Yamamori add that these "life-changing, life-affirming, and future-oriented" Pentecostal believers "are not sitting on their hands waiting for the return of Jesus, nor are they barricading themselves from the world in sectarian enclaves. Quite the opposite, they are dancing to Jesus tunes and figuring out how they can align their lives with a reality that transcends the oppressive quality of much of urban life" (2007, 217–218). Shayne Lee finds it "ironic that Pentecostalism, the branch of Christendom that once harbored ardent secular sentiment, transformed into a Pentecostal movement with the strongest embrace of technology, secularism, capitalism, and popular culture" (2005, 176). This book provides some hints as to what lies behind this irony.

While embracing affinities with the broader consumer culture, Oasis is not consumerist in its approach. As a new paradigm church, it is not a seeker church as described by Kimon Sargeant (2000), that is, Oasis does not attract spiritually seeking baby boomers who join well-programmed, age-diversified churches catering to a variety of lifestyle interests. Instead, Oasis's greatest growth is occurring among Millennials, the post–Gen X young adults in their twenties and early thirties looking for spiritual authenticity mixed with a measure of cool. The average age of the congregation, according to church records, is twenty-nine years.

And while seeker churches are suburban, Oasis feels familiar to urban crowds. Different social classes regularly interact with one another, and many attenders regularly experience sharp rises and falls in their annual income. Oasis is also entrepreneurial and innovative, eschewing any denominational identity while keeping a broadly conservative doctrine. "Seeker churches are generally less charismatic and more middle class" than new paradigm churches, Sargeant points out, yet they "share the same entrepreneurial innovation, contemporary cultural style, empowerment of the laity, and antiestablishment or antidenomination sentiment" (172). Through strategic incorporation of elements from the surrounding cosmopolitan culture, Oasis captures and reinvigorates the urban experience in a spiritually charged ambience that encourages the earnest zeal of true believers who remain intimately connected to the modern, commercialized world.

One striking observation became a cornerstone of the analysis for this book. Over 80 percent of attenders at Oasis are connected in some way to "Hollywood" (a term explored in detail in chapter 2).[2] Regardless of race, age, or church tenure, the great majority has working experience in the entertainment industry. Some are successful. Many are aspiring. And many, having left the business, still carry heartache resulting from disappointing experiences. All of these former and current entertainment people speak of the challenges of making it in the industry (see chapter 5).

A significant theme emerged from a detailed look at the types of people attending Oasis and the lifeworld of the social groups they represent.[3] Whether part of the Hollywood entertainment industry or not, the people of Oasis embody the economic difficulties and ideals of today's aspiring, urban middle class. The theology and structure of the church especially connects with the stories, achievements, and dilemmas of the emerging creative class (Florida 2002).[4]

Comprising as much as 30 percent of the workforce, the creative class is the largest group of professional workers in this nation. It is the result of shifts in the labor market and the changing economic structure of corporations and is defined not by income but by occupations based on artistic, technological, and critical thinking skills. In the development of their careers, members of this class often anticipate long periods of low income despite extensive training and sophisticated skill sets. In this relatively new and growing stratum of the U.S. workforce, many are still figuring out how to live meaningful lives as creative professionals. For believers in the Oasis congregation, the pressing concern is how to live a godly life amidst the uncertainty of their professional demands.

This book, then, began with my attempt to understand congregational diversity because multiracial churches are rare, and studies of them are few. But in exploring the unexpected ways congregational members live out their religious devotion amidst the tensions and ambiguities of modern society, my thinking continued to expand on other significant themes. My analysis here shows that congregational diversity is a consequence of more fundamental dynamics within this interesting congregation. Recognition of those dynamics started early in my time at Oasis.

In the first few weeks at Oasis, I looked over membership records and a 2003 congregational survey. I found that the older the congregant, the more likely the individual was to be African American. Conversely, the younger the congregant, the more likely the individual was to be white. This information, combined with nascent observations, led me to initially focus on affinities between out-of-work actors and African Americans. If participation in the entertainment industry is a common experience at the Oasis (especially among whites), I hypothesized, perhaps affinities between African Americans and Caucasians reflect common experiences in the face of overwhelming and seemingly oppressive social structures. In other words, perhaps there was a parallel between the social experiences of older African Americans in a white-dominant society and younger, out-of-work Caucasians trying to make it in the entertainment industry. The struggle to make it in a system that honors insiders and relationships with the right people seems similar enough for both groups that each would be willing to lend support to the other and share the family-emphasis environment cultivated at Oasis. Also, the consistent emphasis at Oasis on being a champion seemed to address similar deeply felt socioemotional needs for coping, belonging, and achievement.

But I soon saw that the champions of Oasis include more than out-of-work actors and African Americans. Oasis draws people through affinities among more subtle aspects of their identity. While the church appeals to people who are black, white, Hispanic, and Asian, it draws them on the basis of something they already share in their life experiences. What I discovered was that the reasons for the attraction and retention of members and attendees in this racially diverse congregation fell into a distinctive pattern of corporate empowerment.

Oasis negotiates social change on behalf of its members by providing them with a religious identity as overcomer and champion that anchors difficult career choices and failed opportunities. For example, champions have ambition; they are not beaten down but burn with desire to get ahead. Oasis urbanites come to the church borne on the momentum of values from a modern culture that pushes people toward a sense of achievement and accomplishment in the face of obstacles. Oasis grows out of the egoistic individualism that emerges, which is not capable of dealing with the structural inequalities in the broad social system. And while such individualism tends to discount the human need for community, belonging, and solidarity, Oasis cultivates a warm, relational atmosphere of familial support to console and reenergize the weary worker.

Oasis draws on themes familiar to African American churches through a reworking of Holiness/Word of Faith theology, especially in stressing the importance of personal dreams, acknowledgement of frustrations, and encouragement to trust in a powerful God. Oasis has a theology of prosperity that does not manifest in its most crass form (see chapter 6). Rather, Oasis orients its messages and activities toward those with failed ambitions, including out-of-work actors in search of fame, single women who want both a career and a family, and second chancers seeking to remove repressive stigmas imposed by previous life experiences. By intentionally seeking to relate to those in the entertainment industry, Oasis unintentionally captures the historic functions of the black church in a manner that appeals not only to African Americans but also to others experiencing pain, frustration, and oppressive systems (see chapter 7).

The church cultivates a distinctive moral community that empowers highly ambitious fame- and profit-seeking members of the creative class from the entertainment industry who are negotiating between secular success and religious devotion. People who attend Oasis are empowered to cope with disappointment and persist in the hope of fulfilling not only their personal dreams but also a God-sanctioned mission of evangelistic influence that their success will make possible. Through this congregation, they achieve great confidence in a God who wants to use their talents to fulfill cosmic purposes (see chapter 8).

The Challenge of Blending Faith and Fame

Hollywood grew up in the shadow of an idealistic community of churches that had formed a sacred haven of belief and practice in Southern California toward the end of the nineteenth century.[5] Within a few short decades of the following century, a churchly utopia was transformed into the home of the Hollywood film industry. Mechanisms of production and distribution, as well as battles between humanistic ideals and aggressive business tactics, became the dominating forces in the region.

Hollywood today is foremost a moneymaking business, and the pragmatic morality driving a financially successful film is not the same as the religious morality promoted by churches. Understandably, religious leaders were troubled that the influence of Hollywood threatened to surpass the influence of their religion. Although the Oasis Christian Center is a fascinating exception, theologically conservative churches today still express protest and hostility against the evils of Hollywood, and this affects the attitudes and beliefs of believers toward the entertainment industry. A number of factors make the pursuit of fame and profit problematic, especially among evangelicals (see chapter 3). While conservative churches often depict Hollywood as the devil's playground, for example, the evangelistic imperative makes the opportunity to influence millions of people through film and television compelling, and conservative Christians frequently seize the devil's megaphone to promote their own God-oriented message.

Hollywood as the Devil's Playground

On the surface, evangelicals are worried about what achieving fame requires from aspirants in the entertainment industry. Based on my observations at both

Oasis and Mosaic (which also has a high concentration of people in the entertainment industry), evangelicals by and large believe that sending members into
Hollywood is equivalent to sending them into a foreign country ruled by irreligious norms (Marti 2005). Visions of Hollywood evoke backstage shenanigans
involving sex, drugs, parties, and the need to win the favor of those who promote such things. Industry insiders often reinforce this image, as did comedian
Jon Stewart, who as host of the 2006 Academy Awards described Hollywood as
"an atheistic pleasure dome," "a modern day beachfront Sodom and Gomorrah," and "a moral black hole where innocence is obliterated in an endless orgy
of sexual gratification and greed."

So while fame itself might be desirable, to succeed in Hollywood a person
must successfully adopt blasphemous norms, according to the conservative
Christian view. In the process of achieving success, a believer promotes immoral
actions like smoking, foul language, sex outside of marriage, and senseless
violence. Such notions were made explicit in my observations at Oasis when a
pastor publicly spoke of a member who experienced success in the role of a gay
man. The pastoral comments focused on the need to consider whether success
should come at the price of portraying, and thereby promoting, a lifestyle seen
as inherently sinful.

Consider the theological framework of holiness evangelical churches have
historically taught, in which a belief in separation is inherent. The lexicography
of holiness is related to the Hebrew word *qodesh* and the New Testament Greek
word *hagiazo*. Both translate as "to set apart" or "to separate." To be pure and
clean is to be simultaneously set apart or separated from what is impure and
unclean. A familiar saying among evangelicals is, "We are to be *in* the world but
not *of* the world." For the evangelical, pursuit of the sacred involves intentional
separation from profane, nonreligious segments of life, and holiness involves
connection to a transcendent realm separate from the profane. Emile Durkheim
(1995) and Mircea Eliade (1959) both reinforce this binary understanding of sacred
and profane spheres of life in religion. Can holiness ever be achieved in the den
of iniquity called Hollywood? For the great majority of evangelicals, the answer
is a firm no. Holiness is not compatible with the pursuit of fame and profit.

The evangelical objection to the pursuit of fame runs even deeper. The ethos
of evangelicalism contains an inherent tension between self-effacement and self-
promotion. Christian virtues of humility and submission to authority run counter to the self-promoting and attention-grabbing activity essential for success.
The pursuit of fame thus becomes a radically self-centered, self-seeking form of
pride. Rather than self-promotion, many evangelicals concern themselves with
a fuzzy notion of discovering God's will that translates into a deep suspicion
of self-promoting human agency. Waiting on God's will becomes an ideology
of resigned fatalism that views life as just whatever happens to occur. Career-
advancing agency that promotes an idealized self-image is rejected in favor of a

wishful-thinking determinism that vaguely expects breakthrough opportunities to happen through serendipitous encounters. Career success in this framework derives from unplanned, unexpected events.

Furthermore, the adulation of fame is analogous to the worship of false idols, behavior clearly forbidden within Christianity. Indeed, the word "idol" commonly refers to attention-grabbing celebrities like teen idols or the highly rated Fox television show *American Idol*. Such a cult of celebrity has been a central component of the dynamics of the entertainment industry since the 1920s. But for the evangelical, when the love for a person exceeds the love for God, that person becomes a false idol. Evangelicals are to avoid worshipping false idols; conversely, a sincere believer most certainly must avoid being worshipped as an idol.

Most significant within the theological framework of evangelicalism is an inherent connection between the pursuit of fame and the self-seeking rebellion of Satan, God's primary competitor for the soul of humanity. Even if active belief in direct satanic intervention is not as strong as it once was, the mystique of Satan has not waned. Occurring before the creation of the world, Satan's self-seeking ruin is the most significant prehistorical event in Christian theology. Conventional theology has long established a compelling narrative of Satan: (1) God Almighty creates the angelic host; (2) the Almighty appoints Lucifer, the angel of light, to guard the glory of the throne of God; (3) envious of the worship of the Almighty and recognizing his own God-given beauty, Lucifer rebels against God in order to forcibly draw worship to himself; (4) Lucifer takes one-third of the angelic host into his newly formed demonic tribe; (5) the Almighty banishes the devil and his angels, who are then thrown to earth, given considerable power, and, subsequently, vie with God for the souls of humanity.[6] If adulation of fame emanates from successful self-promotion, then a famous person is acting out a form of self-worship. And self-worship is what corrupted Satan. In sum, the abhorrence for self-promotion is embedded in the fabric of evangelicalism because it is central to the story of Satan. Motivated by inappropriate pride, the pursuit of fame is the sin of Satan, since it seeks to rob God of the glory due to him and redirect it to one of his creatures.

Hollywood as the Church's Pulpit

Evangelical Christians may disdain the self-promotion inherent in fame, but their churches desperately desire to wield fame's influence. The use of the mechanism of Hollywood to promote religion is always problematic, because religion is a significant source of profit for the Hollywood entertainment industry. Hollywood is opportunistic: As a profit-driven industry, Hollywood is willing to co-opt any ideology that sells. In 2004, the outstanding financial success of Mel Gibson's *The Passion of the Christ* spawned a variety of other biblical dramas with appeal for religious conservatives. Like the moneychangers in the first-century Jewish temples, studio executives are willing to exploit sincere worshippers for their own financial benefit. And because biblical dramas consistently put storytelling over scriptural literalness, they rarely achieve doctrinal purity.

But church leaders are equally opportunistic, even when filmmakers tamper with religious truth (see chapter 4). Christian leaders leverage any attention paid to Christianity to advance their own agenda. The financial success of Gibson's *The Passion of the Christ* in the United States was due in part to the aggressive support of conservative Christians' buying tickets for their unbelieving friends. Churches across the country showed trailers for the movie in Sunday services and organized groups to prepurchase seats for unchurched friends and family. The same was true for the 2006 film *The Nativity* and the 2007 film *Amazing Grace*. For conservative church leaders, movies like *The Passion of the Christ, The Nativity,* and *Amazing Grace* are not simply entertainment; they are evangelistic tools. Taking nonmembers to see these films is an evangelistic extension of the church's ministry.

Christian groups also capitalize on speculations about the life of Jesus to advance their own brand of religious truth. Consider the substantial attempts to correct the speculations in Dan Brown's bestselling novel *The Da Vinci Code,* which Ron Howard made into a feature-length film starring two-time Oscar winner Tom Hanks. The Roman Catholic Church essentially banned the book in 2005 by asking the faithful not to read it, and the Vatican discourages viewing the film or DVD. The popularity of *The Da Vinci Code* catalyzed a steady flow of Da Vinci correctives consisting of dozens of books and pamphlets, which are fueling an explosion of film-based sermons, Bible studies, broadcasts, and podcasts on the life of Jesus.[7] In a play on the idea that any press is good press, church leaders are glad to have Christianity brought to the attention of the public, since such exposure creates opportunity for invitation, dialogue, and conversion.

As the producer of *The Passion of the Christ,* Mel Gibson is the most prominent example of a Hollywood insider using the medium to promote a religious truth, although his DUI arrest in August 2006, during which he uttered anti-Semitic slurs, may prove a performance that hurts his production career. Gibson is one of an emerging group of Hollywood insiders motivated by religious commitment and channeling their filmmaking ambitions to create products that support and express Christian messages. In this effort, a profound religious imperative is finding an intriguing avenue of expression since fame, like money, is a generalized commodity that can be cashed in for influence. Groups of devout actors, producers, directors, and screenwriters are carving out spaces of sacred activity by embracing the global platform created by the Hollywood industry machine. Channels of film production and distribution are used to dispense Christian-friendly products supported by Christian audiences who are willing to financially support them and bring non-Christian friends along.

Oasis, then, represents one segment of believers in the entertainment industry who view themselves as part of an underground community carrying out a

Christian-based movement to reform and convert Hollywood. Many entertainment industry people who attend Oasis see themselves as part of a network of believers who work and pray together for success in the industry and success in the gospel (see chapters 3 and 4).

Approaching Oasis through Emile Durkheim

This book's examination of Oasis adds significantly to our understanding of American religious life, particularly in the context of capitalistic developments in the new millennium, which are most concentrated in highly urbanized settings. The focus on religion in this Hollywood church extends to a broader focus on the new economic circumstances of a great proportion of U.S. workers (see chapter 9).

Moreover, the explicit focus on the conscious construction of moral community within this church contributes to our understanding of how congregations shape, negotiate, and reshape moral imperatives that provide day-to-day meaning and influence everyday behavior through duty-bound religious identities. This theoretical focus is the primary launch point for my understanding of the Oasis Christian Center.

I trace my initial theoretical influence for the analysis in this book to the writings of one of the earliest sociologists, Emile Durkheim (1857–1917). While I do not attempt to be absolutely faithful to Durkheim's theoretical stance, I gratefully acknowledge that his insights provide remarkable conceptual resources for understanding Oasis and its relationship to the broader social context.[8] In other words, it is not my purpose to apply a "Durkheimian theory" to the practice of religion in the Oasis congregation, but I freely acknowledge that the general direction of my analytical reflections that resulted in this book began with meditating on Durkheim's work.

Durkheim's Religious Sociology

Durkheim is widely acknowledged to be one of the most important founders of the academic discipline of sociology, and sociologists continue to wrestle theoretically with several aspects of his sociological perspective. Yet in casual conversations with colleagues over the past year on the nature of my study and my intention to use Durkheim as a theoretical reference point, I received cautions and even outright advice to not mention Durkheim at all. While all sociologists recognize his historical importance, not all acknowledge the value of his work.

My sociology professors, for example, barely mentioned Durkheim's *Elementary Forms of Religious Life*, published in 1912, a powerful and challenging book. In graduate school, my first instructor in sociological theory showed open contempt for Durkheim. She gave the class less than a week to read the bulk of his first major work, *The Division of Labor in Society*, and then spent a breezy class discussion on the inadequacies of functionalism, a widely discredited manner of theorizing about society loosely connected to aspects of Durkheim's work. For me, that class experience drove a stake into the heart of Durkheim's theoretical promise. I was well into graduate school before I decided to read *Elementary Forms* for myself.

I remember spending many days slogging through page after page of seemingly irrelevant detail on totem rituals of aboriginal tribes in Australia. Viewing religion through ethnographic accounts of the Arunta of Australia, Durkheim looked at what he considered to be the most simple and primitive society in order to examine the most essential aspects of religion. It was not an assignment; no one asked me to read it. Moreover, in reading through the text I had to overcome my own sense of believing that Durkheim was no longer important and that the development in sociological thought over the past century had far surpassed his ideas and made his work superfluous. At the same time, I vividly remember throughout this free, unforced reading turning pages and coming onto remarkable passages providing a young sociologist an enlightened sensitivity to aspects of social life. The insights obtained then suggested plausible explanations for corporate phenomena that other theorists had simply neglected.

That was almost fifteen years ago, and my initial enthusiasm gave way to disappointment as I found Durkheim's reading of ethnographic data flawed, his separation of sacred and profane overstated a presumed universal quality in all societies, Swain's 1915 English translation contained inaccuracies, and, ultimately, many of Durkheim's contemporaries (like Marcel Mauss, Maurice Halbwachs, François Simiand, and Célestin Bouglé) and most later theorists failed to build adequately on his insights. I also discovered that in the century after his death, Durkheim was at the lowest point of his popularity (see Collins 1988). Part of the reason for his loss of status coincided with my first years in graduate school, when Durkheim was introduced to U.S. sociologists as a functionalist and then viewed as a founder of multivariate statistical analysis, which classified him (wrongly) as a positivistic, quantitative sociologist. As Randall Collins noted in 1988: "No wonder then that most of the intellectual factions today have nothing but disdain for Durkheim" (107).

The early development of sociology ignored many of Durkheim's emphases on religion and symbolic processes. Durkheim did not live long enough to independently develop his ideas, and the disruptions of war in the early twentieth century prevented systematic investigation of his unpublished lectures and manuscripts. Scholars with different theoretical concerns either co-opted aspects of his work that served their interests or ignored it completely.

Today, through the work of Jeffrey Alexander and others, scholars acknowledge a decisive shift in Durkheim's perspective that has led to a rereading of his work and to studies informed by this new reading.[9] Durkheim's exploration of religious structures in contemporary modern life were embedded in a series of posthumously published works, and it is in them that we most clearly see Durkheim pursuing his religious sociology. According to Alexander (1988), there emerged in the last part of Durkheim's life an understanding of society that drew greater attention to symbolic processes of human interaction. His interest in religion stemmed not from an interest in church or theology but from his discovery in religion of the prototypical social processes embedded in secular society.

For Durkheim, religious experiences are particular forms of social experiences. In examining religious phenomena, we can explore the preconscious motivations that structure individual action, as well as the emergent, largely unintended social forces that characterize and structure groups. Other prominent sociologists continue to find inspiration for the study of ritual, social interaction, and community through Durkheim (Bellah 2003; Collins 2004; Lichterman 2005). For them, as for me, the major point of departure is *The Elementary Forms of Religious Life*. R. Stephen Warner emphasizes this work as a classic text for the new paradigm approach to American religion and believes that sociologists of religion have too often neglected the theoretical insights available in it (see Warner 1993, 1052; 2005, 284).

Durkheim and the Development of Moral Community

Durkheim lived during a critical period of reconstruction for France's pedagogical system in the late nineteenth century (L. Jones 1999). In France and elsewhere, religion and morality historically have been interconnected. With the dismissal of ecclesiastical power and church doctrine in an emerging civil society, the core problem for Durkheim was how to develop moral frameworks among France's citizens on a secular basis. Without moral codes internalized by members of a society, civilization is impossible; every society must find a means to curb self-absorbed egoistic behavior and create bonds of unity, loyalty, and faithfulness. How would this society create a new base of morality? This problem consumed Durkheim in his empirical work. For him, morality is an emergent property of society external to individuals that exerts a channeling, constraining, and regulative force on personal behavior (Durkheim 1982). In pursuing the issue of moral development, he argued that morality is a distinctive facet of human experience deserving dedicated scientific analysis. He believed the study of religion would reveal principles that could be applied to the deliberate, conscientious construction of a civic moral life.

Looking at Oasis provoked in me questions similar to Durkheim's. How can the seemingly egoistic individuals of today be compelled to accept and exemplify moral standards of conduct? The key to understanding Oasis lies in appreciating the distinctive moral community cultivated through the congregation. While society awakens our ambitions (because it is through social interaction that we become not mere animals but reflective, purposeful human beings), it simultaneously constrains these ambitions (since social interaction cultivates morally binding imperatives that guide both thought and action). Similarly, Oasis promotes worldly ambition, yet involvement in the congregation actively cultivates a public morality, that is, a set of standards for how to conduct oneself with success in the world. Based on his admiration of the medieval Christian concept of duty, Durkheim ultimately attempted to build a new morality on a secular basis.

Similarly, Oasis, like other churches, finds itself in a largely secularized society that has conceded to commodification of labor and the overall capitalistic structure of competition, to hierarchical social classes, and to alternate status levels with corresponding levels of privilege. Oasis reinvigorates a Christian morality that integrates the values and standards of a dominating capitalist structure.

In approaching the morality cultivated at Oasis, I note that Durkheim characterized religious experiences as structured around the sacred and the profane. Caillois (1959 [1939]) explains that Durkheim's concept of the profane implied that which is routine (in contrast with effervescence and charisma) as well as evil (in contrast to good). Durkheim distinguishes between the life of routine and the frenzied excitement of religious ritual. In other words, human beings experience life at two levels: the private, mundane, and utilitarian, and the collective, elevated, and moral. At Oasis, the sacred overcomes the day-to-day drudgery of life outside the spotlight. Cultic experiences at Oasis instill a belief in members about their identity that sustains momentum from worship beyond the church walls. Energizing, collective ideals emerge from the congregation and empower the self for action in the mundane world. The empowered self also overcomes outright immorality, greed, and corruption. The Oasis champion triumphs over the mundane, as well as over the immoral.

Solidarity, religion, and morality are interconnected for Durkheim, as his early lecture notes and his empirical work make evident (L. Jones 1999). Social solidarity, the initial problem of sociology, involves the bonds that unite people and create social groups (Durkheim 1978, 205). Durkheim emphasized that solidarity is accomplished through the development of moral communities. Morality is then an inseparable component of social solidarity. Although the moral discipline of each member of a group is socially accomplished, moral rules are external to each member and experienced as coming from outside them. "There is in [morality] something that resists us, is beyond us. We do not determine its existence or its nature. It is independent of what we are. Rather than expressing us, it dominates us" (Durkheim 1961, 28). Morality itself is to be studied as an independent phenomenon existing beyond each individual.

While Durkheim conceptualizes these processes in abstract and nonpersonal terms, I find his theoretical problem is a practical problem for all pastors seeking to build a morally cohesive community in densely populated, metropolitan settings with people from widely differing social backgrounds. The cultivation of morality is a project for church leaders in all congregations. The problem of creating morality is in part one of creating a new base of discipline, since morality and discipline are interconnected. For Durkheim, in fact, "the fundamental element of morality is the spirit of discipline" (1961, 31). Discipline is natural and necessary to being human. Discipline keeps people from egoistically fulfilling their own desires without regard for the concerns of others or the society as a whole. As a part of their discipleship process, church leaders seek to instill or accentuate disciplines that shape individuals into a cohesive moral community.

Durkheim's work encouraged me to explore at Oasis the ongoing construction of a moral environment that celebrates and encourages ambition while channeling that ambition into disciplined action that is empowered from the sacred community and that simultaneously supports the sacred community. As Durkheim would say, Oasis as a church is a moral community, and it is one that can be discovered and observed. Regarding moral communities, Durkheim wrote: "The moralist can . . . neither invent nor construct them; but he must observe them where they exist, and then seek in society their causes and conditions" (1887, 46–47). Aggressive self-promotion in pursuit of fame occurs in the context of moral community. At Oasis, the moral community is crafted and sustained through corporate gatherings (especially worship), and internalized moral imperatives guide each person's behavior when the congregation is dispersed. Oasis is thus a distinctive organizational culture that draws people of particular life experiences and uses various corporate rituals to shape them for particular types of moral action that empower them for uninspired, mundane activity away from the sacred community.

A familial sense of acceptance and belonging is a vital component of the bond of moral community, according to Durkheim. It is therefore not surprising that alongside the emphasis on ambition, Oasis manifests a strong family focus with an emphasis on the church as "our house." Through the building of relationships, the warmth and openness of praise and worship rallies, and the nurturing experiences of small groups, Oasis creates family-type communities (see chapter 7). A sign in the church lobby reads, "Welcome home."

In a similar vein, Pastor Philip preached a message on the prodigal son (from Luke 15) that exhibited the twin themes of family and ambition that I found to be ever present at Oasis. The story of the prodigal tells of a young man motivated by greed who insists on taking early his share of the inheritance due at his father's death in order to pursue his ambitions. He leaves his family to make his way in the world alone, squanders his wealth, and soon finds himself miserable. Success is elusive. He finally takes a job feeding pigs and, starving, eats the slops reserved for them. He remembers that even the lowest servant in his father's home ate better than he did now. In desperation he returns home. When the father sees him coming up the road, he hurries to place a luxurious robe on his son's shoulders and a golden ring on his finger. The father enthusiastically embraces his lost son and lovingly hosts a feast to celebrate his return. The son thus went from poor and unemployed to prosperous and surrounded by family. Pastor Philip poignantly describes the prodigal's return home, where he receives both wealth and love.

Through its pervasive emphasis on being family together, Oasis creates spaces of community for ambitious individuals who have found their goals frustrating and society's systems overwhelming. Here they gain great confidence that God can, wants to, and eventually will use them to fulfill cosmic purposes as they at the same time achieve personal fulfillment in a world-affirming way (Shibley 1998). "World affirming" means that their achievements are intended to be recognized, measured, and praised by strangers out there in the world, that is, people who do not share their religious values and beliefs. It is a win-win solution; God fulfills his missionizing purposes, and his people live prosperous, fulfilling lives.

Durkheim asserts that beyond restraining self-interest, the fullest development of morality is the ability to go beyond consideration of the self to the consideration of good on behalf of others regardless of personal consequences. He claims that "there never has existed any people among whom an egoistic act—that is to say, behavior directed solely to the interest of the person performing it—has been considered moral" (1961, 58). Hence the distinctive aspect of morality is a concern for the other person since, as Durkheim rightly emphasizes, there is no such thing as a personal morality. Morality is always geared toward constraining disruptive impulses and actions and keeping the social order operating smoothly. In *Elementary Forms*, Durkheim writes:

> However complex the outward manifestations of religious life may be, its inner essence is simple, and one and the same. Everywhere it fulfills the same need and derives from the same state of mind. In all its forms, its object is to lift man above himself and to make him live a higher life than he would if he obeyed only his individual impulses. The beliefs express this life in terms of representations; the rites organize and regulate its functioning. (1995, 417)

Oasis cultivates a morality in which personal success is a means toward accomplishing the greater ends of kindness, generosity, and altruism (see chapter 8). Self-sacrifice is the means toward self-fulfillment. Oasis promotes a moral community that safeguards itself and simultaneously overcomes excessive egoism and utilitarianism. As Lawrence Jones states: "Moral acts are rather those which are 'publicly' useful, addressed to society as a whole, not to its individual members; and the moral life begins when the individual becomes attached to a social group" (1999, 91). Moral ends are not derived privately but collectively, thus, "a moral propensity to sacrifice, to go beyond one's self, to go beyond the circle of self-interest, . . . clears the way for a true morality" (Durkheim 1961, 83).

A Look Ahead

Hollywood Faith is not a comprehensive social history of Oasis as a church, and it is not a how-to manual for spiritual revitalization. This book is a sociological interpretation of a church I believe is significant for understanding vital religious trends today.

In pursuit of understanding religious dynamics in our contemporary capitalistic society, each chapter looks at the tensions and implications of negotiating holiness and the pursuit of fame and profit in this Hollywood church. Each represents an expanding portrait of the dynamics embedded within this congregation. Chapter 2 describes Hollywood as both a dream and a destination by exploring the regional development of the entertainment industry and the symbolic significance of Hollywood as a repository of hopes and aspirations. Chapter 3 focuses on the complex relationship between Hollywood and evangelicalism, and articulates how fame and profit are problematic for evangelicals. Chapter 4 describes an emerging group of Hollywood Christians and how the evangelistic imperative makes compelling the opportunity to influence millions of people at a time. Chapter 5 describes the experience of people of Oasis working in the Hollywood entertainment industry, highlighting the business of celebrity and stardom juxtaposed with the experience of those whose desire to succeed meets with constant disappointment. Chapter 6 further articulates how Oasis accommodates the experience of those in the entertainment industry through co-optation of twentieth-century theological movements like Holiness, Word of Faith, and Prosperity, as well as twentieth-century congregational forms like the seeker church movement and new paradigm churches. The chapter also focuses on the symbolic importance of the Oasis auditorium, the implications of having church in a theater, and the uniquely American transformation of sacred space.

Chapter 7 describes the population of African Americans at Oasis and demonstrates how the outstanding degree of racial diversity in the church is an unintentional result of focusing on outreach to the entertainment community. Chapter 8 synthesizes the life experience of people drawn to Oasis and shows how Oasis succeeds in its vision to cultivate a moral community for champions in life through a strategic reorientation of personal identity. The role of worship music is especially noted as a means of accomplishing this reorientation. Finally, chapter 9 speculates on religion in an era of identity commodification. Branding of oneself is now imperative for workplace survival, and the theology and structure of the church especially connects with the stories, achievements, and dilemmas of members of the emerging creative class who must master self-promotion for economic success. This chapter also speculates on the relation between religion at Oasis and the changing nature of religion in the United States.

The history and development of the Oasis Christian Center is deeply intertwined with the history of Hollywood itself. Since congregations are situated in places, I found that I could not ignore how Oasis is embedded within a large, and very rich, social history. In particular, over the time I spent at the Oasis Christian Center the symbol of the Hollywood star become increasingly important. Passing Jesus' Hollywood star every time I entered and exited the building, I found it to be the cultural mediator between the broader social history of the region and the specific project of identity reorientation occurring within the church. Because understanding the interplay between regional development and the church through the significance of the Hollywood star provides a base for understanding the tensions between Christianity and Hollywood generally and in the Oasis Christian Center specifically, Jesus' Hollywood Star and its significance is the focus of the next chapter.

The Making of a Star

HOLLYWOOD AS DESTINATION
AND DREAM

LYNN: People come out here with dreams.

Outside Destiny Theater on Wilshire Boulevard, Jesus Christ's Hollywood star sits unobtrusively, a bit worn and easy to miss. The star rests among several icons of the Hollywood entertainment industry—less than twenty feet from a refurbished United Artists movie house, less than two hundred yards from the offices of the *Hollywood Reporter*, less than two miles from the newly built home of the Academy Award ceremonies, the Kodak Theater, and only a few minutes' drive from its kindred stars on the pink and charcoal terrazzo Walk of Fame on Hollywood Boulevard. It fails to appear in travel brochures, and no tour busses stop at the sight. Even the occasional pedestrians on this distant boulevard hardly glance down as they walk by.

Despite its inconspicuous presence, Oasis pastor Philip Wagner intended the star to attract attention, and its introduction to the world was anything but quiet. Every Hollywood star has an official unveiling, and Jesus' star was no exception. On Wednesday, July 17, 1998, the Oasis Christian Center hosted a public unveiling for Hollywood's newest star with a gathering of supportive celebrities—Edward James Olmos, Steve Garvey, Marilyn McCoo, and Rosey Grier. Jesus' star featured widely in newspapers, television news broadcasts, and radio talk shows.

But Jesus' Hollywood star was immediately embroiled in controversy. In a July 30 *Los Angeles Times* article headlined "Chamber Fails to Take a Shine to a New Star," reporter Hector Becerra accurately reports that the idea for the Jesus star came from Pastor Philip. After seeing a Walk of Fame plaque for the Reverend Billy Graham honoring his broadcast sermons, he thought, "Why not have one for Jesus Christ?" Having just acquired the movie theater, Philip intended to establish a *Walk of Faith* (note the subtle word change) on the sidewalk in front of the church building on Wilshire between Highland and La Brea avenues to honor ordinary people making significant contributions to society beyond the celebrity spotlight, for example, single mothers who raise their children and send them to college. "I thought we could use the language of the city and give Jesus Christ the recognition he deserves." It was a good

Figure 1. Just south of the famous Walk of Fame, the entrance of the Oasis Christian Center features a specially crafted Hollywood star honoring Jesus Christ. (Photo by Soo Petrovich.)

idea, but apparently Jesus did not go through the proper channels before being awarded his star.

The disapproving "Chamber" in the headline was the Hollywood Chamber of Commerce, and as quickly as the media announced the new icon, it picked up on the controversy that ensued. From the *Toronto Star* of July 31, under the headline "Jesus Christ's Super Star Burns Hollywood Burghers": "The Hollywood Chamber of Commerce is upset that a church near the legendary 'Walk of Fame' has unveiled a star honouring Jesus Christ that resembles the plaques dedicated to hundreds of entertainers of stage and screen." The writer quips: "Hollywood is a tough place to earn your star, even if you are the son of God."

Adding fuel to the controversy was the reaction of many local residents outraged at what they considered a lack of respect for the Hollywood Boulevard star as an established symbol of celebrity. The Hollywood Chamber of Commerce issued a statement that claimed: "There is nothing wrong with creating a Walk of Faith or with the church honoring Jesus. . . . The question is whether they should have created a star similar to ours without first checking with us."

The Hollywood Boulevard star is a brand icon attracting millions of tourists, and the Oasis Christian Center's selection of Jesus sidestepped the bureaucratic nomination process and apparently violated a Hollywood Chamber of Commerce trademark. Within weeks the chamber had extended permission to Oasis to keep the star honoring Jesus Christ and in return had obtained a commitment that future Walk of Faith stars would be a different color and no more than half the size of official Walk of Fame stars. Leron Gubler, the chamber's executive director, told the Associated Press, "We are pleased that we have been able to resolve this amicably." He assured the press that the church had no intention of violating the chamber's trademark, and the chamber had no objection to a church wanting to honor Jesus Christ, but stressed, "We do have an obligation to protect the Hollywood Walk of Fame trademark."

What makes the Hollywood Walk of Fame star such an important piece of intellectual property to the Hollywood economic community? What was the chamber protecting? A repository of the glamour and mystique attributed to the place called Hollywood. The pink-and-bronze stars comprising the Walk of Fame stand at the center of the symbolization of Hollywood promoted by the city's Chamber of Commerce. For church leaders, installing Jesus' Hollywood star reclaimed Hollywood for Christianity; for civic leaders, Jesus' star threatened a carefully cultivated image of the Hollywood entertainment industry. The image of the Walk of Fame Hollywood star needs to be protected because establishing this emblem reclaimed the romance of Hollywood for the city and the motion picture industry. These stars uniquely capture both the destination and the dream of Hollywood. Indeed, the Walk of Fame stars bond Hollywood the physical place and Hollywood the symbolic space.

A Sociology of Hollywood

Hollywood might seem to be an interesting but ultimately inconsequential aspect of modern society, one scholars might easily dismiss. But film scholar Saverio Giovacchini writes simply: "We ought to take Hollywood seriously" (2001, 7). And as Andrew Tudor states in an essay on sociology and film:

> Film, after all, is more than mere celluloid. It is socially constructed within a three-cornered association between film makers, film spectators, and the film texts themselves, and at every point in that nexus of relationships we encounter negotiation and interaction involving active social beings and institutionalized social practices. Sociology is the intellectual resource best suited to probing that particular complex of social activity. (2000, 192)

In understanding the broader context of the Oasis Christian Center, then, I follow Mark Shiel's proposal to seriously consider a sociology of motion picture production, distribution, exhibition, and consumption (2001, 2). Any sociology of Hollywood is much less concerned with the critical study of the products of the institution (movies) than with the analysis of the cultural / commercial institution that comprises Hollywood. The Payne Fund Studies, reported in *Motion Pictures and Youth* and conducted between 1929 and 1932, are considered the first sociological study of films (Charters 1935). These studies focused on the influence of film on human behavior, particularly in leading young people toward delinquency. The narrow focus of that research, the effects of film, was carried on throughout the twentieth century by conservative researchers on the political right sponsored by Protestant reformers and civic leaders, as well as those on the left like the Frankfurt School. Later, the analysis of film influenced by structuralism and semiotics introduced a hermeneutically oriented sociological analysis (e.g., Denzin 1991).[1]

While the analysis of film content is interesting and important for understanding the interactions between film and society, it fails to capture the larger social complex represented by the phrase "Hollywood entertainment industry." The development of knowledge of the Hollywood film industry must look to broader social structures and be both historically informed and empirically grounded. I agree with Shiel that cross-disciplinary readings should address key issues in "the operation of political, social, and cultural power in the urban centers of the present global system" (2001, 2). Drawing a more expansive understanding of sociological dynamics inherent to the entertainment industry will provoke "a synthetic understanding of the objective social conditions of the production, distribution, exhibition, and reception of cinema."

Hollywood: The Place

Even a glance at the phenomenon that is Hollywood reveals that the entertainment industry is a global phenomenon. But despite the worldwide disbursement of the activities that make up the motion picture industry, Allen J. Scott (2005) forcefully argues that the physical location of Hollywood is significant. The geographic area of Hollywood is quite small, stretching from Santa Monica in the west to Interstate 5 on the east, and from the San Fernando Valley to the north to the border of Orange County in the south. The majority of Hollywood activity occurs in this space. In short, says Scott, the significance of Hollywood the region is that it is the "place where the actual creative and physical work of film and television program production is more intensely realized than anywhere else in the world" (xii). Even in the face of competing global production, Hollywood will remain rooted within the greater Los Angeles metropolitan area for the foreseeable future.

Geography of the Entertainment Industry

Today's Hollywood lies on a main passage through the hills leading from the Los Angeles basin to the San Fernando Valley, the Cahuenga Pass, once home to native Indians and a road for transporting cattle and sheep to San Fernando. The Spaniards called the pass El Portozuelo; it was the official connection along El Camino del Rey, the King's Highway, the Spanish Trail that continued up the coast of California. The padres of early religious settlements traveled this road on their visits to the missions scattered from San Francisco to San Diego. In Los Angeles, this important road became present-day Wilshire Boulevard, the street on which Oasis Christian Center is located.

Historians generally agree that the area called Hollywood owes its beginnings to a severe drought (Torrence 1982, 20). The entire Southern California region had been subdivided by the original Spanish land grants around the year 1800 into a few large ranches that each comprised over 100,000 acres. After farmers and ranchers settled in these large tracts, the lack of rain throughout the 1860s resulted in cruel droughts that dried up fields and waterholes. Cattle and horses died. Land values plummeted. In search of cash and unable to maintain their livestock, ranch owners subdivided their land and offered it for sale to settlers from the east. These new farmers began to raise sheep and grow herbs, grain, fruits, and vegetables. By 1870, the Los Angeles population was 5,614. The local population exploded with the discovery of artesian well water and the extension of railroad lines, like the Santa Fe, in 1885. Water allowed irrigation and the expansion of farmlands. Railroads unexpectedly spurred competition as Southern Pacific and Santa Fe fought for bragging rights to the transcontinental railroad empire. Rate wars ensued, and cross-country rail ticket prices plummeted from $100 to $1 between 1886 and 1888. The resettlement rush did not last, but land values were promoted and the local population boosted considerably. Suburban developments took root.

The founder of Hollywood itself was Harvey Henderson Wilcox, a Kansas prohibitionist who settled in the Cahuenga Valley in 1883. He bought and further subdivided the land in the area and opened a real estate office. The name was the suggestion of his wife, Daieda Wilcox, who on the train back to her new home heard an affluent woman from Illinois describe her own summer home near Chicago. Daieda Wilcox promptly bestowed its name on her Cahuenga Valley ranch. When Harvey Wilcox laid out his ranch in a grid to allow for easily identifiable subdivisions for purchase, the name on the map placed with the county recorder in February 1887 was that on the white wooden sign on the front gate of their ranch: Hollywood.

The holly plant is not native to the area, and when Harvey Wilcox attempted to justify the name of his ranch by planting two English holly bushes on the property, they promptly died. As Paul Zollo points out, it was a prescient effort: "It was a historic endeavor . . . , the first-ever attempt to match the *ideal*—the original abstraction of Hollywood, the inaugural illusion—with something authentic. And it failed" (2002, xiii).

The area grew in part because it was about seven miles east of Los Angeles, one of the most rapidly expanding cities in the nation. With 50,000 people in 1890, it was already fifty-sixth largest. By 1900, the population had doubled to 100,000, thirty-sixth largest in the nation. When Hollywood incorporated as its own city in 1903, its civic leaders intended to establish a peaceful community away from the urban bustle of Los Angeles. Instead, Hollywood was annexed into Los Angeles in 1910. Even today, Hollywood is not a city or an incorporated municipality but a physical area designated by the Los Angeles City Council as bounded by Doheny Drive, Melrose Avenue, the Santa Monica Mountains, and the Los Angeles River. After its incorporation, the population of Hollywood grew along with greater Los Angeles, increasing from 500 in 1900 to 5,000 in 1910 and then jumping 720 percent to 36,000 by 1920.

Around the turn of the twentieth century, Hollywood citizens were largely members of Protestant denominations and members of the Progressive reform movement. These Midwestern Protestants occupied the higher economic classes and quickly customized the business and civic life of Hollywood to suit their religious and social values. Leveraging their influence through their positions in the professions and in business, they passed city ordinances to outlaw drunkenness, gambling, and loitering in places like poolrooms, bowling alleys, and shooting galleries (Torrence 1982, 49–50). As the population of Hollywood grew, stores began to carry the latest fashions and styles to appeal to a more cosmopolitan crowd. Cafes, restaurants, boutiques, and hotels lined the streets. For a short time, the area was a holiness-tinged haven shielded from the sprawling metropolis of Los Angeles.

Development of the Motion Picture Industry

The unanticipated transformation of Hollywood in the 1920s went beyond its increase in population and the affluence of its citizens. The quiet suburb of grand homes set among agricultural farmlands witnessed the mushrooming of barn-sized structures for making motion pictures. Rather than a distant, morally conservative suburb of downtown Los Angeles, Hollywood became home to the major motion picture studios of the world.

Motion picture making took root in Hollywood even though film was not invented there nor were the first films made there. Thomas Edison is credited with creating the motion picture (despite other technological inventions in France) because he registered the first patent. Edison developed the first motion picture camera in 1888, the Kinetograph, along with the first motion picture projector, the Kinetoscope. These far-reaching inventions allowed human beings to capture time and motion in ways not possible by the naked eye. Most importantly, the illusion of motion was achieved by moving a series of still photographs of objects in motion. Recognizing that images could be sped up, slowed down, or reversed at will, it becomes easy to understand the power of this technology. Edison's Kinetoscope was made for single viewers, who would experience the illusion of motion pictures as the machine flipped rapidly through still photos. Almost simultaneously, the Lumière brothers' Cinematographe introduced public motion picture projection in France in 1895. The Vitascope created by Thomas Armat and C. Francis Jenkins in the United States in 1896 also allowed communal viewing. Together, these developments represent the beginning of the motion picture experience we know today.

The early inventors reflected on the possible impact of motion pictures. The chief photographic assistant for Thomas Edison who helped create the technology for motion pictures, William Laurie Dickson, believed film would reinforce a practical sense of reality among the masses. Film would ground the exaggerated claims of fantastic storytellers and train people to exercise reason through portrayal of empirical facts. As Lary May summarizes Dickson's thinking: "No longer would history be tinged with the 'exaggerated claims of the chroniclers' minds'" (1983, 22). But Dickson underestimated the flexibility of the new medium. Motion pictures allowed the creation of fantastic environments, which contributed to the cultivation of greater flights of imagination than Dickson ever dreamed. "Dickson soon realized that the experience of watching numerous frames of celluloid spring to life and project on a large screen challenged a clearly empirical view of the world. Images were five times larger than life; they could defy time and space and distort reality" (25–26).

Rather than anchor viewers to pragmatic realities, motion pictures transported them into flights of fantasy. Even today we recognize that depictions by round-the-clock news programming, true-to-life documentaries, and reality television are all manipulated exaggerations of life fitted to concise narratives that lift us from the mundane, take us to unusual places, and highlight tension and drama ordinarily missing from day-to-day existence.

Motion Pictures as the First Modern Mass Media

Movie projection came into its own when Edison invented a projector with a nickel slot that allowed personal viewing of short films. Entrepreneurs offered these machines—nickelodeons—in urban storefronts for a five-cent admission fee, an important source of amusement for laborers along with saloons and street shows, particularly for the flood of immigrants moving into the cities at the turn of the century looking for cheap entertainment. Nickelodeons dominated from 1905 to 1910, much cheaper for theater operators than anything with live performers. They soon fitted nickelodeons with sheets, and then screens, allowing the public showing of half-hour or hour movies for a fraction of the cost of a Broadway play, vaudeville, or melodrama. From devices used to show a few films on bedsheets in storefronts in 1903 grew to more than five thousand movie houses by 1911—before there was a single movie house in Hollywood.

With cheap admission fees and no language barriers, these silent movie theaters provided entertainment mostly to the working class and new immigrants. Motion pictures were considered a lower-class form of entertainment, along with arcades and vaudeville. Yet the novelty of cinema proved both popular and profitable, and despite the lack of respectability, moviemaking and movie showing grew at a phenomenal rate. As motion picture historian Robert Sklar notes, movies "were the first modern mass media, and they rose to the surface of cultural consciousness from the bottom up, receiving their principal support from the lowest and most invisible classes in American society" (1994, 30).

The development of motion pictures occurred at the same time the United States became a predominantly urban, industrialized society, from 1890 to 1910. According to May, a new consumer ideal emerged, encouraging immigrants with wealth and white skin to live in "a modern utopia where the dream could come off the screen and into real life" (1983, 169). Motion pictures became "a medium capable of capturing the beautiful mystery of our very dreams, and of aspiring to the realm of serious art" (Zollo 2002, 22). Social reformer Jane Addams called the movie theater a "house of dreams" when she wrote in 1909 that "'going to the show' for thousands of young people in every industrial city is the only possible road to the realms of mystery and romance" (Addams [1909] 1989, 75).

The now familiar mystique and power of Hollywood grew with the spread of movie theaters across the country. Thousands of theaters had opened by the mid-1900s, and by 1910 there were more than twenty thousand nickelodeons in northern cities. Between 1911 and 1920, motion pictures became the most accessible form of mass entertainment in the United States. By 1920, attendance had increased tenfold: More than forty million Americans went to the movies every week (Torrence 1982, 87). For the first half of the twentieth century, movies were the most popular and influential medium of culture in the nation.

The Center Shifts from East to West

Hollywood developed as an industry as filmmakers learned to produce successive short subjects and newsreels for small theater operations (Bordwell, Staiger, and Thompson 1985). Southern California, the future home of the Oasis Christian Center, was merely a branch plant extension of companies situated in New York (Scott 2005, xii). Soon, Hollywood became its own viable economic and creative site, as hundreds of small firms moved to the region to pursue film production, and the center of motion picture gravity shifted from east to west. Around 1910, two-thirds of the world's motion pictures were made in Southern California. It is in these few years that Hollywood became the movie mecca, and by 1915 the term "Hollywood" represented the people and process of moviemaking in Los Angeles (Finch and Rosenkrantz 1979, 1–14). By 1919, 80 percent of the world's motion pictures were made there. At the height of the studio system in the 1930s and 1940s, 90 percent of all U.S. film production and 60 percent of world film production was based in Los Angeles (Maltby 2003, 121). Motion pictures became established as large, moneymaking enterprises. By 1947, movie studios earned well over one billion dollars, which made the production of films the third-largest retail business in the United States after auto sales and groceries (Davis 1993).

Historians debate how to account for the uniform shift of the industry to Southern California. One popular explanation involves weather. The story goes that in 1907, due to bad weather in Chicago, Colonel William Selig sent a film company to the dry, warm Los Angeles region to film *The Count of Monte Cristo*. Filmmakers like Selig used the simplest of equipment and filmed in natural and urban settings on streets and open fields. The region promised 355 days of useful sunshine. Even interior shots were filmed outdoors using walls without roofs, with the sun remaining the major source of lighting. Taking note of the predictable weather and diversity of landscapes available in the region, Selig returned two years later to build a studio. Lack of weather delays increased the pace of moviemaking and made the process more efficient. Other filmmakers followed, with at least fifteen companies establishing themselves in Hollywood between 1911 and 1913. This figure surged to 37 by 1915 as studios planted themselves in the region.

But weather alone does not explain the radical move and quick establishment of movie businesses in Southern California. Weather had not been a concern previously; the majority of the first studios were located in New York, Philadelphia, and Chicago (May 1983). Also, at least one other geographically closer option existed: A number of filmmakers favored Jacksonville, Florida, over California (Ponti 1992). As an alternative to the weather as an explanation, many historians argue that avoiding costly lawsuits from Thomas Edison's company, located in New York, motivated the move west.

The Edison Company kept a tight control over the basic patents to the most technologically advanced movie cameras and projectors in the United States. The company sold or rented films exclusively to filmmakers and exhibitors who agreed to use Edison's licensed products. Those not licensed to use his technology were prosecuted by the Motion Picture Patents Company (also known as the Trust) on the basis of patent infringement. At the same time, the Edison Company's control over access to cameras and projectors drastically limited the stream of moviemaking. Demand for movies far exceeded the number of films available to exhibit. The motion picture business became dependent on exhibitors, and to meet the demand for more films, independent filmmakers pirated cameras and made their own films. Motion picture companies moved to the West Coast to evade the Trust's litigious grasp and thereby financial ruin. Southern California became a great place both to fight the Trust and to escape until the Trust faded away (Torrence 1982, 70–71). Eventually, when the courts ruled in 1915 that Edison's motion picture patents company was not a legal trust, motion picture producers were free to make their films and create a new industry.

Although avoiding Edison's patent protection lawsuits is a persuasive explanation, it also does not adequately account for the growth in Hollywood of the motion picture industry. Examining the list of the first studios in Los Angeles shows that they were members of the Trust and that most of the early studios retained headquarters in the Northeast and quite accessible to the Trust. Finally, the Trust only dissolved in 1915 after a number of movie studios in the region had already been established. More important than the economics of either weather or lawsuits is the economics of land and labor.

Land, Labor, and Local Business

Hollywood offered studios an excellent business location: large tracts of undeveloped land, cheap (nonunionized) labor, and a booming population. The first founders of film studios in the United States were entrepreneurs, mostly first- and second-generation immigrants fleeing war and oppression in eastern and southern Europe. The success of D. W. Griffith's 1915 film *The Birth of a Nation,* which generated more than $15 million in revenue, greatly encouraged entrepreneurs to pursue film production. Boosters for the Hollywood area like Harry Culver, whose tracts of land eventually became known as Culver City, encouraged these nascent capitalists to move west, believing that movie studios would stimulate more people to relocate there and business would also move into the area.

The international triumph of the U.S. motion picture industry accelerated during this time in part because World War I prevented European filmmakers overseas from developing both their craft and their business. The abrupt stunting of European industry allowed the United States to take over their markets and become by far the most dominant presence in theaters all over the world (Sklar

1994, 46–47). The movie industry was highly portable and did not require access to natural resources or specialized production plants. With railroads having been extended decades earlier to the West Coast, studios could affordably ship reels of film anywhere across the country.

After owning nickelodeons and seeing the profit to be made in motion pictures, immigrant theater owners moved to Los Angeles. Most were Jews who migrated in the late nineteenth century, among them Samuel Goldwyn of MGM fame, who said, "Los Angeles is more efficient for us, more cheap" (qtd. in May 1983, 181). But while many tried, few survived. The major studios that became Hollywood were those that made it through this economically tumultuous time, the Big Eight movie studios that monopolized the motion picture industry—Paramount; Loew's, which became MGM; Twentieth Century Fox; Warner Bros.; RKO; Universal Pictures; Columbia Pictures; and United Artists.

Compared to other groups that migrated from rural areas, these new American Jews were urban and entrepreneurial, characteristics that led directly to their greater success in accommodating to business practices in the United States and in accumulating capital for new ventures (see Glazer 1958; Kuznets 1976; Thernstrom 1973). Max Weber would have called them pariah capitalists, entrepreneurs who took opportunities in marginal trades that were yet to be embraced by members of the dominant society (see May 2000, 57–65). The cohesion and cooperation evident among the Jews of Hollywood like Sam and Jack Warner, Jesse Lasky and Samuel Goldwyn, Sam Katz, and A. J. Balaban were notable. Together they created the new world of studios, stars, and screens.

Allen J. Scott (2005) advances a theoretical argument that emphasizes the uniqueness of particular organizational structures in certain geographic locations.[2] In Hollywood, the distinctive advantage of geography and local labor conditions played into the dynamics of what Scott calls "locational agglomeration." A growing number of individual units of production were able to forge strong functional interdependencies. In other words, the combination of a number of small firms and the diversification of specialized units in an atmosphere of an abundance of labor created a virtuous cycle. The business activities of the motion picture industry remained profitable, and its successes generated more successes. With the establishment of movie studios and their raising of barn-sized structures for filming, motion picture entrepreneurs catalyzed a series of synergistic business ventures culminating in the establishment of a unique labor market.

Rather than a family-oriented residential neighborhood of Victorian homes, Hollywood became a distinctive industrial district. Films were produced by scores of studios, some small and a few large, and all were located in Hollywood around Sunset Boulevard and Gower Street, just two miles north of the present location of Oasis. Other studios were built in a circle around the core of Hollywood, and the texture of the region changed. A prominent political journalist who chronicled the history of California, Carey McWilliams, reminisces on these early days:

> God has always smiled on Southern California. . . . Consider, for example, the extraordinary good luck in having the motion-picture industry concentrated in Los Angeles. The leading industry in Los Angeles from 1920 to 1940, motion pictures were made to fit the economic requirements and physical limitations of the region like a glove. There was one industry, perhaps the only one in America, that required no raw materials, for which discriminatory freight rates were meaningless, and which, at the same time, possesses an enormous pay-roll. . . . Like the region itself, this key industry is premised upon improvisation, a matter of make-believe, a synthesis of air and wind and water. . . . What could be more desirable than a monopolistic non-seasonal industry with 50 million customers, an industry without soot or grime, without blast furnaces or dynamos, an industry whose production shows peaks but few valleys? (1973, 339–340)

The physical characteristics, human capital, and ad hoc organizational arrangements combined into a successful engine for the development of a new creative industry.

The motion picture industry expanded to include studios (film production and editing), actors (screen objects), and theaters (distribution and exhibition). Each studio controlled between five hundred and a thousand theaters through the late 1920s, which allowed them to control the pipeline of production from creation to exhibition. Studios controlled the theaters in downtown areas that took in the greatest revenues through the first weeks of box-office receipts, and then allowed distribution of films for exhibition in small, independent theaters. Indeed, theaters became the chief mechanism by which studios accrued their profits. So, in addition to movie studios, Hollywood built its own networks of theaters, including the United Arts movie theater on Wilshire Boulevard that would eventually become the home of the Oasis Christian Center.

Hollywood: The Dream

In the few years between 1911 and 1925, Hollywood permanently captured the imagination of Americans across the country. Yet, as Scott writes, "Hollywood is a very specific place in Southern California, and, more to the point, a particular locale-bound nexus of production relationships and local labor market activities" (2005, 138). Hollywood is also "the American film industry's synonym for itself" (Maltby 1998, 24). But in another sense, Hollywood is everywhere, and in its realization as a disembodied assortment of images and narratives, its presence is felt broadly across the globe. And in yet another sense, Hollywood doesn't exist except as "an imaginary city . . . in the mind of anyone who has, in his mind, lived there" (Friedrich 1986, xii). "Hollywood was never more than state of mind," wrote journalist Ralph Hancock in 1949 (63). And director John Ford said: "Hollywood is a place you can't geographically define. We don't really know where it is" (Bordwell, Staiger, and Thompson 1985, xiii).

Hollywood, that is, became both a physical site and a place of fantasy—a place of marvelous dreams, dramas both personal and historical, and infinite possibility. Screenwriter Tim McCanlies reflected on his moving to Hollywood in 1979: "I went right to Hollywood, thinking that's where the center of the film business would be, thinking that all the studios must be right there. I was so naïve" (Field 2004, 49). But studios were not necessarily located there; by the late 1970s, Hollywood had already become "an almost mythic place where the movie folk spent money on personal expression" (May 1983, 189). "If you go looking for Hollywood," comments film historian Richard Maltby, "the sign won't help you find it because the place you're looking for isn't really there" (2003, 5).

As Hollywood historian Paul Zollo writes: "Hollywood persists in existing as both an actual place and as a metaphor for the entertainment industry that extends far beyond its physical borders." It is "forever on the map of the world and the human psyche" (2002, xiv). Most importantly, Hollywood is a metaphor, a symbolic repository of hopes and dreams.

Hollywood as a Repository of Hopes

Far more than the motion picture capital of the world, Hollywood became a place of ambition and fulfillment. The symbolic significance of Hollywood as a repository of hopes is fundamental to the orientation of members of Oasis Christian Center. Hollywood is "Her Highness of Hype, dispensator of silver nitrate dreams, merciless siren, enchanting temptress" who signified "to many, . . . the highest hopes, the ultimate attainment" (Torrence 1982, 9, 133). Comedian Jonathan Winters said that for him, "coming from Dayton, this was the dreamland. The place of dreams" (Zollo 2002, 230).

Hollywood's sense of place, rooted in the historical development of the region, is part of the palpable ambiance of Oasis and gives texture to the disappointment routinely found among its members (see chapter 5). The imprinting of the geography of Hollywood on the modern mind began as early as 1915: "The allure of Hollywood began then, as it has ever since, to lure thousands of young hopefuls each week from all parts east to Hollywood Boulevard, which quickly became known as 'the boulevard of dreams' and, as was inevitable, of broken dreams" (Zollo 2002, 22). The phrase "going Hollywood" in the early twentieth century stood for the willingness to give up one's social roots to pursue the promise of fame and fortune amidst the enthralling social mix of the region. "By the early 1920s, when people spoke of American motion pictures they began to use the name Hollywood to describe the place, a people, and as many over the years have said, a state of mind" (xiv). The space of Hollywood took on gravity, a magnetic draw for the ambitions of many.

The interplay between Hollywood as a destination and Hollywood as a dream melded into the geography of Hollywood when movie scenery blended with the urban landscape, beginning most notably with Griffith's construction of ancient Babylon for his 1916 film *Intolerance*. The massive set, including huge columns topped with white elephants, remained standing at the corner of Hollywood and Sunset until it deteriorated many years later. Retaining massive movie sets in its neighborhoods and streets spawned a growing theatricality in the architecture of Los Angeles and the construction of public spectacles for sightseers, a practice now most prominently seen in the storefronts of Universal Citywalk. Even Griffith's original Babylon, complete with elephants and columns, has been recreated just a few blocks north of Oasis's Destiny Theater at the newly constructed Hollywood and Highland plaza.

Young girls especially were drawn to the movie production business of Hollywood for its glamour and fantasy. A few that migrated became famous, more became extras, and the rest became workers and domestic servants in the city. Recognizing the destitution of wannabe starlets, the Young Women's Christian Association (YWCA) sustained a ministry to provide many with a home.

For these and other dreamers, Hollywood represented a triad of luxury, fun, and freedom from the moral constraints of Victorian life, an image it perpetuated through its films. For example, the Paramount Famous-Lasky 1923 film *Hollywood*, directed by James Cruze, showed celebrities enjoying the good life beyond class hierarchies. Such films contributed to the belief that success in Hollywood is possible for anyone with talent willing to take risks and work hard. This is what Scott calls "the romanticized image of Hollywood itself, not as the rather humdrum working environment that it actually is, but as the 'home of the stars'" (2005, 7). Because studios were located so close to one another, it was once possible to see celebrities working, traveling, or eating on the streets of Hollywood, the same streets that now feature the Walk of Fame. Aspiring actors could thrill with the occasional excitement of seeing a real star on the street, but these recognized and highly paid stars were precious few in comparison with the multitudes of people still seeking their big break.

The cultural producers of media who live in Hollywood today continue to emphasize its romantic aura in their artistic endeavors, drawing on local icons and traditions to create a streamlined, popularized, global image. Central to the cultivation of Hollywood's mystique is the movie premier, the source of much admiration and envy in the symbolic economy of Hollywood. The Hollywood premier is one of the most dramatic vehicles for synthesizing all the elements of the motion picture industry. Invented by Sid Grauman at his famous Chinese-themed theater (located just north of Oasis's Destiny Theater), premiers were "designed to be as flashy and glamorous as the movies were magical, . . . providing that rare opportunity for the public to see movie stars in the flesh" (Zollo 2002, 26). Grauman understood with his first premier that the personal presence of the star—in this case, Douglas Fairbanks, star of *Robin Hood*—would be as dramatic as the film itself. A connection was established for the public between the studio and the screen, the actor and the studio, and, most importantly, the actor and the character on the screen. Appearing at movie premiers became one of the earliest defining marks of celebrity.

For many of the ambitious, fame and fortune is bound up with the Hollywood sign, one of Los Angeles' most famous landmarks and visible only minutes' drive from the Oasis building. Although the fifty-foot-high sign on Mt. Lee appears to mark the location of Hollywood, it originally read "Hollywoodland" and was an advertising gimmick by developers to sell five hundred wooded acres of knolls and canyons over the business district in 1924. Many decades later, the Hollywood sign became the principal symbol of the hopes and dreams embodied in the aura of the motion picture industry. Today, tourists still crane their necks to catch a glimpse of the sign, and an aspiring actor on the 2005 reality television show *Fight for Fame* on E! said, "When I was eight and I saw the Hollywood sign, that was it. It got me." Oasis members and other residents still thrill at the sight, part of their local scenery.

Less well known is the despair the sign represents. Actor Lillian Millicent "Peg" Entwhistle moved from New York to Los Angeles, where she failed to repeat her stage success on the silver screen (Torrence 1982, 133). In September 1932, she climbed to the top of the H on the Hollywood sign and jumped to her death. Since then, hundreds of actors have repeated this grim gesture, mocking the promise and hope embodied in the giant letters.

The Dream Threatened

Hollywood's tranquil, cultivated setting began to disappear in the 1930s and 1940s, as new apartments, offices, hotels, and, of course, movie theaters filled in the open spaces. Above all, the construction of the Hollywood Freeway through the Cahuenga Pass cut through dozens of well-established neighborhoods and destroyed hundreds of historic homes. Completed in 1954 and built to accommodate the growing number of industry personnel who had moved to San Fernando Valley for cheaper housing, the 101 freeway ushered in the era of urban commuting. In theory, greater access would allow more people to easily eat and shop in Hollywood; in actuality, it stimulated an even greater boom in suburban shopping malls, movie theaters, restaurants, and alternative sites for entertainment. Hollywood lost its pedestrian, residential, community feel and become a place of office buildings and tourists. The diffusion of office sites, studio buildings, and personnel that characterized much of the area from the mid-1950s directly contributed to the decline of Hollywood.

For years, the dilapidated Hollywood sign mirrored the urban blight that increasingly dominated the region. Parts of letters were missing, and much of the structure had either collapsed or threatened to collapse. The sign had fallen into disrepair. The Hollywood sign that had been the signpost of the area's hopes and dreams now took on tawdry connotations.

Visitors in search of their image of Hollywood found, in addition to the increasingly tattered Hollywood sign, a drab town, decayed buildings, and all-too-ordinary street corners. In the mid-sixties through the mid-seventies, Hollywood accelerated its urban decline by becoming a hotspot for the pornographic industry. "At the feet of the shiny high-rises along Sunset and Hollywood Boulevards lay what was beginning to be called Sin City, in which pornography was the heir apparent. Festering pockets of sex bookstores, sex shops, strip joints, clip joints, sex-movie houses, massage parlors, and the like were catering to a new clientele of drifting dregs from the flower-child Sixties, dopers, dealers, drag queens, pimps, prostitutes, muggers, transients, crazies, and other unsavory sorts, who were drawn to the area like maggots to rotting flesh" (Torrence 1982, 263). Adult movie theaters multiplied, and there soon followed adult bookstores, topless bars, massage parlors, and live sex shows all along Western Avenue and Santa Monica Boulevard (248). Many blamed the increased sex trade for the higher rate of street crime. Youths drawn to the mystique of Hollywood were finding a different type of excitement in sexual and hallucinatory experimentation. The teenage drug scene expanded.

Within two decades, Hollywood was transformed into a wasteland overflowing with drifting, rebelling youth on the run from the conventional norms of Middle America. A carnival atmosphere reigned, and Hollywood's image deteriorated still further. The end result was an economic downturn for the region. Businesses floundered. Tourists turned away, disillusioned. The atmosphere announced tacky rather than glamorous. Tinseltown had tarnished.

The restoration of the Hollywood sign became an important rallying point for the recovery of the romance of Hollywood. Mike Sims of the Chamber of Commerce said, "If you can't save the sign, you can't save Hollywood" (Torrence 1982, 269). Its deterioration reflected the neglect of the Hollywood area; its restoration would express and affirm the resurgence of enthusiasm, energy, and dazzle the area desperately needed. The sign has no practical value, but public sentiment convinced the Los Angeles Cultural Heritage Board to declare it a historic cultural monument. Fund-raising efforts continued through the 1970s and culminated in the unveiling of a newly built sign in 1978. As one local business owner said, "The sign is the hook we needed to hang the restoration of Hollywood on" (274).

The Hollywood Walk of Fame Star and Revitalizing the Dream

The significance of the Hollywood Walk of Fame star is connected to the importance of the symbolism of Hollywood to the local economy, especially the tourist economy. In the late 1890s, tourists arrived to see the hillside Victorian homes of the wealthy. Electric streetcars ran from downtown Los Angeles through Hollywood and on to Santa Monica and the ocean. In Hollywood, tourists stopped to see the extensive gardens and creative work of the world-famous French artist Paul DeLongpre and to enjoy a meal at the Glen Holly hotel. By the mid-1910s, tourists came to watch silent films being made on the streets, a constant source of free entertainment. For years, tourists could spot celebrities walking around or working in public.

Even as the mystique waned, and the excitement and immediacy of classic Hollywood deteriorated into gaudy lights, dirty streets, and tawdry vendors, the desire to recapture the glitz and glamour grew. As far back as the mid-1950s, the Hollywood Chamber of Commerce took the initiative to bring the magic back, at least symbolically.

> Having demolished many of the existent links to its glamorous past, and having masked the former grandeur of many of the boulevard's classic build-ings, they had created a Hollywood Boulevard devoid of any connection to that which gave it cachet, its former promenade of stars. And so a symbolic connection to the stars was created, a physical reminder that this old boule-vard was not simply another busy business thoroughfare in Anytown, USA, but the Street of Dreams itself, the very street where the world's greatest stars once walked. (Zollo 2002, 50)

They had walked here in the 1920s and 1930s, when Hollywood Boulevard was the city's main thoroughfare, and the talented of Hollywood lived nearby. Then, adoring fans thrilled when they caught glimpses of screen stars on the streets, going about their daily life.

The plan to pay tribute to Hollywood's stars culminated in the famous Walk of Fame, as well as a new system of ultrabright streetlamps. A promenade of bronze stars became a symbolic substitute for a time when film screen stars actu-ally lived and worked in the city. The first eight bronze stars were placed in 1958 at the northwest corner of Hollywood and Highland. By 1960, a thousand such stars graced the streets.

The Chamber of Commerce did little else to improve the area for sight-seers until 1975, when the Revitalize Hollywood Task Force emerged to make the area a better place to live and work—and more importantly, to visit and spend. They stimulated the remodeling of old buildings to attract new businesses, as well as the renovation of parks and shopping districts, and the addition of attrac-tive landscaping. Although Hollywood lacked a central focus point for most of the later twentieth century, in 1986 Hollywood Boulevard between Gower and La Brea, several city blocks north of the Oasis Christian Center, was officially designated a historic district.

Today this area features a refurbished Hollywood sign; the Kodak Theater, the new home of the annual Academy Awards ceremony; new shops, offices, and several minor attractions at Hollywood and Highland; and a more earnest effort to keep streets clean and clear of homeless people and public nuisances. The immediate area is still filled with tiny shops touting all forms of kitsch—t-shirts, keychains, shot glasses, and fake autographs. Nevertheless, tourists are likely to experience more of their idealized notion of Hollywood than has been possible in decades.

A core feature of the historic Hollywood area now consists of long avenues filled with the bronze-filled pink and charcoal terrazzo sidewalk stars of the Walk of Fame. These abundant stars, along with the newly constructed plaza at Hollywood and Highland and the restored El Capitan, Chinese, Egyptian, and Pantages Theaters, a symbolic center for the Hollywood dreamland, enchant sightseers and fuel the aspirations of industry wannabes. With more than sixty million visitors yearly, Hollywood is second only to Disneyland in popularity in Southern California.

The Hollywood Star: Rooted in Place, Reclaiming the Dream

The revitalization of Hollywood, the cleaning up of the slums of America's Tinseltown to restore the glory and glamour of the iconic images of classic Hollywood, began at the same time that Pastors Philip and Holly Wagner started their first Bible study. When Oasis refurbished the historic movie house in an art deco theme that hearkens back to the glory days of Hollywood, the restored Destiny Theater mirrored the revitalization of the area (see chapter 6).

The significance of the controversy over Jesus' Hollywood star, then, is enmeshed in the history of Hollywood and the recent attempt to resurrect its romanticized glamour. The Hollywood Chamber of Commerce seeks to protect the trademark of the bronze Hollywood star because it is vital to their business interests to maintain the secularized romance of the region and continually draw tourists (and more businesses) to the region. By installing a Hollywood star for Jesus, Oasis participates in the revitalization of Hollywood, upholding its idealized past and at the same time sacralizing that glamour for the purposes of the church. The prestige of the Walk of Fame stars spills over to the idyllic image of the grandeur of the church, its goals, and its mission, as well as to the largely mythologized ambience of the newly constructed image of Hollywood. Moreover, the redemption of Hollywood from destitution and decay is broadly connected with the wish of the congregants at Oasis to capture the most important and glorious aspects of the Hollywood aura and clean up the industry through the application of an earnest spirituality.

The ambiguous alliance between Hollywood and Oasis signals a new alliance emerging between Christianity and the Hollywood entertainment industry. For many, the bronze Hollywood star has become the core symbol of achievement in the entertainment industry. But this symbol did not always exist; it emerged out of an initiative to capture the romance of Hollywood's golden years and stimulate the local tourist economy. Oasis not only acknowledges but also fully embraces the dream of Hollywood in the installation of its own star-shaped symbol.

3   Love and Hate between Hollywood and Christianity

CHARLENE: Being in the entertainment industry is hell. It is a world all its own. Everything that you could possibly want to do, want to have, get involved with that is negative is there. You can sleep your way to the top. You can have any kind of drugs you want. I mean it's a Sodom and Gomorrah type of thing.

On the hills of the Cahuenga Pass, the corridor connecting the city of Los Angeles to the San Fernando Valley along the 101 Hollywood Freeway, stands a white cross. At night, the solitary lighted cross is impossible to ignore, a clear and unyielding brightness against a vast canopy of black. The cross commemorates the life of Christine Witherhill Stevenson, heiress to the Pittsburgh Paint fortune and generous philanthropist. She dedicated her wealth and creativity to promoting a religious drama of the life of Christ called *The Pilgrimage Play*. The play used words drawn from all four Gospels (in the King James version) and incorporated authentic materials from the Holy Land that Stevenson had bought to add vividness and authenticity.

To build a permanent outdoor venue dedicated to her play, Christine Stevenson recruited wealthy friends and neighbors to form a financial group, the Theater Arts Alliance. The Alliance acquired the property for what is now the Hollywood Bowl but, to Stevenson's dismay, decided the site was best suited for outdoor music. So, although the Hollywood Bowl would feature among its programs annual Easter services, sacred music performances, and religious dramas, it failed to be dedicated to the ongoing performance of scenes from the life of Christ (Smith 1993).[1] Persisting in her vision, Stevenson purchased in 1920 a twenty-nine-acre natural amphitheater in the foothills not far from the Hollywood Bowl. This she named the Pilgrimage Play Theatre (today the John Anson Ford Amphitheater). The lighted forty-foot steel and concrete cross was placed alongside the Pilgrimage Theater in 1923, the year after Stevenson died, the product of volunteer labor, donated light bulbs, and electricity eventually paid for by Southern California Edison. Performances of the play continued until 1964 under that memorial cross. (The play's phenomenal success inspired Cecil B. DeMille's landmark 1927 production of the life of Jesus, *The King of Kings*.)

Standing on a hill overlooking Hollywood, the cross is for some a reminder that Hollywood grew in the shadow of an idealistic community of churches that had formed toward the end of the nineteenth century a sacred haven of belief and practice in Southern California. Stevenson's vision to promote the life of Christ through drama is indicative of the religious intensity that existed in Hollywood at the turn of the century. Her vision also foreshadows the earnest desire of many Christians, like those at the Oasis Christian Center a century later, to promote Christianity through entertainment media.

How did Hollywood stray so far from the values of its immediate religious community? The divide between Hollywood and Christianity was neither necessary nor predestined, and the widespread condemnation of Hollywood among Christian leaders for most of the twentieth century neither uniform nor inevitable. From the earliest days of motion pictures, aggressive debate addressed the nature of film as an innovative medium of communication and its potential for use as a means of evangelism and religious instruction. Oasis participates in this ongoing debate through its ministry and uniquely frames a congregationally based solution to resolve the tension between Christianity and Hollywood.

Hollywood as a Churchly Utopia

The establishment of churches in Southern California was not a smooth process. The region's religious history reveals a surprising swing from midcentury apathy to vibrancy a few decades later. In the mid-1850s, Los Angeles was considered a deeply irreligious town. One historian recounts a Sunday in 1853 when a Reverend Freeman was about to preach the first Baptist sermon in the area. Residents of the town wanted to disrupt the meeting. The pastor went to the pulpit, "calmly drew a gun and placed it on the altar beside the Bible, and, as a further precaution, his two sons took seats in the front row, with pistols protruding visibly from their pockets" (Hancock 1949, 240). A year later the first Presbyterian services were held, but the founding pastor, Rev. James Woods, soon left the city in disgust; coming after him two years later, Rev. T. M. Davis also left in disgust.

Yet Southern California emerged as a surprisingly religious place. The earliest Protestant churches did not meet in church buildings but in renovated buildings formerly used for irreligious purposes. The Reverend Adam Bland started the first Protestant church in Los Angeles by acquiring the El Dorado, a famous saloon. Other church services in the early days were held in storehouses, schoolrooms, and homes. Hollywood's first church structure, the German Methodist Church, was built in 1876 by Rev. George Shultz to house a handful of members (Torrence 1982, 37). Others soon followed, but overall, the city had a small number of meeting spaces, and two or more congregations often used the same space at separate times (Hancock 1949, 241). The challenge of building space and funds for development persists and stimulates the creative use of already established facilities among Southern California churches like Oasis.

Although Los Angeles had no Protestant church before 1850, by the turn of the century it was described as a city of churches (Hughes 1924, 17). From 1890 to 1945, during the birth of the Hollywood film industry, Protestant evangelicalism dominated. With many Protestant fundamentalists and a strong presence of mainline denominations, Los Angeles gained more than two hundred churches. In addition, several important denominations and religious movements were founded there, including the Pentecostal movement, the Church of the Nazarene, Aimee Semple McPherson's Foursquare Gospel movement, the Christian Fundamentals League, and a cadre of independent fundamentalist Christian churches and colleges. By the 1950s, Los Angeles boasted some of the largest congregations in the country, including the First Congregational Church of Los Angeles, Immanuel·Presbyterian Church, and Lake Avenue Congregational Church. In the latter twentieth century, Southern California was the setting for several innovative religious initiatives, most notably the Vineyard Movement (with John Wimber in Anaheim), the Calvary Chapel Movement (with Chuck Smith in Costa Mesa), Campus Crusade for Christ (beginning at UCLA with Bill Bright), and the Trinity Broadcasting Network (with Paul and Jan Crouch at the international headquarters in Costa Mesa). Several prominent pastors and their vibrant congregations—including Robert Schuler's Crystal Cathedral, Rick Warren's Saddleback Community, John MacArthur's Grace Community, Tommy Barnett's Dream Center, and Erwin McManus's Mosaic—continue to spur the development of innovative churches, despite the absence of traditionally defined church property.

Meanwhile, early on, those outside the religious realm "complained that Los Angeles was an excessively puritanical, provincial, and narrow-minded city" (Pitt and Pitt 1997, 429). This was especially true for the growing area of Hollywood, where religion was deeply rooted. When Harvey and Daieda Wilcox established their 160-acre ranch, Hollywood, in the 1880s, they hoped the area would be "a peaceful and sacred oasis where devout Methodists like themselves could practice abstinence and other virtues" (Zollo 2002, xiii–xiv). The Wilcoxes were abolitionists from Topeka, Kansas, dedicated to temperance and absolute moral purity. They and other families sought to create a city that would be a model Christian community. As wealthy residents built palatial homes on tracts of land Harvey Wilcox sold, Daieda Wilcox persuaded them to donate generously to the building of schools, libraries, and churches. Moreover, the local government pledged to provide churches with free land if they located within the city limits (Starr 1985, 284–285).

The founders of Hollywood in fact viewed the city as the moral capital of Southern California (Belfrage 1938, 184). The city was to become a utopia of like-minded Christians who would live in a community devoted to virtuous moral living. Both the sale and consumption of alcohol was prohibited. Strict laws against liquor elevated the possibility of godly living, for nothing was to dilute the power and purity of the Holy Spirit. Longtime *Los Angeles Times* journalist Sam Hall Kaplan called the early Hollywood a vision of a "genteel, Bible-quoting suburb for those wanting to escape the hard-drinking, decadent lifestyle of downtown L.A." (qtd. in Zollo 2002, 6). And the sanctified atmosphere continued well into the new century. A Hollywood minister in 1924 wrote: "It is not a community given up to orgies and wild extravagances of life" (Lindvall 2001, 286). C. Clayton Hutton, a reporter who came to Hollywood in 1928 looking for sin instead found, "to his disappointment, sobriety and sanctity." As he reported: "We who had set out to find the lair of Hollywood's sin listened to the Sermon on the Mount" (Zollo 2002, 24).

Given that "the puritanical atmosphere of Southern California in the early years of the twentieth century made it distinctly inhospitable to the early motion picture industry and the people associated with it," the development of the entertainment industry in the region is surprising (Scott 2005, 13). But the moviemakers did come, and within a few short decades of the early twentieth century transformed the churchly utopia into the home of the Hollywood film industry. Christian settlers and show business profiteers coexisted in an uneasy relationship.

The clash between Christians and the entertainment industry was not confined to Hollywood. Across the country various forms of inexpensive entertainment emerged among the working-class population—dance halls, professional sports venues, beer gardens, bowling alleys, saloons, and movie houses. Movie houses were inexpensive to operate; owners obtained licenses for only twenty-five dollars instead of the five hundred dollars required for vaudeville and stage theaters and encountered little enforcement of health and safety standards (Sklar 1994, 30). With the combination of entrepreneurship and popular demand, theaters mushroomed throughout the nation.

The Protestant Victorian Ideal and Attempts to Censor Films

Victorian culture still reigned when motion pictures emerged, and movie audiences were almost entirely Protestant (Jowett 1999). Religiously motivated responses to this new, powerful medium were inevitable. Terry Lindvall and other historians assert that the entertainment industry "transferred social authority from the church to the larger secular culture. Motion pictures often adopted religious forms and supplanted religious needs to become an alternative 'church' of the twentieth century" (2001, ix; see also Lyden 2003). Hollywood's cultural influence began to overshadow that of religious leaders, prompting a series of efforts to manage and control the content of motion pictures. Thomas Edison, who invented the core technology for motion picture production and exhibition, told heads of the movie industry in 1924: "I believe, as I have always believed, that you control the most powerful instrument in the world for good or evil" (qtd. in Zollo 2002, 18). Christians agreed and came to view motion pictures as distracting people from spiritual matters. They believed that constraining these ungodly forces through boycott or censorship would accomplish the redemption of Hollywood.

Protecting the Vulnerable

The story of religious conflicts surrounding the motion picture industry is largely that of the attempt by Protestants (and, soon, Roman Catholics) to control the messages, values, and lifestyles presented to the American public, especially to children and immigrants being socialized into U.S. society. The antagonism between Christianity and Hollywood, then, is primarily rooted in reaction to film content, which included portrayals of ideals and lifestyles that strayed from traditional values. More troublesome to Protestants was that the audience for motion pictures was limited only by the price of admission. A few cents granted anyone access to a world of immorality.

The earliest nickelodeons catered to recent immigrants and working-class audiences who were not constrained by Victorian-era values. Over half of the four thousand films shown in the United States in the several years before 1910 were produced in France, Germany, and Italy without consideration for American moral sensibilities. Many films were channeled to exclusively male audiences in vice zones of cities and included showings of boxing matches, slap-stick humor, and vaudeville skits that directly affronted cultural authority and middle-class tastes. According to May: "These tales depicted pre-marital sex and even adultery as human weaknesses or even as something to be enjoyed. Rarely was sex condemned outright. Interracial love affairs also received a sympathetic portrayal" (1983, 37). The screen magnified everything, and the emotional impact registered by observers at the time attests to the impact such powerful images made on the audiences. Movie audiences were captivated; Protestant reformers were appalled.

Religious groups joined forces with conservative politicians, journalists, social workers, and various voluntary organizations in public pronouncements and periodic crusades to severely limit the operation of movie theaters. The desire by Protestant cultural elitists to curb the content of motion pictures was part of a broader attempt to reform U.S. society as a whole. Protestant reformers had focused on social problems like prostitution, child labor, housing conditions, and alcoholism. Such efforts were part of the larger Progressive reform movement (of which people like Hollywood founders Harvey and Daieda Wilcox were members) that created national legislation like Prohibition and the raising of the age of consent.

Protestant reformers viewed themselves as protectors of American society, including the moviegoing public. They believed the United States had achieved its high level of industrial and material civilization "because of the inherent superiority of Protestantism and its underlying moral code, which stressed hard work and adherence to a simple, God-fearing, evangelic faith" (Jowett 1999, 17). Protecting Protestant morality was thus important for national survival, and civic and religious leaders demanded children be socialized properly and immigrants acculturated correctly (see Lindvall 2007, 82–92). Yet Garth Jowett (1999) is one of many who cite the presence of Jewish entrepreneurs as owners of movie houses and eventually as leaders of motion picture studios as threatening to the Protestant establishment; this view finds anti-Semitism never far beneath the surface of Protestant concern about the dangers of film.

Then as now, movies were not just a form of diversion but a means of disseminating information about culture, normative expectations, and moral standards. In the minds of reformers, films were active agents of corruption, especially for children and single adults attending movies unchaperoned in dark auditoriums. The Protestant establishment viewed movies as vulgar expressions of unseemly aspects of life, and Victorians feared that movie houses would lure innocent young men and women into red-light districts and infect them with the social ills of the day. Protestants were particularly concerned to control and shape the cultural standards being promoted. In short, "the growing notoriety of nickelodeons brought movies to the attention of the middle-class men and women who serve the institutions of social control—the churches, reform groups, some segments of the press, and ultimately the police" (Sklar 1994, 30).

Public sentiment among the middle and upper classes turned away from films and viewed movie audiences with patronizing condescension. For example, in the 1909 Block v. Chicago case presiding chief justice James H. Cartwright refused to issue permits for two films considered immoral, because "on account of the low price of admission," movies were "frequented and patronized by a large number of children" in addition to "those of limited means" who are unable to attend the productions of plays given in regular theaters. In his role as a civic guardian, Cartwright felt obligated to safeguard these vulnerable populations, including "those classes whose age, education and situation in life specially entitle them to protection against an evil influence of obscene and immoral representations" (qtd. in Jowett 1999, 23). Prominent among reformers was the Reverend William Shaefe Chase, one of the architects of a bill in Congress to establish a national censorship board to be named the Federal Motion Picture Commission. In Chase's view, "the evil motion picture carries its influence to the youngest and most ignorant" (32). Further:

> Here is a new condition with reference to the childhood of our country, a new danger that confronts them. . . . Who do [the filmmakers] propose to have control of this great invention? Who are going to be the people, if this bill is not enacted, who will educate the children of our land? A few motion-picture manufacturers, whose principal motive is making money. (qtd. in Vasey 1997, 23)

Other reformers issued similar pronouncements of warning and danger. Movies were "five times more powerful than any other form of communication" wrote one (May 1983, 53).[2] A professor of philosophy claimed that "pictures are more degrading than the dime novel because they represent real flesh and blood characters and import moral lessons directly through the senses. The dime novel cannot lead the boy further than his limited imagination will allow, but the motion picture forces upon his view things that are new, they give firsthand experience" (40).

One 1907 film, *The Great Thaw Trial*, which graphically portrayed a lurid love triangle, resulted in a call for public hearings on the role of movies in public life. The New York City papers quoted a Reverend Foster's reaction; he said that theaters were able to "corrupt the minds of children" (May 1983, 43). Lurid acts like kissing and deception of parents were condemned. Joseph R. Fulk, superintendent of schools in Nebraska, wrote that "free hours determine the morals of the nation," and that movies "engendered idleness and cultivated careless spending" at the "expense of earnest and persistent work" (40; see also Fulk 1912). He added that "sacred and private" experiences shown on the screen encouraged "too much familiarity between boys and girls" unchaperoned in theaters. Further, Fulk claimed, "the constant playing on the emotions of the child and adolescent tends to overexcite and prevent the development of the emotional life, generating an overwhelming drive for something that stirs and thrills. This growing desire is apt to lead children and adolescents especially away from right ideals and morality. Here lies the greater danger of the motion picture drama" (41).

Prominent middle- and upper-class Protestant women mobilized as moral guardians of the new industrial order. Women's clubs and reform groups sought to protect what they believed to be the most impressionable members of society. Concern for children was paramount—unchaperoned youths attending motion pictures in darkened, unsupervised places—and then for illiterate adults. The patronizing tone is conveyed in the words of Mrs. Everett Hamilton, representative of the General Federation of Women's Clubs, who spoke before the New York State Legislature: "The most important thing is the safeguarding of morals not only of children but also the vast throng of persons, who, while perhaps they are not children in years, may be children in minds" (qtd. in Vasey 1997, 25).

The concern for morality reached the highest levels of government. A study commissioned by President Theodore Roosevelt in Washington, D.C., concluded that films encouraged "illicit lovemaking and iniquity" (qtd. in May 1983, 44). City and national governments were to exercise moral leadership in what they allowed and what they constricted in public behavior. Mayors, judges, and police officers joined the effort to curb the evil influence of motion pictures.

Additional concern arose for single women, whose purity was threatened by darkened movie houses that provided "opportunities for making chance acquaintances and familiarities of one kind or another; . . . the darkness takes away the feeling of responsibility" (qtd. in May 1983, 38). The advent of movie theaters coincided with changes in women's dress, greater mobility of young people, and changing roles for women. But the cult of domesticity still exerted powerful pressure, and a good, moral home headed by a morally strong woman remained the best guarantee of a moral society.

Protestant reformers and public sentiment mobilized local, state, and national governments and law enforcement agencies to consider strict limits on film exhibition. Common across the country at the time were blue laws that prohibited the sale of liquor and kept saloons and other immoral places closed on the Sabbath day, and church leaders debated whether Sunday was an appropriate day for attending movie theaters. With laborers having more freedom for leisure activity on the weekends, churchgoers were forced to choose between church and theater. Organizations such as the American Sabbath Union and the Lord's Day Alliance fought to apply a strict enforcement of blue laws on theaters to prevent the showing of motion pictures or, at the very least, ensure that pictures were religious in nature and that profits were donated to charity (Lindvall 2001, 253).

The most famous confrontation of Protestants attempting to enforce Sunday blue laws took place on Christmas Day, 1908, when leaders from every Protestant denomination asked the mayor of New York City to enforce the power to close theaters due to their violation of Sunday closing laws. Mayor George B. McClellan Jr., on his own walking survey of movie theaters, found many movie houses that channeled people through exits directly into saloons every day of the week. Under orders of the mayor, all licenses were immediately revoked. The police department closed all 550 movie theaters in the city. A lawsuit, led by William Fox, soon allowed the theaters to reopen with an increase in licensing fees, greater police oversight, and restrictions on children's attendance (Sklar 1994, 31).

Unanticipated Alliance between Purity and Profit

The threat of film censorship and theater closures prompted an unanticipated alliance between entertainment and religious leaders. Film producers and theater owners began to consider the possibility that the appearance of immorality was bad for business. In a strategic move, the motion picture industry lobbied Congress to reject bills for national censorship of movies and began cooperating with the desires of reformers by creating their own national censorship board.

Although enforcing morality is frequently cited as the reason for establishing the National Board of Review of Motion Pictures in 1909, motion picture companies voluntarily submitted their films for censorship out of fear that their operations would be uniformly shut down.[3] Censorship added to the financial cost of making films, and the fear among film producers was that they would be subject to a variety of different censorship boards in cities across the country; this would cost them not only in licensing fees but also in the editing and reproducing of motion pictures for exhibition. At the same time, movie exhibitors had begun screening films and cutting out portions of films before showing them both to shorten the program to fit in a two-hour format (economic reasons) and to avoid offending audiences (economic and moral reasons). Motion picture producers were increasingly anxious to find one censorship body to which they could submit rather than numerous local bodies across the country. The risk of losing profits was worth the cost and effort of obtaining a seal of approval before their film was shown to the public.

The voluntary censorship of films in the United States also helped the film industry curb the competition from foreign films. Soon after the formation of the National Board of Review between 1908 and 1914, film producers sought to create uniquely Americanized, wholesome entertainment. The seal of approval granted U.S. films access to more theaters across the country, making censorship a lucrative, rather than restrictive, practice. This early financial success of U.S. films goes far to explain what made Hollywood an "American" rather than a worldwide phenomenon (see May 1983, 60–66).

The National Board of Review (initially the National Board of Censorship) operated in New York. Motion picture executives voluntarily submitted their films for review while balancing concern for the protection of free speech. Now through voluntary participation, the motion picture industry fended off national and state censorship, avoiding costly fees and rejected products. Film producers accepted the system since objectionable films could be fixed before hitting the screens. Because the board censored scenes or, rarely, entire films, the films that did pass and receive the board's seal of approval gained immense moral legitimacy. Although the National Board of Review was not explicitly religious, the majority of members were Protestant (clergy and conservative Christian believers) and membership included representatives from the Federal Council of Churches and the YMCA. Although the board itself was exclusively male, more than a hundred female assistants actually viewed all films and applied conservative moral codes to them. These women in theory represented general public opinion; in practice, they represented middle- to upper-class Protestant, Anglo-Saxon values.

The National Board did not last, discredited as it passed on problematic films and approved morally questionable ones. Reformers like Jane Addams were horrified by the promotion of racial discrimination in D. W. Griffith's 1915 film, *The Birth of a Nation*. Film producers from Protestant backgrounds admitted that films were approved that they did not want their own wives and daughters to see (May 1983, 62–63). Some states continued to set up their own censorship boards to review films—Pennsylvania in 1911, Ohio in 1913, Kansas in 1914, Maryland in 1916, and New York and Virginia in 1922. But standards within each state were vague and often seemed arbitrary, and standards between states often conflicted (Vasey 1997, 66).

The National Board also became less important once filmmakers understood that naughtiness sells and put scantily clad women in their films. When censors attempted to ban them, the subsequent publicity attracted more attention. Mack Sennet, a filmmaker known for his Sennett Bathing Beauties, noted that "women's clubs, reformers, preachers, and the police gave us a million bucks worth of publicity" (qtd. in May 1983, 104). The popularity of risqué films grew, along with a more playful approach to sexuality on screen.

The Grand Social Worker: Movies as a Force for Good

Between 1905 and 1908, some Protestant reformers began to speculate about the power of movies for good and showed great optimism for the possibility that films could contribute to a continuation of conservative, Victorian-inspired, largely Protestant Anglo-Saxon values. Reverend Charles Parkhurst, pastor of Madison Avenue Presbyterian Church, was a prominent member of the National Board of Review. Years after taking part in the closing of New York nickelodeons in 1908, he believed that his crusading had yielded a rich result. Movies increasingly were seen as healthy recreational activity for respectable families. Jane Addams in 1907 wrote: "It is unfortunate that the five cent theaters have become associated in the public mind with the lurid and unworthy. Our experience at Hull House has left no doubt that in time the moving picture will be utilized for all purposes of education. Schools and churches will count film among its most valuable entertainment and equipment" (qtd. in May 1983, 149). Since movies could penetrate the subconscious, they could instill in people the highest moral ideals imagined by the Victorian morality—sobriety, sexual purity, and wholesome family life; movies would become a grand social worker (May 1983, 53). Motion pictures would be enlisted to solve social problems, inculcate positive values, and perform civic functions like teaching history.

Once movies were granted moral legitimacy and movie houses became acceptable for middle- and upper-class clientele, theaters became firmly entrenched as a national public institution.[4] During this shift, the popularity and profitability of films skyrocketed. Most theaters in 1908 held only three hundred people, but theaters in 1912 held over a thousand in luxurious surroundings (May 1983, 66). Between 1908 and 1914, movie theaters appeared in wealthy suburbs of New York, Boston, Chicago, St. Louis, and Atlanta. The advent of sound had unanticipated consequences. Wiring theaters for sound was expensive, forcing the closing of numerous small movie houses. More upscale, larger theaters took their place and changed the perception of the moviegoing experience. It reflected a higher level of status and attracted higher classes and more wealthy patronage.

Perhaps most important in the development of the movie industry, the growth of consumerism altered the values of mainstream society. Fulfillment of Progressive Era values lay not in restraint of self, but rather in the cultivation of leisure through consumption. Americans could enjoy a new, wholesome, family-centered life by attaining a level of wealth that allowed for the playful cultivation of ease. Capitalism and consumption formed an alliance that changed the nature of daily life for Americans in the twentieth century. In the midst of increased mechanization and bureaucratization, the tensions that sprang from automated work were offset by leisurely activities outside the workplace.

When films became mainstream, producers no longer found the National Board's seal of approval necessary for getting films distributed to theater owners. That is, they no longer depended on external review to find acceptability. The rise of the celebrity-driven star system enticed people to see films without regard for their moral content. Also, the moral nature of the stories portrayed on film changed during this time, stressing triumphant heroes and heroines who overcame villains and other dangers.

Motion pictures certainly remained under the watchful eye of Victorian Protestants throughout most of this early period, but the reformers' hold on films crumbled around 1915. By 1920, motion pictures had escaped completely from Protestant scrutiny. Movie theaters had transformed from urban storefront nickelodeons catering to immigrant and working classes to suburban movie palaces in sumptuous buildings. Movie theaters become more respectable, and motion picture studios became more morally sensitive out of eagerness to avoid government oversight and, especially, to boost their financial bottom line. Not until the emergence of another monitoring organization in 1922 would religiously motivated censorship again take center stage.

Film's Initial Embrace by Christian Leaders

Apart from the attempt by mainstream Protestants to control the moral content of films, many church leaders embraced film as a medium capable of powerful religious impact. The attitudes of these early film advocates anticipate those found at Oasis and other Hollywood-friendly churches (see chapter 4). Knowledgeable clergy insisted that the work of censorship boards was not only barring the distribution of immoral films but also raising the quality of motion pictures as a whole. Indeed, progressive clergy believed the degrading effects of film were grossly exaggerated. "While the salient 'hot' issues of censorship and moral reform attract secular perspectives on movies, propagating an enduring fiction that religion and the movies were born antagonists, other data indicate that many men and women of faith, both in the clergy and in the industry, sought a union of art and religion" (Lindvall 2001, x).

The inventor of reel-to-reel film was, in fact, an Episcopalian minister, Reverend Hannibal Goodwin, who wanted to make the Bible come alive and thus hold the attention of children for religious instruction. He found Edison's stereopticon problematic; the glass slides broke easily and were hazardous to the children of his Sunday school. Concern for the safety of children and the imperative of religious instruction through film motivated his invention of celluloid, the core technology that sustains the distribution and presentation of film today.

Early Christian Advocates for Film

A visionary group of pastors, missionaries, and denominational leaders were among the earliest advocates for the use of films (Lindvall 2007). The concern among progressive ministers was less about which films to keep away from the public than about how to promote certain films that should be exhibited as widely as possible. They wanted to generate and support films that highlighted the values and beliefs they treasured, to spend less time judging the content of films and have more time to use the medium for accomplishing their own purposes. Colonel Henry H. Hadley, an early revivalist, exclaimed, "These moving pictures are going to be the best teachers and the best preachers in the history of the world" (qtd. in Lindvall 2001, 4). Around the turn of the twentieth century, the Salvation Army established a Cinematograph Department, and Herbert Booth, son of the founder, claimed to be the first to use film for the cause of Christian mission (Lindvall 2007, 56–57). Film became an evangelistic tool.

Reverend Dr. Harry W. Jones, a pastor from Long Island, took film evangelism to the next level. After seeing a film based on John Bunyon's *Pilgrim's Progress*, Reverend Jones resigned from his congregation: "I realized there I was wasting my time. . . . A religious subject, thus tactfully and reverently treated, in my opinion, will do more to advance the cause of religion to uplift humanity than a thousand eloquent preachers ever can hope to accomplish by their oratory" (qtd. in Lindvall 2007, 68). He obtained a motion picture projector and began showing religious films as his ministry. Among progressive clergy like Jones, motion pictures became a weapon against the immoral influences of secular culture.

Several more prominent clergy embraced the new medium of film to promote religious ideas to the broader population. The evangelist Billy Sunday had his own preaching filmed, with his expressive gestures the point of interest for audiences, as the films were silent. Sunday also appeared in other films alongside celebrities like Douglas Fairbanks, accentuating his relationship with movie stars.

By 1920, Methodist and Episcopalian missionaries were using film widely to spread the gospel message in Africa, China, India, and Malaysia. Many argued that there was simply no reason why every church in the United States should not have a motion picture projector and screen as part of its equipment, as essential as the organ, the pulpit, or the pews. K. S. Hover claimed, for instance, that "Satan has a new enemy," and that "the motion picture has actually become a part of the equipment of the up-to-date church" (Lindvall, 2001, 48). A century later, Hover's claim is true. Through dramatic presentation, film is the handmaiden of theology and expands the missionary work of churches.

Before World War I, the appeal to masses of church-connected viewers came from films containing a large number of religious themes or allusions. Religious films depicting the events of the Passion Week in the life of Christ were produced as early as 1897, and as early as 1900 churches were exhibiting motion pictures not only for their own congregations but also for the broader community. It is estimated that by 1920 more than two thousand churches were using motion pictures (see Lindvall 2001, 229). Another estimate suggests that as many as fifteen thousand church schools and clubs were using motion pictures as part of their ministry (Maltby 1999, 62).

Pastors hoped to accomplish with film what Christine Witherhill Stevenson had intended with her *Pilgrim Play* amphitheater. The greatest difference is that Stevenson fulfilled her vision by dedicating a single geographic site to the dramatic expression of a Christian message and ideals, while the most revolutionary aspect of film is its portability. Christian leaders saw that the new medium would release Christians from particular localities; they could show films anywhere a screen could be put up. In addition, film reels can be shown repeatedly without loss of quality. And the cost of setting up and displaying films is drastically less than the cost of building theaters or paying professional actors.

The Reverend Herbert A. Jump, pastor of South Congregational Church in New Britain, Connecticut, was an articulate early spokesperson for the use of motion pictures (see Lindvall 2007, 59–65). Jump's vision for the use of motion pictures resonates with the practice of contemporary seeker-sensitive churches as modeled by the Oasis Christian Center and, more famously, by Willow Creek Community Church as a tool for appealing to the interests of the unchurched.[5] In his 1911 pamphlet titled *The Religious Possibilities of the Motion Picture*, Jump stressed that Jesus used dramatic stories to convey the essential message of Christianity. He then argued that film is the most important invention since the printing press in the fifteenth century. Films would make the gospel story vivid and, most important, interesting.

> Why is it the people do not come to church? Many of them will say frankly, "your church is not interesting; your service of worship is adapted only to the taste of those who've been trained up to it; I cannot understand your music and cannot keep awake for your sermons; the interest of the clergyman seems to be far more with Johoikim and Ancient Babylon than with the living men in the living issues of today. In a word the church is dull, therefore I stay away." (qtd. in Lindvall 2001, 57)

For Jump, film projectors became consecrated machines that would bring in the unchurched. "The great cry of the unchurched millions ought to ring in our ears permitting us no rest until we have availed ourselves of every conceivable device to attract them to the higher life in Jesus Christ" (Lindvall 2001, 73).

As one of the earliest advocates for the use of motion pictures by the church, Jump articulated several important points. Films can be a source of wholesome entertainment equivalent in value to organ recitals and concert choirs. Films are also effective media for religious instruction. Films highlight and promote missionary activities both at home and abroad. They offer a means for public service by providing education and awareness regarding social issues and social needs. Most important, films provide preachers forceful and engaging illustrations for truths they wish to convey. As a result, Jump claimed, "the motion picture preacher will have crowded congregations, not because he's sensational but because he's appealing to human nature more successfully than his fellow-clergyman, because he's adapting his message to the psychology of his hearers, because he's employing a better pedagogical method" (Lindvall 2001, 71). Jump advocated that everything else in the service essentially remain the same. Hymns would be sung; prayers would be offered. Motion pictures would illustrate and provide modern parables for the sermon that would help people in living everyday life. Bible reading and film exhibition were two sides of the same coin. New technology produced a greater impact than the spoken word alone.

Reverend Jump acknowledged the reticence among contemporary church leaders to embrace this new technology. Foreshadowing Everett Rogers's (1995) articulation of the cycle of innovation, Jump believed that films as a novelty would meet opposition. Yet he combats opposition based on films' supposed frivolity by presenting a vision of the great potential of film for Christian ministry. Sensitive to the fear among church leaders of showing films that compromised moral values, Jump provided an initial list of wholesome, biblically sound films that could be shown in the church. He believed that once films demonstrated their utility for religious work, they would follow the same path that the organ and other musical instruments had taken in church history. As with those innovations, films would become acceptable and sacred. And in a growing number of media-friendly churches like Oasis, Jump's prophecy is being fulfilled.

Film Projection as a Crowd-Gathering Gimmick

It is easy to see movie houses as inherently antagonistic to churches. Clergy in the first decades of the 1900s witnessed crowds flocking into movie theaters every evening, a sad commentary on the numbers who entered their churches. Some church leaders saw the competition for audiences as a battle for the allegiance of people's beliefs and values. Yet many who witnessed the popularity of movie houses concluded that showing motion pictures—*any* motion pictures—would be the key to raising attendance in the church. As one saying went, "Pictures in the pulpit mean more people in the pews." A publication aimed at church leaders advised: "Show movies, survive and flourish. Ignore movies, decay and perish" (qtd. in Lindvall 2007, 96).

Church leaders quickly found that the novelty of motion pictures enticed people into church who would never have attended services. Many saw films as a gimmick; people were fascinated by the experience of watching motion pictures—almost anything that was put onscreen attracted attention. One church in Rockport, Massachusetts, that incorporated films into its services reported an increase in Sunday evening attendance from twelve congregants to more than five hundred (Maltby 1999, 69). With the proper equipment, churches could host free screenings as a supplement to their overall ministries and remain the center of local community life, drawing in even youth, who especially were interested in attending movie theaters in contrast to attending church.[6]

Across the country, churches purchased projection equipment, installed permanent machines in their auditoriums, and integrated film clips into their Sunday services. The Presbyterians, for example, gratefully accepted Eastman Kodak's donation of two thousand motion picture projectors in 1920 and through their use saw tremendous growth in attendance at Sunday evening and Sunday school programs. Short films became sermon illustrations. Other films would be shown before Sunday school to ensure attendance that morning. Some pastors rented equipment and raised giant screens in large, outdoor venues. Increasingly, missionaries used films to record the work of the gospel in foreign lands, showing them to raise compassion in home congregations for peoples in distant cultures.

Why Motion Pictures Failed as Church-Sanctioned Technology

Despite progressive initiatives, churches soon rejected motion pictures. Around 1925 religious leaders became disillusioned with the possibilities of film, and by 1930, they had decisively isolated themselves from the entertainment industry. Rather than integrating film as a staple of congregational ministry, church leaders eventually resisted it on two fronts, economic and moral.

Moral Resistance: Celebrity Scandal

Celebrity scandals in the early history of Hollywood deeply affected the moral evaluation of motion pictures. Church leaders could not reconcile the use of films with the apparently rampant immorality in the movie industry. Much has been made of the scandals of the early 1920s, when Hollywood became known as Tinseltown, Babylon, the Sodom of the Twentieth Century, and the Graveyard of Virtue. The media grabbed hold of any Hollywood rumor to satisfy the insatiable curiosity of the public (see Anger 1973). Lavish lifestyles of successful movie stars fueled celebrity scandal, and popular images of Hollywood emphasized its shallow and morally chaotic nature. The astronomical salaries of top celebrities were as widely known as their indulgence, greed, and immoral excess. Especially between 1921 and 1923, sex, drugs, and murder became the dominant themes emerging from Hollywood.

The first major celebrity scandal implicated Roscoe "Fatty" Arbuckle in 1921. He had been the lovable Fatty, the highest-paid comic of the silent film era, a favorite of children, the subject of good clean slapstick fun, but he was implicated in an alcohol-fueled sexual orgy and a needless death. The popular comedian was accused of raping and killing a twenty-five-year-old woman at a wild party in a San Francisco hotel suite as he celebrated his new three-year $3 million contract with Paramount. In three separate trials Arbuckle was found not guilty, but the stain on his reputation kept him from ever working again.

Other prominent stars marred by scandal at this time included box-office draw Wallace Reid, who died in a padded cell in a private sanitarium for drug addiction. His studio had supplied morphine to boost his energy, hide his exhaustion, and help him maintain a grueling acting schedule. A string of deaths from drugs or alcohol abuse included those of Barbara La Marr, Jack Pickford, and Jeanne Eagels. The mysterious murder of director William Desmond Taylor became another occasion for highlighting the moral atmosphere of Hollywood. Although Taylor had been president of the Screen Directors Guild and was socially very popular, it was discovered that he had abandoned a wife and daughter in New York before coming to Los Angeles. And Mary Pickford, known as America's Sweetheart, spoiled her image when she divorced her husband and immediately married the dashing actor Douglas Fairbanks.

The stain on these and other celebrities labeled movie actors as perpetual symbols of decadence, debauchery, and depravity (Yallop 1976). By 1922, a congressional investigative report spoke of Hollywood as a place of "debauchery, riotous living, drunkenness, ribaldry, dissipation, [and] free love" (qtd. in Clark 1995, 71). Stars were said to earn five thousand dollars a month or more—an outrageous and untrue figure—that they spent on immoral living. Despite movie studios' desperate attempts to stave off further scandal through the introduction of morality clauses in actors' contracts, popular culture had already absorbed the image of wild parties and a common theme of sex, drugs, and alcohol among Hollywood celebrities. Hollywood became a symbol of an immoral way of life.

Economic Resistance: Refurbishing Auditoriums

In addition to religious leaders' moral judgments of Hollywood was economic resistance. The cost of acquiring this new technology was not cheap. When Chester C. Marshall sent out an informal survey in 1924 soliciting opinions about the use of films in church, he found that almost everyone believed films could fulfill a very important function. Yet all felt the expense required to prepare a theater was a major obstacle (Marshall 1925).

With prearranged seating and a central viewing area, church buildings were well suited for film exhibition. The minimum equipment required was a motion picture machine, a projection booth, and a screen. Once a church invested in this equipment, film rentals averaged only a few dollars a day. Still, the cost of appropriately refurbishing a church for exhibition in the era of silent films was relatively high. The projection unit alone cost around $225. And since early projection machines generated a great deal of heat, they required installation of special fireproof booths for around $500 to $700. The building also required additional preparation in terms of ambience and artistic surroundings.

With the introduction of sound, motion pictures became more popular and more profitable for the studios, but more costly for churches. Silent films required only organ accompaniment, and most well-furnished churches had exceptional organs with skilled musicians trained to play them. But the transition to talkies in 1927 made church buildings instantaneously obsolete as theaters. Just as thousands of movie houses across the country were forced to change to accommodate talking pictures or go out of business (which many did), churches continuing to show films financed extensive renovations, which included purchasing new equipment and wiring for sound. Many were unable to finance such expansive modifications and opted to let the new medium pass them by. The religious use of film suffered from lack of financial investment.

Censorship and Bureaucratizing the Religious Control of Film

Once church leaders walked away from involvement in film, censorship again dominated the relationship between Christianity and the motion picture industry. For the studios, censorship continued to be an economic issue, since failure to comply with moral standards led to a decline in profits. But censorship standards between states were not uniform, introducing costly changes to films to ensure their conformity to censorship boards. And since studios were required to pay fees to boards for review, Ruth Vasey points out, "local censorship became equivalent to a multiple taxation on motion pictures" (1997, 17).

In addition to domestic concerns were concerns about the international market. Foreign countries were also scrutinizing films and consequently banning distribution of films from offending movie studios. The Mexican government, for example, viewed the common portrayal of villains in U.S. westerns as Mexican as an insult to their national character and banned films from certain studios in 1922 (see Thompson 1986, 140).

The specter of a collective boycott by women's clubs, church organizations, and anti-vice committees loomed. "With the professional puritans clamoring for a clean-up, something had to be done to improve the movie's image—*fast*" (Anger 1973, 40). On the one hand, audiences responded to those elements that were most resisted by reformers. On the other hand, the imposition of federal oversight would bottleneck profits.

Religion and the Hays Office

Enter the most significant agency of censorship in the history of U.S. cinema, the Motion Picture Producers and Distributors of America, Inc. (MPPDA). Founded in March 1922, the MPPDA was often called the Hays Office, acknowledging the powerful role of the association's president, Will H. Hays.[7] Its purpose was to curb direct censorship under the federal office of the National Recovery Administration (NRA) created by Theodore Roosevelt during the depression by assuring the government that industry leaders were committed to the same morality codes included in Article VII, General Trade Policy Provisions, of the NRA Code. The first line of the MPPDA morality clause states: "The industry pledges its combined strength to maintain the right moral standards in the production of motion pictures as a form of entertainment." When several industry groups disputed the clause, the Hays Office persuaded them that a voluntary industry checkpoint would free the industry from imposed federal censorship. The clause remained a central part of the Hays Office mandate.

The Hays Office is typically considered a type of censorship board, and it exercised considerable influence over the content of U.S. films.[8] But the development of the MPPDA was a function of the interest of major movie producers and distributors to resolve conflicts between companies domestically and overseas. The MPPDA stepped into the unanticipated role of ensuring the moral quality of movies so that movie studios could distribute films both domestically and abroad with the fewest problems with censorship or viewer indignation.

The MPPDA was the film industry's foreign trade representative and acted as a liaison between the motion picture industry and the U.S. Commerce and State Departments to negotiate business practices and transactions between the United States and foreign countries. Its charter did not provide for any influence on movie production, yet the MPPDA gradually extended regulatory oversight of production until it became in the 1930s a centralized agency for scrutinizing the content of films.

Hays maintained an open-door policy and voiced concerns about the moral value of films as family entertainment. He sought to increase the number of affluent middle-class patrons to theaters so that their revenue would positively influence films' moral content.

Most significant, through the MPPDA, censorship remained primarily in the hands of Protestant reformers. Hays's qualifications consisted of critical business and political connections—he was Republican Party national chair in 1920—and especially "his reputation for high morals and his prominent membership in the Presbyterian Church" (Vasey 1997, 28). The concern for public morality expanded to include Roman Catholics, who began to organize more diligently in the 1920s against the negative influence of motion pictures. The efforts of the Catholic Legion of Decency became a powerful and unavoidable force, particularly beginning in 1930 with the construction and enforcement of the Hollywood Production Code.

From 1934 to 1966, it was almost entirely through the enforcement of the Production Code and through censorship that Christians exerted influence on the entertainment industry. Enforcement of the code by representatives from the Roman Catholic Church and the Southern Baptist Convention and leaders from a few other Protestant denominations successfully kept explicit sex, violence, profanity, and blasphemy from the screens. In addition to the Protestant Commission organized by the National Council of Churches, other organizations concerned with the moral content of films included the Daughters of the American Revolution, the Boy Scouts, the General Federation of Women's Clubs, the International Federation of Catholic Alumnae, the Russell Sage Foundation, the National Education Association, the National Catholic Welfare Conference, the National Congress of Parents and Teachers, and the YMCA. The pressure brought by these groups gave Hays more power in the industry to push for compliance.

Attempts to Partner the Church and the Entertainment Industry

Although most church leaders by this time were reticent about involvement with the film industry, Hays tried to stimulate a partnership between church leaders and motion picture producers. In 1923, the MPPDA established a Committee on Religious Pictures to inform the motion picture industry of the needs of churches and to help churches understand the problems involved in meeting their demands. Two years later, the MPPDA established a policy to encourage production of motion pictures for use by churches through the Religious Motion Picture Foundation. Specially made motion pictures with biblical themes and based in historical fact would serve as supplements to sermons. As there was little enthusiasm for the project, it was abandoned. Funds failed to appear from any quarter to support the expense of moviemaking for such a limited audience.

Along the same lines, however, some Christian denominations, especially the Lutherans, Methodists, and Presbyterians, made an effort to coordinate financing, production, and distribution of films for churches in the early 1920s. Alongside them were nonsectarian firms like the Christian Herald Motion Picture Bureau and the International Church Film Corporation. These and other more modest efforts experienced a sharp rise and fall in activity throughout this decade. Both the production and consumption of church films peaked in 1925. Unable to attract enough interest from church leaders to sustain the expense of the endeavor, almost every Christian-sponsored film company ceased to exist by 1930 (Lindvall 2007).

Another attempt at an alliance between motion picture producers and religious leaders can be traced to Cecil B. DeMille's 1927 film *The King of Kings*. A hugely expensive film produced for around $1.5 million, it purported to be a nonsectarian biography of Jesus, nearly the fortieth in a long line of film versions. DeMille's film was intended to be ecumenical, and he initiated production with a religious service that included Protestant, Catholic, Jewish, Buddhist, and

Muslim faiths. He brought clergy on as advisers. The film was marketed through Protestant churches, and publicity included names of ministers who had visited the set while it was being produced. The picture strategically premiered on Good Friday, April 15, 1927, in New York, and later in Hollywood as the first movie shown at Sid Grauman's new Chinese Theater. Unfortunately, it was not a financial success. Religious leaders were not satisfied with its portrayal of Jesus, and despite the attempts to avoid controversy Jewish leaders criticized the film for placing the blame for the crucifixion on Jews.

Although *The King of Kings* was intended to establish a mutually beneficial relationship between liberal Protestant churches and the motion picture industry, such alliances ultimately failed because of a clash of agendas. Religious leaders wanted to shape the content of the films, and motion picture producers merely wanted new avenues to promote and publicize the film. Religiously affiliated organizations served as endorsers of products already made rather than as shapers of films (see Maltby 1999). These and other initiatives to spur the development of films explicitly oriented for use in churches failed.

Morality and the Hollywood Production Code

Ultimately, the alliance between purity and profit was ingeniously achieved through the cultivation of what would be known as The Code. In 1930, Martin Quigley, an influential Catholic layperson, and Daniel A. Lord, S. J., a Jesuit priest from St. Louis University, created the Hollywood Production Code. Although on the surface it was intended to enforce the religious morality of motion pictures, it also cleverly accommodated box-office demand for provocative films and the desire for profit among motion picture producers. The Production Code did not remove sex and crime completely from motion pictures but provided a formula that minimized them, keeping them within middle-class moral boundaries.

The Production Code laid the foundation for the future cooptation of Hollywood by industry-friendly Christians like those at Oasis (see chapter 4). As historian Robert Sklar explains: "Their solution allowed for a fairly wide leeway in depicting behavior considered immoral by traditional standards—adultery or murder, for example—so long as some element of 'good' in the story balanced what the code defined as evil. This was the formula of 'compensating moral value': if 'bad' acts are committed, they must be counteracted by punishment and retribution, or reform and regeneration, of the sinful one" (1994, 174). In the words of the code itself: "Evil and good are never to be confused throughout the presentation." Guilt must be punished and viewers must not be encouraged to sympathize with any form of sin or crime.

The Production Code, then, was not imposed on Hollywood by intrusive outsiders but played an integral part in the broader context of the motion picture industry regulating itself in anticipation of higher profits. From the standpoint of studio executives, the emphasis on proper morality in films was a bow less to morality per se than to the profit motive. With the rise of Hollywood scandals, "stacks of uncomplimentary press notices continued to pour in; pronunciations rang out from the pulpits. It was not divine wrath magnates feared, but retaliation at the box office" (Anger 1973, 40).

A top priority was removing from films the possibility for public offense both at home and abroad. Avoiding overseas censorship was vitally important; as much as 35 percent of gross revenue in the motion picture industry came from foreign markets before World War I (Thompson 1985). "Just as the American industry had to persuade its domestic audiences that its products were harmless and morally sound, its domination of the markets of the world depended at least in part on its ability to convince its foreign customers that its output was inoffensive and ideologically neutral" (Vasey 1997, 8). Business relations demanded that the motion picture industry find ways to monitor itself before lawsuits or public outrage ruined it financially. The solution paved the way for Christians who would see Hollywood as a means for accomplishing the worldwide work of God to reconcile humanity to himself. Hollywood could become a site for the sacred, and work in the Hollywood industry could be seen as a sacred calling.

Isolation as a Forerunner to Participation in the Hollywood Industry

The historic antagonism between Christianity and Hollywood was not inevitable. Yet despite early, tentative alliances between church and film, the Christian church by the 1930s abandoned its involvement with the motion picture industry. At this time church leaders overwhelmingly walked away from relationships with the Hollywood industry and voluntarily isolated themselves from the new medium of film. Commenting on such amusements as dancing, playing cards, and attending the theater, the influential preacher R. A. Torrey would confidently state: "No one can indulge in these things and know the radiant Christian life" (Lindvall 2001, 119). Evangelist Jack Linn claimed that "a Christian cannot even darken a movie theater, and at the same time fellowship with Christ" (254). Christian participation in the motion picture industry, either as producer or as patron, was effectively stopped.

The most dramatic shift in the history of motion pictures—the transition from silent to sound—parallels the withdrawal of Christian interest in film. Movies became even more popular and their impact on culture more powerful after the transition, but the potential partnership between Christianity and Hollywood disappeared. In the end, Hollywood is foremost a moneymaking business, and the pragmatic morality driving a financially successful film is not the same as the religious morality promoted by churches in the region. Understandably, religious leaders were troubled that the influence of Hollywood threatened to surpass the influence of their religion. Ultimately in the minds of Christian leaders, films accommodated too much to the secular world. Although films had the potential for good, their potential for evil was greater.

Reverend C. F. Wimberly proclaimed that films appealed to the basest nature of human beings by "offering quick thrills to an increasingly pleasure-mad world" (Lindvall 2001, 109). Rather than films bringing the sheep into churches, films were stealing the sheep away.

Charles Johnson Post, writing for the *Christian Herald* early in the history of Hollywood, lamented that churches had passed up their opportunity to create substantive films.

> The churches were in a position to have stepped in—in the early days—and controlled the motion picture industry from the distribution end at least, i.e., the placing of films before the general public. And this in turn would have been a powerful factor in influencing the kind of film pictures that would have been produced. The churches should have used it as they used and use the printing press. . . . Instead of supplying a vital public need and themselves regulating the supply they lagged until they could furnish only denunciation. They have prayed for relief in a censorship when the work was in their own hands to make for progress and idealism. (1922, 466)

Decades would pass before a new dialogue on the use of film for Christian purposes would emerge, before ministries like the Oasis Christian Center would boldly move to integrate faith with involvement in the entertainment industry.

4   Save the World,
Starting in Hollywood

> DAMION: One of the things that's big on my heart
> is to be here in Hollywood now and to be trying to
> work in the industry and be a light of Christ and
> show people the idea that they have about Christi-
> anity isn't necessarily right.

Jesus' Hollywood star installed in front of Destiny Theater represents a bold
attempt to reclaim the entertainment industry for sacred purposes. But it is not
the only one. Oasis Christian Center is part of an informal network to reform
and redeem Hollywood.

Until the 1970s, it was unimaginable that one could be a conservative Christian and work in the Hollywood industry. In 1923, evangelist Jack Linn echoed
the sentiments of many conservative Christians when he labeled the Hollywood
industry the "Devil's Incubator," explaining: "I cannot speak for all, but I personally never knew a Christian actor, and if there were many moral ones—I mean
of clean, upright lives, free from the abuses of the day—I never met them."
Specifically, he felt "safe in saying that Christians are not actors or actresses, and
once converted they immediately quit" (Lindvall 2001, 275).[1] Christians of Linn's
persuasion believed Hollywood represented an uninhabitable spiritual climate.

Yet, attitudes are rapidly changing in the currently emerging drama of conservative Christianity and Hollywood, and Oasis is one of several ministries that
encourages and further stimulates the development of Christian actors, musicians, artists, and filmmakers. Pastors Philip and Holly Wagner and other church
leaders see the entertainment industry as a strategic place of ministry. One Oasis
staff member said, "If we have people in this business who are standing up for
God and living a life that is, you know, celebrating Him and also being true to
Him, what an impact that could have on this city." While the pursuit of fame
and profit inherent to the business are problematic for evangelicals, the evangelistic imperative makes the opportunity to influence millions of people at a time
compelling. These Christians expect to redeem Hollywood not as protesting
outsiders, but as productive insiders.

The shift in the relationship between conservative Christianity and Hollywood is occurring in two arenas—attitudes toward film content and participation in film production. First, Christians like those at Oasis are abandoning

their roles as watchdogs of film content and embracing their roles as creative interpreters. Many Christians, especially evangelicals, are not afraid of film and are eager to connect with popular culture. These Hollywood-friendly Christians are moving past the condemnation of films as immoral media and advocating a fresh use of films (whether made by people of faith or not) to advance spiritual, moral, and Christian themes. They are intoxicated with film's potential to distribute God-sanctioned messages to the masses.

The enforcement of the Hollywood Production Code and its embedded morality laid the groundwork for this hermeneutic embrace. Studios appeased the public's appetite for all manner of film content while satisfying religious conservatives by harnessing lewd or immoral actions on screen within explicit moral frameworks that reinforced right and wrong. This imposition of (at times artificial) moral frameworks set the stage for later conservatives to see films as inherently possessing deep moral structures to instruct the masses. Rather than vile and immoral, even the most objectionable film content is viewed as providing insight into the soul of popular culture and projecting spiritually astute messages of comfort and warning to the world at large. Through the skillful application of proper exegesis through books and sermons, church leaders are coaxing popular movies to reveal God-approved messages.

The second arena in which the relationship between conservative Christianity and Hollywood is shifting is in filmmaking itself: An increasing number of Christians are going beyond spiritual analysis of film to becoming filmmakers. For most of the history of motion pictures Christians have discussed the use of film as outsiders, and some church leaders early in the history of motion pictures lamented that the isolation and indifference of religious institutions left the medium of motion pictures entirely under the control of those who use it merely as a source of profit. Almost a century later, the discussion is changing. Christians are being urged to enter the Hollywood industry itself—a move that industry pundit David Bruce of HollywoodJesus.com has called a spiritual shift in Hollywood—and they find peers at churches like Oasis.

Another industry insider, Ted Baehr, points out that "a growing number of Christians these days have stars in their eyes; . . . 30 years ago there was a suspicion of the entertainment history in the church, now there's a keen interest in mass media entertainment" (2005, 1). A new generation of Hollywood Christians promotes the entertainment industry as a viable and important means to advance spiritually motivated content and thereby stimulate a spiritual revival. This new breed of Christian emphasizes that believers should be actively involved in creating the products of Hollywood.

In short, while conservative Christian arguments for and against motion pictures have not changed much in the past century, what has changed is the role of conservative Christians in the dialogue, with more and more participating as interpreters and producers rather than merely observers of the industry.

Hollywood Christians like those who attend the Oasis Christian Center are becoming not only religiously astute analysts of film but active participants in a loosely networked group of entertainment industry insiders reinvigorating the dialogue on the relationship between faith and film. Hollywood is the newest mission field, and these believers are taking occupational roles to create and distribute Christian-friendly content through mainstream media to affect popular culture for Jesus. And their influence is only now beginning to be felt.

Organizing the Mission of Hollywood Christians

Hollywood's Christians today are organizing to help aspirants navigate entry into the industry. Along with the many nonreligious guides to success in Hollywood (e.g., Buzzell 1996; Rodriguez 1996; Goldman 1984; Lumet 1995), specialized Hollywood Christian career guides are emerging. One such guide, Ted Baehr's *So You Want to Be in Pictures? A Christian Resource for "Making It" in Hollywood*, is an inspirational tour de force, which, according to the book jacket, "is a must read for any Christian aspiring to effectively reach the world through the media." Endorsed by a variety of Christian leaders that includes the president of the Southern Baptist North American Mission Board, the book is aimed at the faithful who have a calling to take on a career in the industry. Its goal is to show readers "how to use your faith to change the culture of Hollywood and the mass media of entertainment" (Baehr 2005, xiii). The book opens and closes with Scripture, contains an opening prayer, and maintains a conversational attitude addressed to industry aspirants. Baehr also encourages aspirants by including an extensive list of Christians in the entertainment industry with some of their accomplishments.

Such guides provide advice on paper, but the most important contemporary efforts consist of emerging organizations that bring the community of Hollywood's Christians face-to-face. Workshops, conferences, networking events, and focused programs provide information, training, fellowship, and excellent networking opportunities for Christian actors, writers, producers, directors, editors, agents, managers, and executives (Goodale 2001; Lindsay 2006a, b, 2007). Through participation in Hollywood-centered ministries, experienced Christians mentor other believers into the workings of Hollywood (even internships in studios) while encouraging them to sustain their moral integrity and vital spirituality.

Act One, Inc.: Training for Industry Success among Christians

Established by former nun Barbara Nicolosi in 1999, Act One, Inc., is one of the most prominent organizations inspiring believers to invest their talent in the Hollywood mission field. (Others include Inter-mission, Actor's Coop, Associates in Media, Catholics in Media, Intervarsity Christian Fellowship–Arts/Entertainment, the Los Angeles Film Studies Center, Mastermedia International,

Media Fellowship International, Open Call, and Premise.) Believing that spiritual change in Hollywood must come from within the industry rather than be imposed from without, Act One dedicates itself to training artist-apostles for the mission field of mainstream Hollywood. Although the organization has existed for only a few years, its alumni are scattered throughout the industry, gaining work, selling scripts, and earning awards. Several prominent Christian writers, directors, and producers are Act One faculty members who provide workshops and mentor others.

Much of the ideology of the group is encapsulated in *Behind the Screen: Hollywood Insiders on Faith, Film, and Culture*, edited by Act One associate director Spencer Lewerenz and Nicolosi (2005). The consistent theme of this volume is that Hollywood is a powerful medium for changing culture and that Christians can take on influential roles within the industry if they are talented and willing to work hard, and if they pursue the highest level of artistic quality in their work. Through the faithful effort of talented Christians, films can become a new form of public art used by the church in the same way "the great artistic achievements of the Middle Ages, the cathedrals, were located at the center of the community for all the people to use. Images in stone and glass presented the Christian story for all to see" (May 1982, 101).

If Christian filmmakers do not create films explicitly expressing Christian ideas, what differentiates theirs from humanistic films? By Act One's standards, religiously motivated films are similar to highly noble secular films. Act One wants to make the secular religious by making movies that carry religious messages. Overall, Act One makes conservative Christianity less problematic by promoting more general spiritual or humanistic themes. Christian dogma is routinely substituted for generalized spirituality or humanism.

The move toward using non-Christian stories and mythologies for specifically Christian purposes relates to Durkheim's reflections on Jesuit pedagogical methods in education in the late nineteenth century (Durkheim 1977, 233–51). Confronted with the laicizing policies of the Third Republic, which removed ecclesiastical authority and established state schools, religious schools in France were forced to accommodate to a secular regime. Durkheim describes how the Jesuits succeeded in their mission of providing Christian frameworks in a pagan culture by combining "the strictest personal orthodoxy with an indulgence toward the ideas and tastes of their opponents" (Jones 1999, 63). To accommodate the new concern for a distinctly civic morality, the Jesuits mined the mythology of the Greeks in order to continue to support what they believed to be essentially Christian values—humility, truth, and beauty. They understood that "to guide their age they would have to assimilate its spirit." In particular, "the Jesuit interpretation of Greco-Roman antiquity deliberately excluded everything specifically Greek or Roman, substituting an idealized, ahistorical civilization in which individuals were reduced to symbols of Christian virtues and vices—Achilles representing courage, Ulysses wily prudence, Numa the archetype of piety, Caesar the man of ambition, and so on. These general, unspecific 'types' could then be used to simplify the precepts of Christian morality" (64). Similar to the Jesuits' strategy, Act One operates in a subversive manner by connecting with broad humanistic goals readily assimilated into the Hollywood entertainment machine.

In a very real sense, Act One is attempting to raise a new form of religious authority that would communicate through the medium of mainstream film. Because the church as a whole has rejected Hollywood, programs and initiatives like Act One feel free to entrepreneurially stake a claim on how Christianity should be propagated in the modern world. Their influence is propelling others to reconsider the role of faith in the industry.

The Hollywood Prayer Network: The Power of Spiritual Gossip

The Hollywood Prayer Network (HPN) is another prominent conservative Christian organization. A nondenominational ministry endorsed by evangelistic organizations like Campus Crusade for Christ and by prominent Christian leaders like Bruce Wilkinson, its motto is, "Through prayer for Hollywood comes cultural revival." The group coordinates prayer for all aspects of the entertainment industry. A core theme is, "Stop protesting, and start praying." HPN pursues prayer in the belief that God intends Hollywood to be lovingly saved rather than hatefully condemned.

HPN began in 2001 and already has more than three thousand members. Through its Web site (www.hollywoodprayernetwork.org) and monthly e-mail newsletters, it regularly publishes lists of people and productions to pray for, along with monthly prayer requests, praises, news, and updates. HPN has more than four hundred one-to-one prayer partnerships, a program by which Christians outside the industry commit to pray for a specific Christian in the industry. HPN also creates Incognito Prayer Teams who pray anonymously for various media professionals. And the network provides bright red, oval-shaped prayer stickers for television remote controls that read, "Remote Prayer—PRAY FOR THIS SHOW."

The most impressive resource HPN distributes is *The Media Leader Prayer Calendar*. Published by Mastermedia International, this free, multicolumned brochure lists influential people in the Hollywood entertainment industry to pray for every day of the year. Larry Poland, the founder of Mastermedia International, explains the reason for putting out such a calendar:

> Perhaps at no time in American history has such a small number of men and women wielded such awesome and continuing influence over so many others as do the leaders of our media. Yet, the few hundred people who control film, television, the Internet, and other media are mostly unknown to

the American people. Because they are unknown, these leaders are seldom the object of the most powerful force on earth—the power of prayer to the living God. If the Scriptures had been written in this century, would not the exhortation to pray for those exercising governmental influence over us have been expanded to include those exercising media influence? I think so. (Poland 2005)

The calendar is divided into four quarterly brochures in order to keep the information continually updated. Media leaders are writers, directors, studio executives, and media personalities who "deserve our prayers" and are "one miracle away" from a transforming faith. A separate list of "cultural influencers" consists of celebrities with a dominating presence in the national culture, musical groups that have broad appeal, and popular television programs. Christians are to "pray that those seeking or needing a relationship with God will find him and the peace, healing, and hope which he provides," as well as "that Christians in media will lead godly, exemplary lives and that they will have loving boldness to express their moral convictions in their marketplace."

Oasis Christian Center: Spiritual Formation in Hollywood-Friendly Churches

Alongside parachurch organizations and resources like HPN, Mastermedia, and Act One are Hollywood-friendly churches, and the Oasis Christian Center is acknowledged to be an important example of those encouraging work in the entertainment industry. (Others include Bel Air Presbyterian Church, Malibu Vineyard, First Presbyterian Church of Hollywood, and Mosaic in Los Angeles.)[2] Many members came to Oasis on the basis of its reputation. On visiting the church, Tim, Jarrell, Brandy, and Brent each discovered Oasis leaders had backgrounds and relationships in the industry. As Brent said, "Maybe they're not actually entertainers themselves but they might be working for a film company or production company doing TV, doing music, you know, whatever it may be." Tim met another believer on a movie set and was surprised to find someone who was a Christian. He said, "That's doesn't happen often enough in Hollywood, you know." Jarrell said that in his first week as an extra on a movie set, "This girl told me about it, and I visited." Brandy had tried several other Hollywood churches before committing to Oasis. The church's services feature skits, films, improv theater, dance teams, and professional-quality music up to "the Hollywood standard," Brent said. "That's very attractive at this point now." For these and others, Oasis is a place especially for those in the entertainment industry.

Seeing Film through Spiritual Eyes

The first and perhaps most critical shift in conservative Christians' historical approach to the motion picture industry is in the moral revaluation of film content. Rather than using a decadent lens that immediately rejects films on the basis of violence, sexual activity, or the use of four-letter words, a number of Christians are advocating that films are secular expressions of biblical truth. For these Christians, movies provide a window into the American psyche and contain aesthetic, coded messages addressing spiritual longings in modern society. The first impetus for seeing film through spiritual eyes came from writer, producer, and publicist Malcolm Boyd.

Praeparatio Evangelica

Working in the entertainment industry until his ordination as an Episcopal priest, Malcolm Boyd was one of the first to argue for a reconsideration of film content. He argued that Christians must pay attention to significant cultural events in the world, especially the release of motion pictures. "The church must understand what the world is thinking, doing, talking about, being entertained by, voting for. Only then may the church—which is certainly in the world if not of it—speak to the world in dialogue, in intelligible communication, indeed, in the compassion of involvement" (Boyd 1958, 122).

Boyd's framework emphasizes the involvement of the Christian in absorbing the products of Hollywood. Understanding the products of the Hollywood industry is a form of *praeparatio evangelica*, preparation for evangelism. For Boyd, the greatest challenge for the Christian in the face of secular entertainment is to know how to interpret it.[3] *"The development of a Christian interpretation—and the sharing of it with others—is today a major frontier of evangelism"* (126, emphasis in original). Boyd acknowledges that over the twentieth century the motion picture industry became a network of cultural producers who both reflect and influence the values of the mainstream culture. He believed the process of creating artistic works constitutes a type of religious experience for secular humanists. Specifically, creative work evident through movies and television represents deep angst within humanity, questioning life's meaning and the goals of human existence.

Access to the creative works of motion picture producers thus allows discovery of the deepest questions of humanity. Boyd believes it is the task of Christians to help people realize the dynamic answer to those questions through the word of God. But not until the 1990s did church leaders take up Boyd's challenge.

Pastors and Film Exegesis

Harking back to the early days of film, progressive churches like Oasis are once again bringing Hollywood films into the sanctuary. The use of films in worship services is now a staple of many contemporary pastoral sermons. The equipment required for projecting lyrics of praise songs and salient points from sermons is the same equipment used to show films. In the twenty-first century, quotes, scenes, and plotlines from blockbuster films are replacing the historical illustrations in sermons in place since preaching manuals recommended their use in the 1800s. Erwin McManus, pastor of Mosaic in Los Angeles, was trained to use historical events to illustrate his sermons but has used films instead since the early 1990s. "No one knows world history anymore. Now they know films."[4] Pastors are actively co-opting nonreligious media to further religious goals and messages, using clips from blockbuster films to illustrate biblical truths and drive points home. At times, they build whole messages on a discussion of popular films.

Pastor Philip Wagner preached a sermon series at Oasis Christian Center in 2006 called Oasis @ Movies, for example, that focused on messages from films that connect with the Bible. He is one of many evangelical preachers across the country who see their role as accurately exegeting biblical truth from popular films for both believers and nonbelievers. Along with sermons on *The Lord of the Rings* and *The Da Vinci Code*, Pastor Philip connected stories projected on screen with stories from the Scriptures. He and a growing number of other church leaders find the gospel in any good film with ambiguous content, among them *The Fugitive*, *Forest Gump*, and *Pulp Fiction*, by placing their stories into a religiously framed meaning context (see Marti 2005, chap. 4). Pastor James Emery White of Mecklenburg Community Church in Charlotte, North Carolina, the former president of Gordon Conwell Seminary, created a four-week film series explicitly around the four highest-grossing films of the previous year—*The Passion of the Christ*, *Shrek 2*, *Spiderman*, and *The Lord of the Rings: Return of the King*. Each week he gave a full synopsis of the film and provided a steady stream of connections to spiritual themes. Other examples from across the nation are easy to find.

The primary difficulty with using film as a religious medium is that film is notoriously ambiguous to interpret. And it takes a tremendous amount of faith not in God but in a stable hermeneutic that exists within all human beings to believe any modern-day filmgoer will resonate with the religious themes a pastor says are imbedded in a film. The church service is a controlled environment that frames the sermon, which helps a congregation see what the pastor wants them to see in each film. Sermons can be framed within an overall context of the preacher and the church; however, a film shown in a movie theater is not similarly framed. Movie theaters are sites for exhibition; movie audiences do not represent a community structured around shared values. Films are shown without introduction and without a clear interpretive framework. The challenge for pastors like Pastor Philip is to find the affinities between the symbolic resources available in the Christian theological tradition and the symbolic universe established in any major motion picture.

Fortunately, blockbuster films offer preachers a vast array of rhetorical affinities because of the many symbols, meanings, and values embedded within them. The gospel message according to evangelicals is sufficiently broad to connect with the multivalent symbols, meanings, and values in blockbuster films. Such films offer preachers like Pastor Philip an almost endless resource for connecting ancient biblical ideals with contemporary popular culture. Maurice Halbwachs (1992) provocatively describes the nature of tradition in any theological system as offering many points of contact that allow masterful preachers to play with the steady stream of stories and images available through the Hollywood production machine. The pastor giving a sermon can highlight a particular idea and then show a film clip illustrating that idea. For example, *The Matrix* series, *The Star Wars* series, *The Lord of the Rings* series, and the growing *Chronicles of Narnia* series all offer rich, sprawling narratives of global battles between good and evil, which partly explains their great popularity as preaching material. And blockbuster films like the adaptation of John Milton's *Paradise Lost* planned for 2009 highlighted within sermons provide evangelical churches a resource for what they consider their most important mission: bringing in nonchurched people to their services. By bridging the sacred and the secular, preachers routinely show how popular entertainment enjoyed in the visible world points to spiritual dynamics in the invisible world.

Not only do pastors utilize symbolic affinities to theological truths, they also borrow the prestige of blockbuster films to support the status of the Christian message. Evangelical churches pursue converts in worship services with an eclectic mix of philosophical argument, personal testimony, popular science, and elements of popular culture, the most important being reference to motion pictures. Pastors borrow movies' success to give legitimacy to their own message. They believe unchurched people are more willing to attend a church that talks about film than a church that talks only about the Bible. What results is a patchwork quilt of arguments, allusions, and associations to wear down and draw in the seeker.

Resources available to Christian leaders for spiritually understanding film are surging. Dozens of new books carefully exegete the spiritual meanings of nearly every major Hollywood film.[5] The Church Communication Network (CCN) hosted a Narnia Outreach Training seminar, billed as an opportunity for leaders to learn how to use the film as an outreach opportunity; CCN urged them to "invite your community to explore its messages of reconciliation and forgiveness, love and grace." Other companies are helping studios connect with churches, since affirming Christian values in mainstream films boosts commercial success. Grace Hill Media markets itself as helping Hollywood to reach people of faith and creates resources for marketing films like *Cinderella Man* and *Kingdom of Heaven*. The company advised Sony Pictures on marketing *The Da Vinci Code*—a trickier task, as it is adapted from a novel that challenges the basic tenets of Christian faith. The comedy *Evan Almighty*, which adapted the story of Noah's ark, was bolstered by an "acts of kindness" campaign through ArkAlmighty.com and advertised to churches through Christian publications. Twentieth Century Fox has launched a newly branded distribution channel, FoxFaith, along with a Web site to promote a stream of new productions of Christian and family-friendly movies; the site includes a church resources link suggesting Bible verses to discuss in conjunction with scenes from the films.[6]

With and without the help of these resources, church leaders are reframing films produced for profit as religious authorities in their own right. It is interesting to find believers like screenwriter Tim McCanlies saying that "Christians do not have a monopoly on God's Word" (Field 2004, 60). A theology of film is being constructed such that non-Christian sources reveal God's truth, a notion Sheryl Anderson, a Christian media executive, supports: "We have to be willing to see Christ everywhere, to look for his message everywhere. We have to be willing to write and to watch stories of redemption, charity, and love and celebrate the Spirit inherent in them" (Lewerenz and Nicolosi 2005, 140). The spirit of God is inherent in non-Christian films because the truth of God can be drawn out of them through a spiritual analysis. Such efforts are accompanied by a profound belief that nonbelievers are able to recognize biblical truth even though they may not know its true, transcendent source. By paying attention to significant films, preachers can keep themselves in dialogue with the spiritual truths they believe are already being apprehended and can build on those insights in their sermons.

Changing the Morality of Hollywood Films: Patronage versus Boycott

This new open attitude toward film content affects the strategies conservative Christians are adopting to influence future film development. Earnest attempts to affect films' moral content through boycotting have most notably been aimed in recent years at Martin Scorsese's *Last Temptation of Christ* (1988) but also at the gay-themed *Priest* (1994) and the irreverent comedy *Dogma* (1999).

The boycotts, protests, and controversy that swirled around *The Last Temptation of Christ,* the most notorious depiction of Jesus in modern history, became a cultural phenomenon. The film veered from the biblical narrative, following the speculation by Kazantzakis, who wrote the novel on which Scorsese based the movie, that Jesus was sexually tempted in his relationship with Mary Magdalene. Christian leaders who attempted to steer the faithful away from the film were frustrated that the machinery of the entertainment industry could so easily and so widely promote a heretical vision of the Christ.

Boycotting has been advocated by denominational bodies, including the Roman Catholic Church and the Southern Baptist Convention, and by nonprofit organizations like the American Family Association. Campaigns organized by the Roman Catholic Legion of Decency have generated millions of signatures on petitions against films deemed offensive, and leaders of both Protestant and Jewish groups overwhelmingly supported these campaigns.[7]

Yet boycotting has fallen out of favor in recent years and patronage encouraged instead. Rob Briner, an advocate for both Christianity and the Hollywood industry, criticizes the use of boycotts against the industry by Christians: "Let's be honest: all our protests have done is make us feel good about standing up and being counted. They have not cleaned up Hollywood, nor will they. The studios just don't care. What will ultimately speak to them is profit" (Briner 1993, 91). His words echo those of other Hollywood insiders who understand Hollywood as a business. Dean Batali, a prominent Christian writer and producer, encourages Christians to pursue patronage: "Let them know when you see something you don't like, and send them praise when they deserve it" (qtd. in Lewerenz and Nicolosi 2005, 13). Barbara Nicolosi, another Christian Hollywood insider, writes: "Our fears and misconceptions have us standing on the sidelines, cursing and boycotting and begging for favors from the pagans who have paid their dues and have the power to green-light stories for the screen. The whole church needs to brood over what it means to be the Patron of the Arts in a Post-Christian setting" (117).

Patronage in this view is the active support of films that are morally acceptable, and it is a shrewd strategy that addresses what is most important to movie studios: financial profit. To make an impact on Hollywood, Christians need to make an impact on producers' bottom lines. Movie patrons have the freedom to determine what they want to see and what they will avoid by their choices at the box office. The Hollywood industry understands these choices as patron sovereignty. Movie producers are ultimately concerned about profit, so money made at the box office is the single greatest determinant of the future content of motion pictures. Films that attract revenue on the basis of the moral approval of social and religious conservatives encourage the industry to continue developing such films. Most recently, the strategy of patronage has promoted films like the apocalyptic *Omega Code* (1999), the animated *Jonah: A VeggieTales Movie* (2002), and the controversial *The Passion of the Christ* (2004), as well as the adaptation of the C. S. Lewis novel *The Lion, the Witch, and the Wardrobe* (2005), the retelling of the Christmas story in *The Nativity* (2006), the biblical drama of Esther in *One Night with the King* (2006), and the spiritually motivated antislavery campaign of William Wilberforce in *Amazing Grace* (2006).

The strategy of patronage is not new. As early as 1916, Christian writer Orrin G. Cocks gave his own practical suggestion for influencing films: "Go to them; don't stay away," and let the owner of the theater "know when you are pleased. Speak to him about the future shows. Support the decent, conscientious men; and there are many. Discriminate between houses, if necessary" (qtd. in Lindvall 2001, 146). In his role as president of MPPDA in the 1920s and 1930s, Will Hays actively promoted patronage as a way of influencing the content of films. He hoped that by persuading members of the affluent middle class (estimated by Hays and his committee to be around 40 percent of the American public) to attend films, he could force motion picture producers to take into account the nature of audience demand in the moral content of their films.

In 1925, the Reverend C. L. Collins also stressed patronage as the avenue of change:

> If Christian people always absent themselves from the picture theater, the management is left with nothing but the baser element of the community for his patronage and he must cater to them or go out of business. It seems to me, therefore, that the moral and Christian people hold the question of better or poorer pictures very largely in their own hands. . . . We can help create and foster a virile public sentiment that will demand good pictures and none other. . . . We should boost and boost hard whenever a notably good screen production comes along. . . . If we want the motion picture business turned over to the devil, lock, stock, and barrel, let Christian people boycott it. But our boycott would not put the motion picture out of business. Such action on our part would simply compel all connected with the industry to make pictures to suit people of low morals or of no morals at all. Just as the Church, long ago, began to make use of the best in music for the glory of God, so would I have us make use of the best of the art of the motion picture for the glory of God and the good of man. (qtd. in Lindvall 2001, 312)

Similarly, in 1929, Rita McGoldrick of the International Federation of Catholic Alumnae suggested: "Producers who show . . . that they are making a sincere effort to raise the standards of the screen entertainment deserve the endorsement and cordial support of organizations such as ours" (qtd. in Vasey 1997, 79).

More recently, Jonathan Boch, a Christian leader who connects Christians with mainstream media that agrees with their values, has put forth the same argument in what he considers a fairly simple plan to revolutionize the Hollywood industry: "Go to *more* movies. Yup, that's it. Go to more movies. No boycotts. No press conferences. No marches. No posters or flyers or mailers or phone calls. No citizens or blockades or protests or picketing" (qtd. in Lewerenz and Nicolosi 2005, 191). If Christians attend more films, Boch's thinking goes, they could become the largest moviegoing market in the world, and the Hollywood industry will have to be attentive to their desires. As Ted Baehr sums up the notion: "Every time you buy a movie ticket, it is a vote to the producer to make more of the same" (2005, 226).

Films as Moral Mouthpieces of Popular Culture

How did film content become saturated with moral messages and amenable to spiritual exegesis? After all, Hollywood is a capitalistic enterprise, a "commercial institution, engaged in manufacturing and selling a specific product in a capitalist marketplace" (Maltby 1983, 10). But Hollywood has also been a moral battlefront since its earliest days, although the most important early conflicts were not religious but political, battles between the pursuit of a humanistic agenda for social change and the pursuit of financial profit.

Politics and Morality in Early Hollywood

In the beginning, Hollywood consisted of a large collection of progressive filmmakers who sought to educate and uplift a working-class audience. The development of a cinema with an intentionally broad base of relevance to large audiences meant that film could become a medium of communication for the masses and an instrument for positive social change. Studio heads did not operate in an intellectual or political vacuum but relied on a network of writers and directors who created the films they sold and distributed. These early writers and directors were not particularly religious but often were members of the American left, willing to sacrifice financial security to promote their political beliefs. They understood film to be a medium of moral influence on mass popular culture that could shape the values and norms of the broader society. The moral orientation of these European antifascist refugees from totalitarian regimes impacted the overall development of cinema.

The first true advocates for film were not Protestant reformers but progressive political agitators. Antifascists mixed with radical urban intellectuals to create films that would educate and stir up the masses for patriotism and social reform in the United States and abroad. "A good Hollywood film was to promote social engagement in its audience by tackling the issues of the day and proposing progressive solutions" (Giovacchini 2001, 47). With their strong advocacy for social change in the 1930s and 1940s, the political and intellectual debates in Hollywood mirrored debates in New York. A 1943 Writers' Congress assembled on the campus of UCLA brought together Hollywood writers, studio executives, European refugees, and university professors to discuss the potential of American films for advancing democratic ideals. The entertainment industry mixed Hollywood New Yorkers and Hollywood Europeans to produce a leftist political orientation that hoped to cultivate a progressive mass culture through the medium of film.

The early history of Hollywood is characterized by idealistic film producers fighting alienation, big business, and the loss of worker autonomy. Faced with the strength of fascist governments oversees and powerful monopolistic conglomerates domestically, these filmmakers worked for freedom from political control and economic oppression. In the 1930s, the pervasive anti-Nazi sentiment bridged the political gap between right and left, cultivating a political unity among filmmakers to promote American-style freedoms. A deep democratic commitment led them to adopt a shared mission: keeping the masses politically and intellectually engaged through film. Off the set, organizations such as the Hollywood Anti-Nazi League and the Hollywood Democratic Committee created alliances to support the presidency of Franklin Delano Roosevelt, mobilize against fascism, and create cinematic outlets for contemporary political issues easily accessible to the U.S. public.

President Franklin D. Roosevelt set up the Motion Picture Bureau of the Office of War Information (OWI) not only to censor films but also to mobilize the film industry to shape U.S. public opinion to support the war. After the nation's entry into World War II in December 1941, the federal government enlisted a willing Hollywood workforce to produce propaganda for the war effort through several agencies, including the Army Corps' 834th Signal Service Photographic Detachment Unit. Antifascist networks of filmmakers like Col. Frank Capra were absorbed into the war effort, some taking official positions in government. The goal was simple: to produce films that would mobilize public opinion against fascism. Examples include *The Informer* (1935), *Blockade* (1938), *Juarez* (1939), *Confessions of a Nazi Spy* (1939), and *The Grapes of Wrath* (1940).

Movies as Messages for the Masses

Before film, artists and intellectuals with broad social ideals mourned the limited audience for their ideas that stage plays offered. Audiences were fragmented— particular groups went to particular forms of entertainment. The wide distribution of motion pictures provided the solution. Furthermore, the desire for a larger audience led to a unique crafting of films with high aspirations that still connected to popular culture.

That film is a medium for mass audiences was not inherent in the technology of filmmaking and exhibition; rather, film became a mass medium as a distinct historical development. Film styles came to reflect the aims and ideals of the earliest filmmakers, committed to the propagation of political ideals intended for the American (and Americanizing) audience. "Classical Hollywood movies were broadly designed to be consumed by people of all sexes, all ages, and all levels of experience" (Vasey 1997, 4).

Intellectuals stepped away from producing art for the cultural elite and toward addressing Americans as a whole, regardless of social class, race, gender, or cultural, religious, or political inclination. Together, these filmmakers created a style of film Giovacchini (2001) calls "Hollywood democratic modernism." For example, films produced for the war effort used the notion of "the people" to indicate the audience. By emphasizing "the people," the filmmakers refused to distinguish contingents of viewers and thus homogenized the audience.[8] Ruth Vasey (1997) points out that this desire by Hollywood filmmakers to be viewed and understood regardless of the viewer's cultural background stimulated innovative thinking on how to construct and market movies internationally. Meanwhile, European filmmakers, particularly in Germany, did not share this democratic desire to appeal to the masses. Avoiding a mixture of "low" and "high" culture, early German filmmakers remained part of the educated elite in their promotion of *Kultur*, which implied a deliberate separation of social classes on the basis of cultural sophistication and taste.

The hybridization of elements from low and high culture produced a medium of communication with relevance to broad audiences.[9] A smooth story-telling style evolved that presented characters onscreen with whom the audience could identify. Politically motivated filmmakers saw the seduction of escapism as the primary threat to social change through film. This concern propelled them to avoid rooting their stories in fantasy; their films involved a firm conviction of reality shared by all people, an intertwined concern for aesthetics and politics, and plots consisting of compelling personal stories told through sequentially arranged scenes. The thrust of films shifted from presenting abstract ideas to engaging the emotions, often featuring an independent protagonist who overcomes obstacles by combining talent with tenacity. Hollywood created a style of universal images and narratives accessible to the broad mass of Americans. U.S. cinematic art became popular art, paving the way for the cultivation of film as a universal medium of communication. This politically motivated style of filming dominated moviemaking throughout the latter twentieth century, and it is the style largely accepted in the growing Hollywood Christian community.

Our commonsense understanding of film as a mass medium, then, rose out of filmmakers' attempt to convincingly convey progressive political messages to a mass audience. The institutionalization of cinematic style arose out of their passionate concern to shape the hearts and minds of ordinary people. Despite their noble intentions, Hollywood became a profit-intensive business (Gomery 2000; Guback 1969; Wasko 1982). By the end of the 1940s, these high ideals had diminished and Hollywood was dominated by a few corporations aggressively pursuing financial profits.

The crucial insight that emerges is that the development of Hollywood and the motivation for those who were involved in early cinema did not revolve solely around financial success. The migration of New York intellectuals and of antifascist Europeans brought to Hollywood a concern for international politics, a desire to spread a form of democracy, a commitment to fight against totalitarianism, and support for the U.S. war effort, values the early filmmakers imported into their artistic work. Although later generations of filmmakers would be wary of promoting such ideals, for this early generation the mass marketing of their purpose-driven entertainment was good. This ideal was eventually amended for religious purposes.

Hollywood Christians and Aesthetic Stimulus for Religious Revival

The desire by Hollywood's early intelligentsia to shape the minds of audiences to make them receptive to particular ideas has a direct affinity to the desire by evangelicals to reach a broad audience with the appeal of the gospel message of salvation in Jesus Christ. The parallels are remarkable. Specifically, the Christian use of film today and the progressive use of film in the 1930s and 1940s mirror each other in the type of stories that come out of agenda-driven films: (1) a softer narrative propelled by a clear protagonist; (2) a strategic mixture of propaganda with entertainment; and (3) the inclusion of news and documentary footage that roots the story in a realistic setting (Giovacchini 2001, 11). This form of storytelling is important to Christians because they seek to transform the basis for personal morality.

Mass appeal was the inherent goal in the development of the aesthetic of cinema. Movies could reach the masses, and Christians and filmmakers shared a similar concern for stimulating societal change through mass-consumed cinema from Hollywood's beginnings. Both humanists and Christians believed film to be a medium that could promote messages that catalyzed positive social, spiritual, and moral change. The co-optation of Hollywood by the Christian church suggests that the film industry has long been successful in creating films that reach all people with seemingly universal messages.

In contrast with Hollywood humanists—and I define a humanist as a person who promotes a universal morality emphasizing rational self-determination through democratic forms of government—today's Hollywood Christians are not concerned with changing the political system per se, nor are they, like their Protestant reformer counterparts, fighting against broad social ills such as poverty, abuse, or exploitation. Rather, these Hollywood Christians want to elevate the overall moral environment of the country and turn it against intense sexuality, senseless violence, and antireligious sentiment. The social change through film they advocate involves less a shift in the structures of society than a shift in the essential ethos of mass culture that would make it more agreeable to conservative Christian beliefs and virtues. Disseminating a Christian-inspired moral framework would presumably lead to a growth in wholesome families, neighborhood church attendance, and overall devotion to the Christian God.

Most significant, the Hollywood Production Code institutionalized in 1930 that allowed evil, lewd, and immoral activities onscreen as long as religiously conservative morality wins out seeped into the fundamental ideology of the Hollywood Christian. The uneasy alliance between evil (filmmakers who know that sex, violence, and the baser elements of human life attract box-office profits) and good (Christians who promote conservative moral standards) was initially struck to appease film's moral censors and keep movie producers in business. Today, conservative Christians intend this uneasy alliance to serve a subversive purpose: to introduce good morals into a medium that seems in the minds of many believers to have largely abandoned them. The compromise reached for political reasons in the early development of the Hollywood industry has become the conservative Christians' strategic plan for reforming Hollywood.

Hollywood versus Christian Religious Films

Before contemporary conservative Christians became actively involved in filmmaking, Hollywood occasionally produced religious films, including the widely recognized epic Bible films like The Ten Commandments, David and Bathsheba, and Samson and Delilah, as well as pastor/priest films like Going My Way, The Bells of Saint Mary's, and Boys' Town. Although such films appear acceptable to

Christians, their substance is peripheral to Christian concerns. Although set in religiously tinged environments, these films scarcely represent the teachings and doctrines of Christianity. A Christian journalist, Arnold W. Hearn, for example, found Cecil B. DeMille's *Ten Commandments* "another lavish cinematic spectacle, lacking either religious or dramatic significance" (qtd. in Boyd 1958, 26). These movies often emphasize sensuality and greed while using special effects to interject divine intervention. As one critic, William Lee Miller, wrote in 1953: "They make mention of earth and hell, but the message comes straight from Hollywood" (62).

But these films were never intended to promote religion. At times filmmakers included Christian leaders in the production process in hopes of both publicizing the film and avoiding any backlash over controversial subjects—clearly the case with Cecil B. DeMille's flashy epic *Ten Commandments*; DreamWorks first animated feature, *The Prince of Egypt,* a semifictionalized account of Moses; and New Line Cinema's *Nativity Story.* On the surface it would appear that previewing films to church leaders would reduce revenue since a preview not only might keep some people from the box office but also runs the extraordinary risk of cultivating resistance to a film before its release. However, experience has shown that including religious leaders in dialogues about the content of a film— honoring a variety of religious voices—makes them more likely to embrace it and to further promote it upon release. In this way, filmmakers are attempting to sidestep the informal yet still powerful censorship of public opinion.

Some films promote religion despite the nonreligious intentions of filmmakers. *Jesus Christ Superstar* (1973), for example, which was not intended to promote religious devotion and not produced by Christians, inspired an entire generation of believers. Suited to the culture of its day, it featured a multiracial cast, progressive values between genders, and a hip rock-music soundtrack. The success of *Jesus Christ Superstar* fueled the Jesus movement by boldly demonstrating how the life of Christ could be told without the trappings of traditional religion but rather in a manner that was culturally relevant and aesthetically pleasing, and that incorporated the full array of contemporary media. Other important films not made by Christian filmmakers that nevertheless stimulated the connection between Christians and films include *Chariots of Fire* (1981) and *The Mission* (1986). Believers were amazed that films with such popular appeal could portray sincere believers and earnest missionaries true to their faith.

The existence of financially successful films focused on the Christian faith provided evidence that explicitly religious themes and the profession of faith on film did not automatically mean the loss of a mass audience. These productions paved the way for the birthing of the modern Hollywood Christian. Filmmakers not associated with the Christian faith were producing films that inspired believers, but could Christian filmmakers produce films that would inspire those outside the church?

The Passion of the Christ: A Breakthrough Film for Faith

Mel Gibson's 2004 film *The Passion of the Christ* decisively sanctioned the promotion of religion among industry insiders. With the success generated by *The Passion*, Gibson holds first place in the hierarchy of conservative Christians in Hollywood. Although his celebrity is tainted by anti-Semitic slurs he made during a DUI arrest in 2006, Gibson's film achievement remains a model and inspiration.[10] As an independent project produced for only $30 million (cheap by modern standards and mostly financed by Gibson himself), the film took in $26.5 million on the first day alone, and $125 million in the first five days. Until then, mainstream Christian films were dogged by lackluster sales at the box office, the gold standard of success in the entertainment industry. The film ultimately brought in $370 million in domestic ticket sales and $610 million worldwide, becoming one of the top-grossing films in history.

Many insiders were surprised when Gibson decided in 2002 to reject other moviemaking offers and direct his own film. *The Passion* went against the common wisdom of how to build a blockbuster film, which holds that any retelling of the story of the life of Jesus is risky. Gibson based his film on the Gospels as well as on diaries from St. Anne Catherine Emmerich. Equally disastrous, the dialogue would be in the original Aramaic and Latin rather than in English. The casting would avoid recognizable superstars. Since no studio would fund the project, Gibson put up $25 million. Asked by a journalist if he expected a profit, he answered in Italian, "Sará un film buono per l'anima ma non per il portafoglio" (This film is good for the soul, not good for the wallet; qtd. in Epstein 2005, 292).

The film is deeply personal for Gibson and the result of a decade-long spiritual journey. After now highly publicized struggles with drug and alcohol abuse, Gibson began reflecting on the suffering of Jesus Christ. "Eventually, you realize you need to change your life, or it can go down the tubes. It's that point where you go, 'I need help.' I used the wounds of Christ to heal my own wounds" (qtd. in Field 2004, 4). Drawing inspiration from *The Dolorous Passion of Our Lord Jesus Christ* by Anne Catherine Emmerich, he wrote the film with Benedict Fitzgerald, a Roman Catholic who had recently returned to the faith. Both experienced a profound spiritual renewal rooted in the Roman Catholic Church. During filming, every morning Gibson brought a priest onto the set who offered Latin Mass, the Eucharist, and confession for any of the cast and crew who wished to participate. In a promotional brochure for the movie distributed at a Global Pastors Network conference in Florida, Gibson said, "I hope the film has the power to evangelize." He also shared that he personally evangelized on the movie set and saw both agnostics and Muslims convert to Christianity.

The film was an important component of personal faith not only for Gibson but also for hundreds of thousands of others. Paul Dergarabedian, president of Exhibitor Relations, a box-office tracking service, was quoted as saying: "It's not just a movie. It's a religious experience for many people" (Field 2004, 2). The film was widely publicized in churches, and Christians embraced it as an important aspect of their own evangelistic mission. Although Gibson provided a series of free showings throughout the country to select church leaders, conservative journalists, and Christian audiences (as well as Jewish leaders, due to the anti-Semitic controversy prior to the release of the film), churches rallied to financially support the film through a grassroots media campaign. Movie trailers were shown in Sunday morning services, and believers bought tickets for their families and friends. Some churches bought out whole theaters, seeing the showing of the film as an aspect of their own ministry. *The Passion* was successful despite its shunning by mainstream Hollywood industry and claims that it was anti-Semitic. Churches and religious leaders have promoted other films, including *The Cross and the Switchblade* (1970), *Joni* (1980), *The Omega Code* (1999), *Jonah: A VeggieTales Movie* (2002), *The Lion, the Witch, and the Wardrobe* (2005), *The Nativity* (2006), *One Night with the King* (2006), and *Amazing Grace* (2006). But nothing in the history of the relation between Christians and films comes close to their overwhelming support and the financial success of this Christian-created film.

Most important, *The Passion* symbolizes the triumph of faith in the movie industry, although it is ironic that the film is rated R. Christians long considered an R rating as connoting gratuitous violence and sexuality. Gibson's film has become the most successful R-rated film of all time. Barbara Nicolosi, founder and executive director of Act One, which trains Christian scriptwriters for the Hollywood industry, claims that in the spring of 2004, Gibson's film "went off like a light bulb in the collective consciousness of the Christian Church, awakening every one to the power of cinema to spread the Good News" (Lewerenz and Nicolosi. 2005, 115). After a lengthy gestation period, the Hollywood Christian was born.

The Birth of the Hollywood Christian

The impetus for legitimizing participation of Christians in Hollywood had been building steadily. Believers who are entertainment industry insiders agree that most Christians still shun Hollywood as an immoral, dangerous place. But viewed as a strategy for evangelism, Hollywood Christians see such isolation as deeply flawed. Lewerenz and Nicolosi believe, for example, that "casting Hollywood as the enemy has only pushed Hollywood farther away. And the farther Hollywood is from us, the less influence we have on our culture" (2005, 8).

Jarrell, one of many Hollywood Christians I met at Oasis, came to study and work in Hollywood. "Christians in general, especially in mid-American small towns," Jarrell told me, view things that come out of Hollywood as evil. Consequently, those who work in the Hollywood entertainment industry believe Christians to be condemning of their work. He said those who work in Hollywood "have a negative view of Christianity and don't like it." Industry insiders have said to him about Christians, "All you people say is 'You're bad, you're wrong, you're going to hell.'" The stigma attached to Christians drives Jarrell in his personal mission to Hollywood. "One of the things that's big on my heart is to be here in Hollywood now and to be trying to work in the industry and be a light of Christ and show people the idea that they have about Christianity isn't necessarily right. And that's why to me the most important thing is to show the love of Jesus. And that's what my thing is I'm working on."

The basic belief of Hollywood Christians like those at Oasis is that "whoever controls the media controls the culture." Because film as mass media is the most important medium for shaping values in U.S. society, Hollywood Christians believe that to engage with American culture, they must engage with the entertainment industry. According to Alex Field, who has written a book about Christians in the film industry: "The truth is that every day, films are changing people's minds, stirring up controversy, unearthing compassion for various causes, and inspiring people to make big decisions that ultimately change their lives" (2004, xi). Film has captured the masses, and Hollywood Christians are saying that film can either be a new opiate that dulls people's moral senses and obscures their vision of God's work or it can catalyze their spiritual perception and lead them to religious conviction. Although Lewerenz and Nicolosi themselves "left the business of defining human experience via the mass media to people with the secular worldview," Nicolosi laments the absence of Christians in the industry: "We need to be in the middle of the industry, on the lots, on the sets, and in the network and studio offices, working side by side with those who do not share our worldview, so as to bring God where he is not" (Lewerenz and Nicolosi 2005, 8, 118). Although the church has placed itself on the margins, it can be brought back to the center. Christians can infuse new stories with a redemptive Christian worldview (Baehr 2005, xiii). A wave of new talent will strike down the giants of secularism and immorality.

Modern Advocates for Christian Filmmakers

The most urgent modern call for Christians to integrate and influence the mainstream culture through film came from an explosive 1993 book entitled *Roaring Lambs* by Emmy award–winning television producer Bob Briner. Published by Zondervan, a prominent Christian publisher, the book reads like a prophetic manifesto for Oasis Christian Center. Briner's books, which include *Lambs among Wolves* (1995) and *The Final Roar* (2000), inspired a new generation of Hollywood insiders and insider wannabes to see the evangelistic mission of Christ extended into the entertainment industry.

Briner is frustrated with what he considers the whining and complaining of the Christian world. Not only does it fail to evoke change, it removes credibility: "When Christians criticize, carp, and complain but offer no alternatives, the world rolls its eyes, snickers, and moves on" (1993, 41). He emphasizes that it is time to stop sitting back and complaining and instead step up to professional involvement in culture-shaping industries. He finds the church "almost a nonentity when it comes to shaping culture," a role it has "abdicated" (30, 13). Rather than isolating themselves from popular culture, he advises, Christians should participate in it and make it better.

Briner observed that evangelicals accorded higher status to Christians who chose sacred professions as ministers or missionaries than to those who chose secular occupations and came to believe that evangelicals should remove "the dichotomy between professional Christians and Christians in the professions" (1993, 21). Shaping culture occurs by successfully accomplishing professional creative work, Briner believes, and to be effective evangelists in the modern world, Christians must pursue excellence in creative occupations where they can be recognized and respected as professionals. The church needs to be involved in this culture's creative communities, and Briner gives special emphasis to the Hollywood industry: "Why not believe that one day the most critically acclaimed director in Hollywood could be an active Christian layman in his church?" (33).

Christians should be able to take on roles outside Christian professions that permit them to carry on vibrant, intentional Christian lives. Why is this important? Because, as Briner understands, in modern society people are defined by their work. Evangelism is increasingly based on credibility derived from excellent work within secular occupations. Briner applies to the professions the great commission Jesus gave his followers: "Go into all the world making disciples" (Matt. 28)—"I envision a whole new generation of roaring lambs will lay claim to these careers with the same vigor and commitment that sent men like Hudson Taylor to China" (1993, 178–179). "At the very least," he insists, "the young people of the church should be made to see that their careers, whatever they may be, are just as vital, just as much a concern of the congregation, and just as much a part of the mission of the church as those of the foreign missionaries the church supports" (50). Regarding Hollywood, he concludes: "The movies can be both an important mission field and an important vehicle for the gospel message" (94).

Precursors to the Hollywood Christian Reform Movement

One of the distinctive media accomplishments of the twentieth century is the proliferation of religious celebrities. It was thought that shows sponsored by God should be as lavish as those from the devil (Braudy 1986, 510). One popular preacher who went on the road, Dwight Moody, put on shows that rivaled those by Barnum and Bailey. Later, through radio and television, certain religious personalities rose to the prominent attention of millions, along with their message, their devotion, their antics, and their follies.

The introduction of radio, film, and television outlets created space for a new breed of Christian ministry through mass media. Some of the pioneers of religious broadcasting include Aimee Semple McPherson, Norman Vincent Peale, Fulton Sheen, and Billy Graham. These among others became major religious personalities whose devotion and sainthood were widely publicized. For example, Aimee Semple McPherson, founder of the Foursquare movement in 1927, was the most prominent preacher to shamelessly utilize the dramatic arts being popularized in Hollywood. Mixing Hollywood and the Holiness movement, Sister Aimee's preaching was a dramatic storytelling, often with costumes and props, and she is still considered one of the most compelling preachers in the history of Christianity. Sister Aimee held very conservative beliefs, including a belief in the eternal damnation of people who did not accept Christ, but she did not shrink from incorporating media techniques that drew crowds. She used cheerfulness and optimism to invite people into her church rather than scaring them with the fear of hell.

Sister Aimee built Angelus Temple in 1923 with a seating capacity of over five thousand, participating in the design of the auditorium to ensure that the seating, staging, and lighting mimicked movie palaces. There she acted out adaptations of Bible stories or stories from popular culture, including the Lone Ranger, the Wizard of Oz, or the Trojan horse, with a good dose of humor along with a high dramatic flair for getting her point across. Whether wearing a football uniform, donning a police uniform and riding a motorcycle, or staging some other attention-grabbing message, she drove home Scripture with metaphor. She often used the names of current movies as her sermon titles, including "One Foot in Heaven" and "Keep 'em Flying."

One of the most accomplished and acclaimed religious celebrities of all time is the Reverend Billy Graham. He began preaching in the 1940s with the explicit intention of expanding his audience and never shied away from utilizing media to extend the message as far as it could go. He acted on the premise that the opportunity for religious broadcasters to appear in the homes of millions would be one of the greatest triggers of a religious revival in this country.

Both Sister Aimee and Billy Graham were precursors of a breed of televangelists who took to the airwaves from the 1960s forward. Oral Roberts, Jimmy Swaggart, Jim and Tammy Baker, and Robert Tilton would be among the many Christian ministers to move toward televised ministry programs. The establishment of the Trinity Broadcasting Network by Paul and Jan Crouch would greatly expand the number of televised ministries, and eventually cable and satellite television provided opportunities for multiple channels of dedicated religious programming. Yet these dedicated media were segregated from the mainstream Hollywood entertainment industry.

Hollywood Filmmakers versus Anti-Hollywood Filmmakers

Hollywood Christians like Bob Briner are very critical of Christian moviemakers who reject the Hollywood system. Anti-Hollywood filmmakers believe Christian films should be made only by Christians and for explicitly Christian purposes. For example, filmmaker Byron Jones of Garden City Pictures accuses the new crop of Hollywood Christians of being Hollywood wannabes: "Many producers have tried to give the glitz of Hollywood and do a crossover film. But each time the message has been lost. The Gospel is so well hidden any sinner can watch the movie and not feel convicted. Christian films need to be less about the glitz and more about the message" (qtd. in Field 2004, 66). Anti-Hollywood filmmakers make their biblically oriented films directly available to audiences through independent channels like Christian bookstores; viewers buy them because they know such films must meet a standard of conservative Christian acceptability before they are allowed in the stores. Terry Lindvall called these "tribal films, told and retold within their own community to carry on its traditions and values" (2007, 1).

Hollywood Christians make a sharp distinction between films that are story driven and those that are message driven. They insist that anti-Hollywood Christian films are too heavy on message to be good movies. Christian screenwriter Janet Batchler finds that "most 'Christian' movies today fall under the definition of propaganda" (qtd. in Field 2004, 182). Similarly, Thom Parham sees these films as contrived: "Audiences are not allowed to make the connections; they are told what to think." The problem is, he goes on, that "this approach, no matter how sincere, rings false to audiences and leaves them feeling manipulated" (qtd. in Lewerenz and Nicolosi 2005, 53).

Many Hollywood Christians see such films as simply bad. "A lot of Christian entertainment is such bad quality, so sappy and one-dimensional," Susan Isaacs, actor and Christian screenwriting instructor, told me in an August 2005 interview. "If you want to be a preacher, go be a preacher; but if you want to be an artist, know your art." In sum, "Christians aren't being persecuted in Hollywood; they're committing suicide." There is an overarching impression that Christian filmmakers are "untalented, unfunny, uncreative, and less than technically savvy" (Field 2004, 82). Simply stated, "Christian film" has come to mean inferior work and has contributed to making the word "Christian" pejorative as a description of any piece of media.

It may seem unfair to characterize explicitly Christian films as of low quality, but to date these films have failed to attract the financing and talent of major Hollywood studios. This is what makes Mel Gibson's *The Passion of the Christ* significant. The film affirmed and encouraged Christian filmmakers to join the mainstream to fulfill the deepest values of their religious faith. Yet these religiously motivated filmmakers still struggle to live up to the standard Gibson set. Even mildly Christian-themed films are highly scrutinized, and message films made for mainstream audiences are still highly susceptible to being stigmatized as veiled forms of proselytizing. For example, the 2006 film *End of the Spear* about missionaries killed in Ecuador received scathing reviews in which the film was called "a thinly disguised Sunday School lesson in faith" and "crypto-Christian claptrap."[11]

The core of the debate over Christians in Hollywood boils down to whether Christian filmmaking is a niche industry intended for Christian audiences and sold through Christian outlets or whether Christians are intended to work alongside non-Christians in the mainstream entertainment industry with large-budget films aimed at mass audiences. Do believers make "Christian films," or do they make films that happen to be Christian? Does a Christian filmmaker have to produce "Christian film"? Is it morally acceptable for a Christian filmmaker to make mainstream films?

Ralph Winter, a prominent Christian producer and an active member of his Presbyterian church, has an impressive string of film credits, including four of the *Star Trek* films, all three of the *X-Men* films, both *Fantastic Four* films, and the remake of *Planet of the Apes*. Although Winter struggled with whether he could both work in the industry and be a loyal follower of God, he has become a prominent spokesperson for the power of mainstream film and a role model for many Hollywood Christian hopefuls at Oasis. For Winter, film is a holistic medium for a holistic message that speaks to the entire human condition. He is critical of Christians who ask, "If you're not making movies about Jesus or the end times, what good are you?" (Field 2004, 36). Instead, he emphasizes that films can portray deep human longings that are ultimately satisfied by God. Joining the new breed of Hollywood Christians, he believes a successful filmmaker does not force upon an audience a doctrinal belief system that must be accepted or rejected. He advises industry aspirants:

> Write stuff and produce stuff that will stir up cravings inside of us, because that's the DNA that God's put inside of us. You stir that stuff up, and that's where people want to go to church. That's when they want to talk about the good news. That's when they want to find out, *how do you get through this? How do you do this?* And when we stir up those cravings, we can point into the other resources, and we can share that good news with them. (qtd. in Field 2004, 39; emphasis in original)

Winter believes the world needs good stories told with aesthetic excellence that stimulate reflection on important human issues while avoiding preachy overtones. For him, the most accessible way to address the marketplace of modern society is through the Hollywood entertainment industry, because film and television programming have become a universal point of contact. The pinnacle upon which to stand and share the message would be the blockbuster film. If the gospel message could seep into blockbuster films, spiritual transformation of the entire society would inevitably follow.

Hollywood is the site of Ralph Winter's career and of his missionary efforts. And he is not alone. Hollywood Christians working in the mainstream entertainment industry like those at Oasis do not work on Christian projects; instead, they enter Hollywood as the world's most important mission field. For example, the Hollywood Prayer Network produced a video called *The Hollywood Crisis,* a fifteen-minute documentary challenging the church to embrace Hollywood as a mission field. Hollywood Prayer Network leaders Karen and Jim Covell stress that "every day, young Christians are coming to Hollywood, convinced God has called them to be missionaries in the entertainment industry" (qtd. in Lewerenz and Nicolosi 2005, 83). Sheryl Anderson, a television studio executive, writer, and producer said, "I came to Hollywood because God gave me the gift of storytelling and I wanted to use it as fully as possible" (140). Television writer and producer Dean Batalie pleads: "Come to Los Angeles to help make a difference. Or perhaps I should put it this way: PLEASE PLEASE PLEASE PLEASE PLEASE! (I'm really lonely.)" (19).

Hollywood Christians advocate a less than straightforward approach to Christian filmmaking. "Being too blatant with what we're trying to say always backfires," Monty Kelso states. "It just doesn't have the same effect as a more subversive approach. So taking the subversive approach in a positive way, not a hostile takeover, just being subtle and subversive and how we perpetuate the Gospel truth, I believe, is going to be the success of the film in the future" (qtd. in Field 2004, 66). Sheryl Anderson calls this "stealth theology," defined as "theology to get to people in unexpected ways, it surprises them, and it sneaks up on them while they think they're simply entertaining themselves" (137). Stealth theology is equivalent to Jesus' use of parables, Anderson suggests: "He took complex theological concepts and turned them into clear, entertaining stories that even a child could understand" (139).

Craig Detweiler, a professor of mass communications at Biola University, advises Christian moviemakers: "Don't spoil the film to try to over-explain everything. Maintain the mystery" (qtd. in Field 2004, 86). The goal is to make films spiritually relevant, not explicitly dogmatic. Another successful filmmaker, Richard Linklater, provides similar advice:

> The suggestion here is not that relativism should be the Christian standard, thereby forgoing absolute truth, but that Christians direct non-Christian viewers to ask questions and then find the truth on their own. Providing concrete answers in the film implies that the filmmaker is somehow an expert with hard evidence, an assertion that audiences naturally treat with a large amount of incredulity. Filmmakers should not be in the practice of throwing out complexity in favor of "dumbing down" their movies to bring forth a message. But if audience members can be inspired to search for truth themselves, now there's a goal for Christians to aspire to! (131)

Hollywood Christians are "tentmakers," a term applied to missionaries in foreign countries who hold paid jobs rather than raising financial support. (Use of the term in this context was inspired by the reported practice of the Apostle Paul of making and selling tents to sustain himself rather than soliciting funds from other believers.) Filmmaker David L. Cunningham is an interesting example of this new breed of modern missionary. As a descendent of a long line of clergy on both sides of his family and the son of Loren Cunningham, founder of the missionary organization Youth with a Mission (YWAM), Cunningham sees himself as a missionary in Hollywood. "Through storytelling, [I try to] hopefully rock them, inspire them, challenge them, whatever it may take, to in some way get them closer to an understanding of why they are on this planet" (qtd. in Field 2004, 146). He recruits potential missionaries by inviting interns who raise their own support to his sets and allowing their Hollywood jobs to serve as missionary training.

An increasing number of Hollywood aspirants are being funded as domestic missionaries. Karen and Jim Covell of the Hollywood Prayer Network are not alone in urging Christian leaders to see Hollywood as a mission field and to send more missionaries: "We should encourage talented people who are grounded in their faith to come work here in the entertainment industry" (qtd. in Lewerenz and Nicolosi 2005, 85). Nonprofit organizations like Arts and Entertainment Ministries, founded in 2004 by Joel and Michelle Peluse, are among many that collect and administer financial support for mission-driven believers to pursue a career in the industry. Because success in the industry is difficult and Los Angeles is an expensive place to live, these organizations urge pastors and churches to financially support aspirants to the media. Even traditional missionary organizations are experimenting with personnel initiatives involving film and new media.

Seeing Hollywood as a mission field is an acknowledgment that Hollywood itself is not good. Even among mainstream Christian filmmakers Hollywood is still believed to be an evil place. But they avoid getting dirty by sacralizing their work as an extension of God's mission on earth. As Dean Batali, executive producer of Fox's *That 70s Show*, writes: "I sympathize with viewers who were disgusted with the foul language and sexual content on many television shows. That's one of the reasons I came to Hollywood—to try to influence the content of TV shows" (qtd. in Lewerenz and Nicolosi 2005, 16).

Christian filmmakers can be a part of changing scenes or rewriting scripts in a way that achieves a higher level of Christian morality. Hollywood Christians seek to change the medium of film by promoting stories that lead people toward spiritual questions and spiritual yearnings. They also attempt to transform lives through their evangelistic efforts with people in the media industry. "How do we change the media?" ask Karen and Jim Covell. "We change the hearts of the people creating the media" (qtd. in Lewerenz and Nicolosi 2005, 86). To this end, part of the job of Christians who work in the entertainment industry is to be active in evangelizing others in the industry on a personal, relational, one-to-one basis.

5   Celebrity, Heartache, and the Pressure to Make It

BRENT: I moved to LA to be in the industry, to be successful, meaning fame and fortune.

Back in 1924, a Hollywood minister wrote: "The lure of the screen brings thousands of girls and boys to Hollywood from every part of the world. They come at a constant stream from cities and villages and countryside of America and Europe, come with dreams of fortune and fame, wholly ignorant to what awaits them and destined to disillusionment if not utter failure and shame" (Lindvall 2001, 284).

The failure of thousands to find employment in Hollywood created a significant problem, as misery and destitution among this newly settled breed of worker grew steadily. Every day, men and women eagerly lined up at the corner of Sunset Boulevard and Gower Street in hopes of entering the industry as movie extras (Torrence 1982, 87). Few succeeded. As early as 1921, the Hollywood Chamber of Commerce created advertisements to discourage people from coming. When a movie studio advertised for thirty-five extras, and 3,500 people came in response, the chamber took a photograph of the mob to use as a warning to others with glamorous ambitions about the scarcity of work. Alongside this picture of the horde clamoring outside a building marked Employment Agency, the text of one ad reads:

Don't Try to Break into the Movies
IN HOLLYWOOD
Until You Have Obtained Full, Frank and Dependable Information
From the
Hollywood Chamber of Commerce
It May Save Disappointments
Out of 100,000 Persons Who Started at the Bottom of the
Screen's Ladder of Fame
ONLY FIVE REACHED THE TOP

Yet still they came. As the same Hollywood pastor lamented in 1924: "They come by every train, happy, carefree, unsophisticated, never dreaming of failure but hurrying to meet it" (Lindvall 2001, 245). Studios in the 1910s and 1920s gave more opportunities to women than most other industries, and advice books and articles especially aimed at women provided counsel for aspiring starlets to guard against financial trouble. They were encouraged to bring at least two thousand dollars, enough money to survive at least a year without additional income (Sklar 1994, 75).[1]

Although the business aspect of the industry has changed, exacerbating what has always been a difficult long-term career path, people move where the jobs are, and Hollywood still has the highest concentration of film industry work in the world (Scott 2005, 128; also see chapter 3).[2] At Oasis, Bridgette, a member, said church attenders "are normally young people who come to this area to be in the movies or TV or music or whatever." A staff member noted that "just about every single person is involved in the entertainment industry in some fashion as a singer, dancer, musician, actor, actress, fashion designer, . . . everybody seems to be doing something." Some are working in the industry; others are still finding their way to steady employment—as Brent said, "still pursuing their careers."

Another Oasis member, active in the industry, Donna looks young for her age. "Don't print my age," she told me, "because I'm an actress. If I wasn't an actress, I would wear it on my t-shirt. Okay? I swear to you, I would walk around with it advertised on my forehead." Her age matters in an industry where the appearance of youth is valuable; I had similar requests from other actors, some refusing to tell me their age at all. In fact, entertainment industry workers in general frequently refrained from telling me their age. One frequent Oasis attender said that at first he thought only young people were concerned with keeping their age secret, but he saw later that it was a widespread practice.

Donna, who is white, started modeling and acting in commercials to help pay for college. "I was working six days a week. I did dozens of national commercials, films, TV series, cable, tons of print work, just worked like crazy." Her success continually pointed to Hollywood, "because out here is supposed to be the big thing. They were flying me back and forth for screen tests, so I thought, 'Okay, I have to move to California.'" She moved to Los Angeles, where she "basically camped out" in the living room of the one family member who lived in the area until she could settle down. "I came here with no job, no apartment, no car. I sold everything and left everything and came here to start fresh. It was pretty risky."

Moving to Hollywood and Looking for the Big Break

Among the members at Oasis, moving to L.A. involved sacrifices for the sake of the dream. "No one from Los Angeles is here," said Rodrigo, a Hispanic. "They are from all over the place, all over the world, coming here for one reason—wanting to get a big break so they can become a big star." Damion, an African American, said, "I went through a struggling period and stuff. I was on food stamps and all that. But, hey, it didn't matter because it was happening."

One person described sharing a Hollywood apartment, "a big single, and I had a foldout bed and a kitchen that had a door and my roommate and I would take turns sleeping on the floor." Most moved to California with very few friends and little money. Rocco, an African American, said, "I came with six hundred dollars or so in my pocket, no job. Here I am, let's do it." Such willingness to sacrifice is part of the reason for the persistent labor oversupply for occupations in the entertainment industry, the result of "the large numbers of aspirants willing to make significant sacrifices in the short term for the sake of potentially massive monetary and psychological gains in the long term" (Scott 2005, 128).

Not a single person I spoke with at Oasis came to Hollywood to begin a career; each was already involved in entertainment in some way. Moving to Los Angeles was merely the next step toward being more successful, more fulfilled, and better off. Industry aspirants all show great enthusiasm for the potential of their own work. One woman said to me, "Being a performer has always been my dream. Always." Lynn, a Hispanic in her early twenties, was one of many who said some variation of "I'm going to make it as an actress." Lynn has found her niche. "I love it," she said. "I love this town. I cannot imagine myself living anywhere else really."

Danielle, who is white, worked at a marketing firm after college. Doing commercials, she developed enough contacts to allow her to launch freelance projects, which led to her first big break: producing a motion picture. Building on that success, she moved to Los Angeles. Reggie, also white, majored in theater in college, so moving to Los Angeles from the East Coast was an anticipated career move for him. He soon landed a position at a television network. Another young man had been in Hollywood less than a month but arrived knowing he had secured a part in a motion picture. Over and over in their stories, moving to Hollywood is prompted by a need to achieve greater exposure. Greater attention will provide greater income, greater stability, and greater prestige.

Understanding the Hollywood Labor Market

The bitter reality most Oasis members quickly discover is that no film company exists merely to fulfill the naïve dreams of the starstruck. Motion pictures are commercial entities. As Peter Kramer points out: "The unchanging main objective of the American film industry . . . is to make money by telling entertaining stories to paying audiences" (2000, 63). Since Hollywood is first and foremost a collection of profit-maximizing businesses, aspirants' dreams and hopes always come up against a financial bottom line.

At the same time, Hollywood is the center of one of the most complex local labor markets in the world. There are two phases of labor in the history of Hollywood, the classic studio system phase and the modern disaggregated production phase.[3] Under the classic studio system, a highly efficient and streamlined process from production to distribution to exhibition of production, workers were permanent employees of a studio and earned a regular wage (Hampton 1970 [1931], 305–307). The classic studio film factory brought together different tasks and different types of workers into a single establishment. Economics forced studios to consolidate from more than sixty in 1912 to the Big Eight in the 1920s. By controlling the production, distribution, and exhibition of films, movie studios early on formed an oligopoly of financial control over cinema. By 1937, about 90 percent of employment in the U.S. motion picture industry was in Southern California (Scott, 2005, 25–27, table 2.1).

The second phase of the Hollywood labor system began when a Supreme Court ruling in 1948 in a federal antitrust case (often called the Paramount suit) forced studios to disaggregate production, distribution, and exhibition. The business climate of Hollywood saw "a dramatic rise in competitiveness, uncertainty, and instability in the motion picture industry, followed by the breakup of studio-based mass production, whose peculiar process and product configurations could no longer sustain profitable operations" (Scott, 2005, 36). Studios divested themselves of aspects of the production process, cutting overhead by avoiding long-term financial commitments. An entirely new pattern of production emerged, with its dominant characteristic being a move away from permanent employment and long-term contracts to short-term employment and project-specific contracts. The disaggregated model for motion picture making that emerged out of sheer economic necessity became the norm.

The key production features of what is called the New Hollywood emerged in the 1980s (Christopherson and Storper 1986; Storper and Christopherson 1987; Storper 1989). Firms strategically locate in Los Angeles to benefit from the clustering of creative industries and the spatial concentration of the labor markets (Scott 1988a, b; Storper and Christopherson 1987; Florida 2002). The clustering of firms supports highly complex short-term projects and constant readjustments between projects over time. Hollywood now consists of a network of projects and people centered on the production of mass entertainment for fame and profit.[4]

The burden of creating exciting, marketable, profitable films shifted to independent, entrepreneurial producers. Producers assembled the parts by packaging directors, actors, screenplays, and production components and selling them to studios for distribution. Hired by producers to manage film production and bring screenplays to life, directors became a more important base of power (see Staiger 1982). The flexibility benefits studio heads, who are free to accept or reject films on the basis of profitability alone. Producers are forced to create films that sell. Actors, directors, and production people all live amidst a constant swirl of project requests that give them a few days, weeks, or months of work at a time.

Overall, this loosely networked structure makes for a much more flexible, economically adaptable system of production, but it comes at a price for the worker. With the shift of economic organization, "the local labor market became increasingly flexible and volatile, so that workers caught up in it today are subject to extremely high levels of risk in regard to remuneration, benefits, job prospects, and so on" (Scott 2005, 117). This is evident at Oasis. Regardless of past successes or years of experience, no industry worker at Oasis has job stability. Typical of working in Hollywood today, they bounce from job to job, subject to fluctuations in production schedules and the availability of work. Employment is decentralized into a number of small firms. The majority of industry workers are now temporary or freelance. Workers take on assignments from production companies as short-term employees hired from project to project. Industry workers are not tied to studios but have freedom and flexibility to respond to opportunities as they come, although the most sought-after workers negotiate commitments for a series of overlapping projects.

These dynamics make a career in the entertainment industry for attenders at Oasis highly precarious. The distinctive clustering of creative industries in Los Angeles continues to draw talented scriptwriters, directors, producers, actors, and members of a host of other industry-related occupations because their work is highly valued (Scott, 2005, 7; Florida 2002; Menger 1999; Montgomery and Robinson 1993). With the steady influx of new workers, industry firms continually refresh their base of talent. But what is most efficient for motion picture studio executives is not the most efficient for the average worker in the Hollywood industry. Workers are free from a controlling studio atmosphere, but no one works with long-term security. Even when the overall industry seems to be thriving, most individual workers are not. This deeply affects the day-to-day life experience of members of Oasis, in particular their understanding of themselves and their attempts to manage the trajectory of their lives.

The Special Case of Actors as Laborers

With the disintegration of the studio system, actors became subcontractors with the freedom to join a variety of productions but also dependent on their image and reputation to secure a steady series of income-generating gigs. This freedom brings with it a high level of anxiety. The actors of Oasis Christian Center spend the majority of their time not in front of a movie camera or at publicity events but looking for work, preparing for projects, traveling, networking, and planning for the future.

In spite of the popular belief that actors command a great deal of power in the Hollywood industry, in actuality actors are quite low in the hierarchy of Hollywood workers. Beginning actors understand that establishing themselves in the profession starts with successfully joining a union.[5] The first goal is to get their SAG (Screen Actors Guild) card, proof that they have qualified for membership, paid their dues, and committed to work on productions that abide by SAG rules. The direct benefit to actors is that they are paid competitive wages and can anticipate a good working environment. Joining the union is basic to making a decent living as an actor.

Stories of multimillion-dollar movie roles receive great media attention, but they do not represent the work of the vast majority of actors and other industry players in the day-to-day business of making movies. The breakup of the studio system that allowed stars to negotiate among the studios resulted in a meteoric rise of salaries for those at the very top. At any one time in the film industry, these top actors comprise a few dozen people with shifting fortunes, both rising stars and old stars making comebacks. But few actors command large sums for their work; the great majority are grateful for any work at all, hoping to build a record of employability. Precious few actors are able to leverage their celebrity into high salaries or shares in film profits (McDonald 2000).

Of the eight thousand actors who are members of the Screen Actors Guild, less than 1 percent have received multimillion-dollar fees. Desperation for work, along with the desire to work seamlessly from one project to another, leads actors to accept very low wages. At the bottom are screen extras, who comprise as much as 90 percent of all working actors. Extras live on minimal pay (fifty dollars per working day is not unusual), as well as the hope of being noticed for larger projects. It is estimated that 85 percent of actors are out of work at any time (Wasko 2003, 43). The difference between high-ranking actors and low-ranking actors is "the break," an outstanding opportunity that introduces actors into networks of influence such that they are sought after for particular roles.

Stars, then, are not just clusters of symbols and media images that demand interpretation; they are laborers (Clark 1995; King 1986; Prindle 1988; Ross [1941] 1967). It is not common to view actors as workers because the most prominent among them are treated as royalty in the popular press and general imagination. Blessed with wealth and fame, the most notable celebrities of our time occupy the media stage long enough for us to see them as people of privilege who conduct their vocation as a type of leisurely hobby. They are media personalities, not workers. That actors are primed and poised for the camera creates the illusion even among technicians and set workers that actors are pampered and spoiled. But if we take more than a casual look at the actual life experience of an actor, the dimension of labor looms large.

Pursuing Fame as a Means of Managing Career Risk

Actors at Oasis are not the only ones who see work in Hollywood as an inherently risky business. While the ultimate goal of those working in Hollywood is to make a financially successful film with a compelling story line, the great majority of films fail to make any money at all (Prindle 1993; Wasko 2003). Indeed according to Scott, they have shown a greater "propensity over the last half-century to become ever more unstable and risky" (2005, 9). Every movie is a gamble, but the rare hits (less than 10 percent of all movies produced earned over 90 percent of the profit) more than make up for the losses. Only one in ten films ever recovers its investment domestically; four out of ten never recover their original investment. And for workers, one great success does not guarantee continued success. One analysis of directors, screenwriters, and producers showed that one screen credit is more often followed by continued anonymity than by more screen credits (Weiss and Faulkner 1983).

The uncertainty of work in Hollywood leads to an emphasis on the pursuit of a specific form of prestige among Oasis workers. Today, celebrity making is an established commercial enterprise. It has become important for stars to protect and control the projection of their own public persona. While studios commonly used publicists by the late 1920s, celebrity making has recently become so lucrative that books like *High Visibility: The Making and Marketing of Professionals into Celebrities* (1997) provide how-to steps to accomplish it.

Joshua Gamson (1994) describes self-promoting celebrity as part of the dual job of an actor. An actor is a worker who has the capacity to play a role, but the actor is also a celebrity with the capacity to command attention. Actors actively cultivate this capacity by spending up to 50 percent of their income on personal publicists who market their brand as a person to attain a name that can be cashed in. According to Gamson: "Day to day industry activities are logically geared toward building and profiting from the attention-grabbing capacities of performers" (62). Will this face sell? Since the successful promotion of a star's image has the most direct consequence on the bottom line of movie revenues, studio executives have spent much more time on honing and promoting star images than on developing the working conditions of actors (see Clark 1995, 19).

Not only actors, but series creators, writers, directors, producers, cinematographers, film editors, animators, studio executives, models, musicians, light specialists, sound technicians, and agents all seek to manage the risk of their uncertain careers by cultivating celebrity status. A person may earn well on a single production, but long-term success depends on the ability to string together a series of employment gigs that each pays a substantial sum. Many workers at Oasis reflected on this circumstance, including a veteran television producer who said, "I had a job that was going to pay me some really great money, and it just went away. I don't know what my next job is. I don't even know how much more money I have." The pursuit of stringing together credits and production experiences leads to seeking celebrity as a particular type of reputation building. A reputation becomes invaluable for long-term survival.

The Hollywood-speak that distinguishes workers according to the level of their prestige is "above the line" and "below the line," terms that refer to their place on the list of budget line items. Above the line refers to individual line items consisting of names of specific people whose fee for services is individually negotiated for a particular project—often the teams that write, perform, and produce the film, with the iconic titles of scriptwriter, star, and director. Essentially, to be above the line is to have a name corresponding with a reputation or valued skill that lends the production a greater chance of financial success. Steven Spielberg and Tom Cruise, for example, are above-the-line workers whose line costs are variable and negotiable. While above-the-line costs are the fundamental units that initiate and propel a production, no film can be made without below-the-line activities—functions (including equipment, transportation, and technical personnel) that need to be accomplished to complete a project and that are remunerated according to standard schedules, collective bargaining agreements, and personal standards.

The work histories of Oasis congregants very much reflect Hollywood's two-tiered, have and have-not economic system. At first glance, most appear to come from middle- or upper-middle-class backgrounds, but my interviews reveal a wide range of economic backgrounds and situations, and I often heard tales of fluctuating fortunes. Members frequently speak of severe swings of economic ups and downs—the result of their chosen careers in the entertainment industry or of unchosen life circumstances—significant fluctuations between working-class wages and upper-class income. Moreover, the stories of the few people who were successful enough to be above the line and visited Oasis or who moved above the line while they were members suggest these workers become less involved with the congregation than do below-the-line workers. In a form of self-segregation, above-the-line workers find that their social networks and demanding schedules keep them from steady involvement in this congregation.

Oasis is a church of below-the-line workers. For example, Lauren and her husband both work for Avid, editing film and video. She considers them both below-the-line workers as computer people. Their functions are not listed by name in a film's budget. To be fair, the overwhelming majority of Hollywood workers are below the line. Few become celebrities, and whatever level of celebrity they may attain is often short-lived. Nevertheless, the key to a sustainable career in the entertainment industry is to achieve a level of celebrity that keeps work prospects flowing.

In the end, the pursuit of fame in Hollywood is less about building one's ego and more about the pursuit of long-term financial stability. The goal of becoming a celebrity rests on the need to manage uncertainty and create a flow of work. Workers at Oasis who have moved beyond pursuing their dream in the abstract are acutely aware of their status within the industry. Typical was one model-actor who said, "I'm a little guy doing a few commercials [or films, videos, projects] here and there." They grasp how economic privilege and social capital give one access to financial benefits and career opportunities. There is a great difference between working a few gigs in the industry and enjoying steady work, good wages, and prestige among one's peers. It is not major celebrity that becomes the goal, but enough celebrity to keep paying the bills.

Facing Reality in Hollywood: Disappointment and Heartbreak

An understanding that, for workers in the entertainment industry, motion pictures are commercial entities explains much of the heartache and disappointment routinely revealed by workers (and potential workers) at Oasis. Denny moved to Hollywood to pursue a career in the entertainment industry, had some success as a character on a television show, made good money, and was achieving a measure of fame. Then the writers wrote his character out of the show. After that, he started getting some small roles in commercials and feature films, but the work dried up. "It just went bad," Denny said. "I mean, we got zilch." Roles failed to come. "I ended up broke, on the street, having to move in with a friend after being homeless for about six months." He sought government help, "getting some general relief." When Denny was broke, homeless, and alone, a friend said, "I know things are kind of bad for you, but come and check out the church I go to." That was his introduction to Oasis.

Like Denny, many at Oasis talk about coming to a point where their career success seemed assured, and then experiencing an abrupt change in their situation. "I remember one day driving down Pacific Coast Highway in my brand-new luxury car," Rodrigo said. "I was driving and thinking, 'I've done okay with myself. My life is not bad at all. I've been able to do this on my own.' Then I lost my job." He was angry. "Why am I out of work? Why is it that my market value is not what I thought it was?"

If one is fortunate, one is able to sustain work at one company as Alesha does as a film editor; she works for a company that takes on many jobs for different studios in film and television. But most cannot, and discouragement among industry workers is universal.

Disappointment comes in many forms. For example, the need to support oneself and one's family often comes up against the reality of earning a steady income. Santiago told me he considers his current job outside the industry as just paying the bills. "The fact of the matter is that I would like to be in the entertainment industry. But then you have to bring home the bacon." Recent financial difficulties at a production company for which he worked forced staff cuts. He found other work, but the core decision remains whether to work in the entertainment industry. "I'm married; I have kids. Yes, I have my dream with entertainment, and I will do that on the side. Practically, I get a job, interview, whatever, and work."

Frustratingly common among workers at Oasis is a feeling of personal disregard and financial exploitation. Several spoke of unwanted sexual encounters. One person said he was constantly "getting hit on by men and women. It was such a whacked-out town. . . . I had a production assistant try to jump me in my trailer. I had to run out of there." Others spoke of working extensively on a project and "getting stiffed." In the business, people often agree to staff a production that is supposed to pay everyone at the end of the shoot, so weeks or months can go by without income. These workers risk not getting paid at all for the gig once the set is wrapped, since producers quickly disappear into other projects.

Aspirants who come to the entertainment industry with Christian convictions also experience distress at betraying standards of conservative moral purity. Damion told me, "I was very successful in Hollywood and acting and everything but I honestly and truthfully put everything before God." Others are disgusted with having fallen into personal temptation. I met Tyler as he was preparing to leave Los Angeles. Tyler talked about what he called "the way the media is in L.A. with all the temptation"; he said, "I have a lot of friends that I've met in L.A. stuck in the drug scene and stuck in casual sex. I am really at a place in my life where I'm trying to build up some strength against those things, so I think I might need to stay away right now until I can build up more strength to be around that more successfully." For Tyler, "there is so much temptation and confusion going on in L.A. It's just a hard place for me to live right now."

Other Oasis members told similar stories. "I completely left church and God and everything and had years of wild, crazy living and doing everything I knew not to do," Jennelle said. "I was singing and trying to be this real famous, you know, 'diva,' I think is the best word. 'I'm a star. It's me; they are all looking at me.' And they all weren't." Reflecting on temptation in the industry, Bridgette said, "It's hard. It's really, really, really hard," and "a lot of people fall. You are seduced spiritually, financially—it's a very seductive business." Charlene spoke of the temptations in biblical terms. "Being in the entertainment industry, that is hell. It is a world all its own," she said. "Everything that you could possibly want to do, want to have, get involved with that's negative is there. You can sleep your way to the top. You can have any kind of drugs you want. I mean, it's a Sodom and Gomorrah type of thing." She spoke at length about the constant threats to one's personal morality. "The lure of succeeding the wrong way is just there. It's so in front of you. You have to make some serious choices every day to not go this direction. To behave yourself. To not go along with somebody if you don't believe in what they do, but you want to be close to them because you know that they can help further your career. It's a struggle. Every day it's a challenge."

. Disappointment also comes with the reality of industry work as unsteady and difficult to find. "Money comes and goes for me," one attender said. A church staff member told me that Oasis assists people every day who hit rock bottom while trying to make it in the industry. Rodrigo said, "They come in and say, 'I'm broke. I don't have any money. I need your assistance.' When I ask what happened, I hear them say, 'I'm broke because there's no work in my industry.'" Nicky, who has had moderate success as a producer for commercials, videos, and independent films, nevertheless experiences dramatic financial ups and downs. Shortly after she began donating money to Oasis, her income took a huge upswing for about three years. Then the bottom fell out. "I lost my house. I lost everything." Industry changes were at least partly to blame. "The actors went on strike, which took a big chunk of my work." Contributing to her work instability was a production that went bankrupt, and that meant Nicky and many others would not get paid. She started doing more low-budget jobs. Relational difficulties compounded the problem; she separated from her husband. "I lost him. I lost my house. I lost friends. I lost every penny I had." The church provided financial help. "It wasn't a lot of money, but it was a lot then. It was what I needed to eat at that time."

Although Nicky always felt financially challenged, today, she says, "What I thought was severe then wasn't anywhere near what I have gone through in the past few years." Now she wonders what to do with herself. "Here I am getting older, and I can't even figure out what to do next. Should I get out of the business? Is this the right position for me to be in? Should I be doing something more noble?" She lives with disappointment and fear for her future. "It's not that I don't trust in God and not that I don't think that he's going to come through for me, but today I am really frightened that I'm going to be walking down the boardwalk with a grocery cart." At the end of our interview, she asked me to pray that she would get out of her financial rut.

In contrast, even regular, well-paying jobs lead to disappointment if they are not directly related to the entertainment industry. Some Oasis attenders, like Tammy, have been fortunate to work a series of jobs with several prominent companies. She said, "I've been blessed with work. It just kind of comes to me. But at the same time, it's not exactly what I want to do, but I do it." Tammy feels emotionally drained, stuck in a job she hates:

> I had a little breakdown about a month ago. I told my supervisor, "You know how you do something and you tell yourself you're only going to do it for a little while and it's like you can deal with it for the time being?" And he said, "Yeah." And I said, "I never expected it to go this long." It's not my kind of environment and it's not very creative. But because of different life events, I've had to do that. It's been a blessing in so many ways because it does provide me with income and insurance and some flexibility, so that's been a blessing. But, there comes as point where you're burnt to a crisp.

Damion, who now holds a regular job in a children's hospital, used a biblical comparison for his job away from the entertainment industry: "Jonah is in the whale's stomach, saying, 'God, I've got a feeling you want me to go this way, but I'm going to go over here because there's no way that I should be doing something else. I think I need to be up in Hollywood just doing my thing.' But

God tells him, 'No, there's a big need. You need to touch some lives over here.'"
Damion saw his success in the entertainment industry as resembling the whale,
chewing him up and spitting him back out into working with children. He said,
"Then you get locked into a new place, and you're like, 'Oh, okay, this is where
I'm supposed to be right now.'"

Many spoke of taking temporary jobs while pursuing a career in the industry. Mike in his early twenties was waiting tables in Burbank, and Aaron in his
thirties "was working downtown . . . and going to auditions." Stories are common of waiters, clerks, couriers, fitness trainers, and others who say, "Actually
I'm an actor." Occupations with high turnover and flexible hours become essential for accommodating the segmented nature of industry work. As one woman
said, "In acting, you have to have a flexible job." Working these jobs leads aspiring and out-of-work actors to concoct cover stories, a tactic common among all
temporary workers (Henson 1996). The cover story creates for oneself and others an alternative identity that explains how one finds oneself in a stigmatized,
low-level job.[6] For example, although Connor introduced himself to me as a disc
jockey, he then told me he was working as a customer service representative for
a department store.

The embarrassment of working highly routinized or highly bureaucratic
jobs leads these workers to reinterpret and rationalize their work lives. For
example, Mike told me, "I quit my job as a waiter. And the day I went in to quit,
they told me I was going to be fired anyway." He said, "They didn't get me, and
I didn't get them. And so it was like I had no job." Other people tell of having
just finished a gig, or developing a new project, or being "between shows." The
cover story provides important information in a social situation, staking their
claim to an alternative master status that forms the basis of their true identity,
which survives between the often wild cyclical swings of industry activity. "I'm
working here, but I'm actually . . ."—pick one: an actor/producer/singer/song-
writer. In this way, aspirants to the entertainment industry cloak themselves in
their career dreams, craft an identity to match those aspirations, and nurture
relational communities like Oasis in which others are doing the same. Their
friends nurture their hopes by accentuating and reinforcing the identities they
most want to embrace.

Cumulative negative experiences in the industry change initial excitement to frustration and fatigue. These weary workers become disenchanted.
Heather talked about the importance of the Oasis ministry for "healing a broken heart because of the fact of the business I worked in." Matt "was . . . so
disillusioned with the people in the city," he said, "I lost my heart. . . . That was
me as a young, insecure, unsafe person trying to find some kind of identity,
trying to get by on my looks or whatever, thinking I could be somebody, you
know. No training, just like, 'I want to make some money, I want to be famous.'
That old thing."

Finding Oasis

Uncertainty and heartbreak motivate industry workers to cultivate relational networks for both professional and personal reasons. In terms of gaining work, networking is not optional; indeed it is a necessity for success in the entertainment industry (Batt, Christopherson, Rightor, and Jaarsveld 2001; Faulkner 1983; Menger 1999; C. Jones 1996). Networking is especially imperative among the workers at Oasis, since every person I met had moved to Los Angeles with high ambition but an extremely limited social network. Every person came to Los Angeles with only one key professional contact or one significant gig, which each expected to be a launch point for others. Often, the church became important because it immediately expanded the base of professional networks. Always, the church was an important base for friendship, personal help, and emotional support. One staff member said, "It's a sense of community here too. People call me, and they are like, 'I don't have a place to live right now and my credit is really bad.' So they can come into the Oasis, and we say, 'Don't worry, because we have people who are in the position to help.'"

A Very Small World

The community of Oasis is embedded within many aspects of the Hollywood entertainment industry, and the church has a reputation as a haven for industry workers. As Bridgette said, "We are in Hollywood. And one person tells another person." A staff member concurred: "It spreads by word of mouth. They will have a friend that comes to visit saying, 'I'm going to this really cool church, and it's good.' So then they'll come and bring their friends."

Many attenders found their connection to the Oasis through a friend at work. Charlene met a group of Christians at a work event who asked her if she had ever heard of the Oasis Christian Center. A friend of Lynn's asked her to try it out because she heard it was supposed to be great for actors. Reggie was a Christian looking for a church and asked around his studio. Jarrell, who graduated from college and moved to Los Angeles immediately to get involved in the film industry, said, "These girls told me about it. I met them on a TV show as an extra." Tim was invited by a member of Oasis who worked on the same set to come to church. Pointing to a girl next to him, he said, "She pulled me into this community, and this is my second time here." Although he was not accustomed to an evangelical church service, he said, "I really like to be open. As Roman Catholics people feel like we are very closed off, you know; but I am very liberal and I actually went to a Kabbala service, Jewish mysticism, one Sunday. Then I went to the Buddhist, you know, . . . chanting deal." At Oasis:

> As soon as I came and I saw the mix of people and that everyone was kind
> of on the same vibe and had that good energy, and I just started calling it
> my church. And as soon as I started calling it that, sure enough, I go out into

Hollywood and start meeting people and they are like, "Oh, where do you go?" And I go, like, "Oasis." And you know, like, "Me too." And this week, I ended up meeting some people who were in the congregation. So I knew I had made this my church.

Chad came to Oasis by invitation from someone in his acting class. Oasis is the first church that he came to. Introduced by another professional musician to Oasis, Tyler almost immediately was involved in playing in the praise and worship band for the services. Patricia, despite a friend's wanting her to attend Oasis, did not attend regularly until she met people from the congregation through her work in the industry. She said, "At the gig, I'm like, 'I recognize you from somewhere, but I don't know where.' And then my friend is at the gig with us and he is like, 'Why is our bass player from Oasis in your band?' And I was like, 'That's where I know you from.' Very small world."

Networking for Personal and Professional Survival

The church is comfortable with being a network base. Church leaders promote a vision to reach people involved in the industry, especially if they are not already committed to the Christian faith. Entering entertainment industry networks provides the opportunity to evangelize on a relational basis, a value central to the church. Those outside the Christian faith and involved in the entertainment industry are understood to be a specific target group. One staff member summarized Pastor Philip and Pastor Holly's vision for the church:

> God knows Philip and Holly's heart and how they just love everybody, and they have an extrasensitive place in their heart for people in the entertainment business, with both of them having been in it. Especially Holly, having seen the wrong choices that people can make and how they can get off track. But also seeing how amazing the flip side can be if we have people in this business who are standing up for God and living a life that is, you know, celebrating him and also being true to him. What an impact that could have on this city! So they see that and know that, and so if we could all just get that as entertainers, L.A. would be a completely different place.

Another staff member said, "Our pastor's vision of our church is to reach the unchurched, and many people in the entertainment industry are unchurched. They come into our church knowing absolutely nothing about Christianity, nothing at all, haven't picked up a Bible in their lives before, still not knowing that what they are doing is actually not a healthy thing and that there is a different way of doing things." Another staff member summed up the Oasis mission to the entertainment industry: "It's a group of people that needs to be ministered to, and we all do that."

For many associated with the industry, the ministries of the church provide opportunities to connect to the personal and professional network of people at Oasis. Chuck auditioned for a church play when he first visited and won a key role, after which he progressively became more involved at Oasis. Brent, who is very active in the worship services as a musician, spoke of the strong ministries in the church, including audiovisual ministry, skits, short film, improv, dance team, and music. "All of these different ministries are becoming so strong and professional, a standard that is in Hollywood, up to that standard," Brent said, making Oasis attractive to other professionals. Lynn said, "When people come in, they see the praise and worship, the choir, the band, the dance, the drama, the video team, the editing. There's a lot for that kind of people."

The professional networking of relationships at the Oasis works in two directions: people in the industry introduce others at work to the church, and people at church help connect church members to knowledge, opportunities, and relationships out in the work world. Relationships formed at the church thus contribute to the professional networking so vital to success in the entertainment industry. Rocco said that "some relationships in the church have been valuable" to him, in particular another talent manager in the church who gave him useful advice. Rodrigo told me that when people found themselves without work, the church helps them connect to opportunities. "If you care about people and you know about what's going on with someone, you say, 'Hey, you know so-and-so is without work.' So somebody gets on the phone, they start calling people, and they find that person work—help people out."

Certainly, attenders cultivate relationships for personal as well as professional reasons. When Donna first came to Oasis, she was impressed. "It was really cool, being that I'm an actress as well, that it was in an old theater." She immediately made a friend also involved in the entertainment business. At Destiny Theater, she said, they "were standing outside looking at the star of Jesus Christ that we have out front. And you know me, being the actress, pointed and said, 'I'm going to have one of these one day." That Christmas, her friend made her a special gift; it was a Hollywood star with her name on it. "He had one made with the Scripture, 'Those who are wise will shine like the brightness of the heavens, and those who lead many to righteousness, like the stars for ever and ever.' He gave it to me and said, 'You can quit trying to get that star. Here's your star.'"

When Lois started attending Oasis, her relationships expanded, and when she had a serious accident, she said, "People came to the hospital room right after, taking care of me. It was amazing." Oasis members came to her home with food, contributed financially, and were "there for me in every way." She said, "You never know when you're going to have a crisis and need people, and it's kind of nice to have them there." While she was out of work, friends from the church contributed groceries and spare cash. Although her accident prevented her from working, it did give her time to paint. Her home became her studio, and she received generous commissions to do portraits within the congregation and sold others.

Many especially appreciate how Oasis allows people to connect, free of work agendas, with others in the industry. Charlene distinguished the warmth of the church from the professional warmth she experiences in the television industry. "I know what genuine warmth is as opposed to the phony stuff. In the industry, there are people that would welcome you, but it's all a part of a script." Jennelle explained that

> people in the entertainment industry want to feel accepted and not like they are weird or something. And I don't think churches as a whole do a good job of making creative people welcome. We can tend to be a little strange, a little odd, a little eccentric. And we try to be, sometimes. We try to be weird. That's why we came out here and we do this crazy stuff and at the same time, though, we still want people to accept us how we are. And I think they can get that at the Oasis. We don't care what you are wearing or how you are dressed.

The pressures of maintaining an image are softened. Noel said that "creative people" believe they are "so different from everybody else. But when they come here, it's like, 'I'm actually embraced, and it's okay.'" She includes herself as a person involved in the creative arts who finds it uncomfortable relating to people in mainstream culture yet comfortable among attenders at Oasis. "I'm an actor by trade, and here it's okay. Back where I came from, I felt weird. I'm not, like, out-there crazy, but it's just different."

Creating a Spiritual Connection at Oasis

Christians who arrive at Oasis find acceptance for their ambitions and sympathy for their heartaches. An older woman said, "Our church is right here in Hollywood. Pastor is a kind of guy that makes it okay for us to be in the entertainment industry. It's okay. We can come here, and he's not going to make us feel like we are horrible human beings." Some believers spoke of loneliness and spiritual crises in coming to Hollywood. Rocco is a talent manager who arrived in Los Angeles with a spiritual yearning. It was always his intention to find a good church. He said, "I really felt it was important." Living in the city, Rodrigo said, "God was talking to me and saying, 'Hey Rodrigo, you know where you can find me. You know where I am, you know where to go.'"

Bill moved out from the East Coast to pursue a career as a model and actor. His religious background was Roman Catholicism, but he was no longer active in his church. Although he felt that he had disconnected from God, he said, "I definitely had a hunger for God and wanted to know more. . . . I knew even as a teenager that there had to be more to this whole God relationship than stained glass and dipping my hand in holy water once a week." Soon after arriving in

Los Angeles he recalled walking the streets of Hollywood looking for a church, "to open the door and go in there and just kneel and just pray. Just in my little Catholic way, talk to God, be still, say some Our Fathers." From a hotel room, he "stole" a Gideon Bible, which became important for his spiritual quest. "I had my Bible, I'm in Hollywood, I'm reading it, not knowing but just seeking and must have been in my own way praying and seeking God." Another night, Bill met a Christian on the street who asked him about his beliefs. "I think I'm a Christian," he said.

> "I'm a good guy. Da-da-da-da." I remember him lovingly just blowing that out of the water with the Word, you know, and inviting me to receive Christ and have a relationship with him, the way just laid out, which I had never heard, obviously. I remember thinking and even saying to them, like, "Here? Praying here? Doing that?" You know, thinking, you can't do that on the sidewalk. So I repeated a prayer after them.

I realize that Bill is telling me his conversion story. He is visibly moved. "Even as I say it, I can almost feel it again." Rather than having some vague sense of comfort of going to heaven based on good deeds, Bill found a new comfort and freedom. "For the first time I felt like I had a relationship with God as my Father, and it was awesome. I just felt like the roof was off my car and there was this wind"—he made a blowing sound—"back and forth and I remember being so amazed." It was during this time friends introduced him to Oasis.

Yet not everyone arrives at Oasis as a Bible-believing Christian. Bridgette worked at a motion picture studio and had a friend who attempted to evangelize her. Bridgette said, "I wasn't buying it." She kept asking questions, and her friend would try to answer using the Bible. "I just drilled her for a year." Tim decided to commit to Oasis because of the messages that seemed relevant to his involvement in the entertainment industry. But his commitment is not exclusively to Oasis. "I told my buddy at the Buddhist church, 'I'm going to come back.' I'm not closing myself off to any other spiritual awakenings that might be available, you know, out there. But when people ask me where my church is, I'm going to say 'the Oasis Christian.'"

Doris felt disoriented during her first visit to Oasis, where she came with a friend. She said, "I would never have walked in here had it been a fundamentalist church." Regarding Christianity, she said, "All I knew about Christianity was just rules, regulations, straightening out. There was never anything taught to me about love and caring and God wanting good things in your life. It was always about what you shouldn't be doing and how you should act and that wasn't what my life was about." She remembered the service: "People were raising their hands, clapping and singing and smiling and looked happy. I thought, 'What are they doing? What kind of place is this?'" The first hurdle for Doris was believing that these people were really happy, "because I didn't believe anybody was really happy. I thought Holly was insane. I was like, 'That woman isn't for real. There's no way anybody is that cheerful and nice.'" That night, Pastor Philip "was doing a series on the supernatural rejection of debt and the message that night was 'Let the Lord be magnified in his pleasure and the prosperity of his servants.' And I'll never forget it. It's Psalm 35. And I was having severe financial problems at the time." The message moved her. "I felt very uneasy, and I felt all choked up. I was completely confused when I left and cried and went through this whole emotional thing." Doris had never read a Bible in her life. "Whatever he said was right on the money with what I was living at the time. I started asking [my friend] a million questions."

Doris kept coming back every week. Soon, she went down during the altar call. She made it halfway down the aisle and was sobbing. Pastor Holly approached, asked what she did for a living, and then asked her if she would feel comfortable talking with somebody in her line of work, someone "that could possibly help you and explain how this goes?" And Doris told her, "I don't know if it would help me or not. All I know is that my life as I knew it just fell apart." Pastor Holly introduced her to a successful film producer, and they began meeting. Soon, she went forward to commit to Christ at an altar call, became more involved at the church, served in ministry, attended Bible study, and eventually joined as a member.

Negotiating Fame and Profit amidst Disappointment and Heartache

As a church, Oasis intentionally strives for relevance to those in the entertainment industry, where success is measured in fame and profit. When Hollywood workers start attending Oasis, they view the industry as an arena of opportunity for the accumulation of wealth and fame. But the common experience of disenchantment with pursuing fame provokes them to embrace broader ideals. Their motivations undergo a transformation. This profound reorientation appears consistently in the compelling life stories of Oasis attenders.

6   Religion

> NOEL: I don't know how to explain it. It's different,
> but it's good.

From the beginning, Oasis included attenders from the entertainment industry. Philip Wagner had started dating Holly in 1984 when he was invited to teach a Bible study in the Beverly Hills home of a successful producer. The study took place in a spacious room displaying an Oscar on the mantel, a quiet, powerful presence impossible to ignore. Proclaiming the success and prestige of a talented celebrity, the Oscar was a source of pride and envy. This icon represented the hopes and dreams of attenders and offered tangible hope that since one believer could attain this measure of success, so could others. And it defined a special bond between people to this community.

Attendance at the study quickly surged to over fifty people. In six months, they moved to a larger facility. "Some well-known celebrities were coming," Holly said. "The joke was we would find out if they were coming for the Oscar on the mantel or if they were really coming for the church." She laughed. "We found out it was the Oscar they were coming for." The first church service consisted of sixty, which fell the next week to thirty. The third service dwindled to twenty, and soon they were down to ten. Alluding to an Old Testament warrior whose army was drastically reduced before an important battle, Holly called the ten the basis for Gideon's revival, from which they would grow their church.

Twenty years later, more than two thousand people regularly attend Oasis services, and their venue, Destiny Theater, is ideally located to serve workers in the entertainment industry. As one member said, "We are in the middle of Hollywood, basically." Motion picture and television production companies with their affiliated employment networks form a belt running east to west, from Santa Monica to Burbank, and the center corresponds to the heart of old Hollywood a few blocks from the theater. Indeed, every geographic analysis locating industry work in the region situates Destiny Theater in the geographic center of the Hollywood entertainment industry, whether the mapping includes studios, sound stages, television production facilities, set design and construction sites, peripheral service firms, patterns of residency among workers, or the offices of agents, casting directors, and managers who place them.[1] For Oasis congregants, home, work, and church are located within twenty miles of each other.

More important than the optimal physical location, an intimate connection exists between the style of Oasis's ministry and the life circumstances of its attenders. Philip and Holly built a church that would appeal to industry insiders like themselves. Although the ministry of the congregation is not limited to those who work in the industry, the converted movie house successfully gathers industry-related believers in the intimacy of a physical site where the beliefs and practices enacted through the church resonate with their experiences, reinforce their shared status, and accentuate a corporate bond appealing to their hopes, dreams, and ambitions—and does so using theological and congregational innovations developed in the last century.

Philip and Holly's Journey to Destiny Theater

Pastor Philip, a brown-haired Caucasian, son of a Baptist pastor, and raised in the South, stopped attending church as a young man to have what he called his "little Jonah experience—you know—pursuing other things" and work in the music industry. Then he was caught up in the Jesus movement. Philip took his love for music into a professional ministry, recording albums for Maranatha Music and playing for church youth groups around Southern California. Eventually, he became an assistant pastor at a church described by another Oasis pastor as a "hippie, Jesus-generation, Calvary Chapel offshoot with an L.A. style." Philip left the church after a scandal involving another pastor and joined a Vineyard church. He met Holly, a blonde-haired model and actress, just before starting the Beverly Hills Bible study. Holly had grown up in various countries, as her father's work in the petroleum industry took the family across the globe. She attended college with the intent to enter medical school. Acting was a hobby, and she started modeling to earn extra income and have some fun. Success in Dallas led to work in Los Angeles, where she did "a bazillion commercials" and regular roles in television series and films. She continued working until the church moved to the theater in 1997.

At the beginning, Philip and Holly combined their experiences in the entertainment industry with their extensive church backgrounds to start their new church. Still, they say they had no idea how to do church. Holly said, "Philip came out of the Jesus movement where if you just strum a guitar and preach Jesus things ought to happen." They struggled for two years until they discovered Church Growth gurus Donald McGavran and Peter Wagner, who were based at Fuller Theological Seminary in Pasadena. In the 1980s, Philip and Holly joined legions of other pastors attending newly designed Church Growth seminars who came away saying, "Oh! You can strategize for growth." The new motto for growth-oriented pastors like Philip and Holly became, "The message is sacred, but everything else is up for discussion." From 1987 to

1997, they became attentive students of growth-oriented models of ministry around the country.

Overflowing with fresh paradigms about Christian leadership, Philip and Holly implemented a deliberate style. They established classes to instill values for highly intentional local church ministry. They demanded excellence from their volunteers. They designed groups with greater sensitivity to age strata and life circumstances. The ministry became "targeted." They incorporated contemporary praise music. They advertised on the radio with lines like, "Are you suffering from a broken heart?" They rented a billboard that read, "Looking for Love?" with an arrow pointing to the site of their weekly services. When it seemed advantageous, they emulated the practices of prominent evangelicals (John Maxwell, among others) who advanced an aggressive, strategic approach to church leadership.

Their strategies worked, despite the strained circumstances of rented facilities, limited budgets, and a highly mobile population. They grew the church from two hundred to four hundred attenders. But for this pastoral couple, the corporate model of following trends, marketing ministries, tactically planning for weekly excellence, and sequentially moving to larger locations grew tiresome. And the final move to the theater was not planned but rather forced upon them. Oasis had been renting a community center on Wilshire when the property was sold to make way for a fast-food restaurant. Many members were angered with the loss of the building, yet the need to move necessitated creative problem solving. They made a bid on a dilapidated theater two blocks east of the community center. The single-screen, nine-hundred-seat, art deco–style movie house at 5112 Wilshire Blvd was vacant and for sale.

From Movie House to House of Worship

The history of Destiny Theater is enmeshed in the history of Hollywood as a whole. By the 1920s, movie theaters were firmly entrenched as a national public institution (May 2000, 101–102). They had transformed from urban storefront nickelodeons catering to the immigrant and working classes to suburban movie palaces in sumptuous buildings that drew in the middle and upper classes.[2] Movie palaces were richly textured, elaborately decorated spaces, an escape from the drudgery of day-to-day working life. They consumed the largest portion of Americans' entertainment budget, and Los Angeles, along with New York, Chicago, and San Francisco, boasted more than five hundred theaters with 1,500 to 3,000 seats each, about one seat for every five people in the city (May 1983, 165). Hollywood itself had the highest concentration of movie screens in the world (Torrence 1982, 247).

By the 1930s, movie theaters transformed again, from ornamental cathedrals with massive seating capacities to smaller houses of five to eight hundred seats. Embracing the new American practicality, they were functional and streamlined, eliminating gaudy artistic statues and symbols in favor of simple lines and structures.³ Faux finishes were exchanged for steel, glass, and concrete. Private boxes made way for common seating. Proscenium arches and stages disappeared, replaced by flowing designs and a screen closer to the audience.

The United Artists Four Star Theater that became the home of the Oasis Christian Center was built at this time. It is a modern structure with a playful art deco style that underlines functionality and form rather than lavish taste. The lobby is simple and straightforward. It has no balconies or private areas. Two aisles allow entrance and exit between steadily sloping arrays of theater-style seats. A common entrance and exit reinforce egalitarianism and stress the unity of the crowd. Rounded outside corners create continuity between the interior of the auditorium and the busy street outside.

When the Four Star was built next to the Miracle Mile in the 1930s, Wilshire Boulevard was the longest and widest boulevard in the country, comparable to New York's Fifth Avenue, Paris's Champs-Elysées, and Chicago's Michigan Boulevard. The comparison today seems exaggerated; nevertheless, a grasp of the street's historic importance helps explain how this movie theater would have been built, seemingly strategically, on this spot. By the 1950s, the Miracle Mile, a successful commercial development, boasted a densely populated region of fabulous homes and scores of apartment complexes. It was the pride of Wilshire Boulevard and the central focus of Los Angeles' commercial, celebrity, and metropolitan image (Hancock 1949, 150).

With this location, the Four Star survived as a single-screen movie house longer than most. The growth of drive-ins and the rise of eight- to fifteen-screen multiplexes and megaplexes with sixteen or more screens contributed to the tremendous expansion in total numbers of movie screens in the United States, as so-called four-walled theaters experienced financial difficulties and closed. Hardpressed to remain financially viable, most single-screen theaters like the Four Star before the VHS rental era featured either dollar shows of late-run movies months after their initial release or adult pornographic films. Obscenity laws and the growth of VHS video recordings shut down most in the 1960s and 1970s. But the Four Star still played many first-run hits and exclusive engagements like *The Graduate* and *The Lion in Winter* before succumbing to national trends that indicated the lowest U.S. theater attendance in history.

United Artists pulled out of the Four Star in the 1970s, which followed the fate of other single-screen theaters by becoming a house leased for porn films. The theater switched to second- and third-run double features in the 1980s and 1990s, as well as classic, foreign, and independent films that played to scattered crowds at reasonable prices. The theater would open for several weeks, then close, and then reopen again in a downward cycle of revenue.

Eventually, the Four Star fell into disrepair and was sold to Oasis in 1997. One longtime member said, "When we got it, it was the grungiest place. And you

Figure 2. A modern movie house with a playful art deco style, the former United Artists Four Star Theater on Wilshire Boulevard is now home to the Oasis Christian Center.
(Photo by Soo Petrovich.)

were sort of tiptoeing around. There were rats' nests. There were holes in the floor. And you didn't want to touch the seats or the chairs. People came that first day and went 'Ugh.'" But even before its full rebirth as Destiny Theater, the two-block move to the Four Star fundamentally crystallized the identity and mission of the congregation.

Creating an Arena for Spiritual Champions

Philip admitted that after working so hard to purchase the theater, he and Holly wanted a break. "If I wasn't pastoring this church, I don't know if I'd be attending here." Yet this weariness led to a realization. After spending so many years imitating other churches, Philip and Holly created a church for themselves. "We spent thirteen years being small and unclear and figuring out who we are," said Philip. The rundown theater mirrored the exhaustion of their ministry, but the new space prompted new thinking. "Why don't we build a church we would want to join?" Holly said, "We decided we were just going to be who we were." She added, "The fact it's a theater fit our personality."

As they refurbished the building, they renovated their own ministry styles. Each would symbolically feed on the other. Holly said, "We don't want a stained-glass and crosses everywhere kind of culture. We decided to build the church that we liked—with drama and dance and not the stuffy teaching style." Drawing on their experiences and memories in the entertainment industry, Pastors Philip and Holly created a church that reflected valued aspects of their own identity that would appeal to others. They were not concerned about protecting parochial religious territories like denominational affiliations, doctrinal perspectives, or eschatological viewpoints. Defining the church as "what we do together," they cultivated an affective connection among members at once casual and homey while encouraging them to pursue lives of spiritual significance. Moreover, by taking the pressure off themselves to model other people's success, they laid the foundation for a "come as you are" ministry that would emphasize the love and acceptance pervasive in the experience of attenders today.

"Let's Be Entertaining": Transforming Sacred Space

In the new building on Wilshire, they saw the refurbished theater as a public extension of their identity. Instead of organizing the public ministry of the congregation around pew and altar, the scenario became stage, screen, and audience. Meeting in a stylized art deco theater accentuated the symbolic connection between the worship of the congregation and the emblematic core of the entertainment industry. Moreover, the year they acquired the theater was the same year they amended their philosophy of ministry, expanded Holly's platform presence, and institutionalized their outreach to the Hollywood community through the installation of the Jesus Hollywood star.

In the architecture and design of the building, physicality suggests spiri-tuality. A young white actress who had just moved to Los Angeles recalled her first visit: "I just remember walking in, and it was just a cool look. Just that it's a theater." A musician thought to himself, "If it's like this physically, then there must be something spiritually going on here that really I can fit in with." An African American actor said the church is reaching people who are artistically inclined because, after all, "this is L.A." Oasis continually uses the atmosphere of the building to accentuate the congregational connection to the Hollywood industry. As Philip explained, "It was not traditional, it was very artistic and creative."

The core of Hollywood is entertainment through media arts, so it is no surprise that Oasis embraces music, video, and the spoken word along with dance, drama, and graphic arts to convey its message. One example is in the use of multimedia screens for announcements. The announcements at Oasis are called Oasis Info and presented in *Entertainment Tonight*–style, two-person video messages that comprise a series of ten- to twenty-second commercials that are short, flashy, and fun. The embrace of new technology appears seamless in the converted movie theater. Moreover, the church produces media-friendly products—books, videos, CDs, and DVDs—to accentuate their relationship to the entertainment industry and take advantage of what they consider to be a powerful medium for communication. Jarrell talked about some of his friends who use their creative talents for the church. "They shoot little videos here and there, and they're just loving it. They are doing something they really love and they are serving God while they are doing it."

Oasis regularly features ministry highlights cultivated specifically for indus-try-oriented attenders. Both Philip and Holly often preach sermon series devoted to applying biblical principles to artists in the industry. References to involve-ment in the entertainment industry are frequent and common. In addition, 24/7 is a regular ministry to creative artists, with an assigned pastor and special meet-ings. Flyers in the foyer advertise workshops like these:

COMEDY IMPROV
A veteran in the business, Kelly loves the comedic arts and has a knack for encouraging and pulling the best out of others. Whether you're a beginner or a professional, this group will help you build confidence, unlock your cre-ativity and have lots of fun in the process! Every Tuesday @ 7:00 PM

WRITE ON! SCREEN AND TV WRITERS
Chris has been a screenwriter for many years and currently has a film in production. The goal of this Christ-centered group is to provide personal support and professional development for film and television writers in all stages of their careers. Participants also attend film screenings and seminars together. Once a month Tuesday @ 7:00 PM

In the messages and in the ministries of the church, the focus on the entertainment industry is explicit. Jarrell feels Oasis does things from "an entertainment point of view." He said, "They try to entertain because they have the understanding of how people in the entertainment industry are and what they understand. They know how to reach them." A middle-aged television producer said, "Everything we do is very entertaining." The notion of entertainment is reconstructed to become not a means for self-promotion but a tool for drawing attention to the church as a whole, creating public ministries that generate interest, allow for whimsy, and attempt to keep in step with the style of popular media. Philip said, "I don't like to be bored with the gospel and I don't think it's boring. So let's rethink how we are representing God."

According to Philip, Holly's acting talent also "comes in very handy" because "our style, our focus, is to try to minister to people in a creative, entertaining way." Holly said, "I bring my own energy and personality and creativity." One attender, describing Holly, said, "You know how she is, just kind of wild and spunky and very outgoing." After her marriage to Philip and the start of the new church, Holly continued to work through the late 1990s. This long success combined with her perky optimism remains an important asset for the church. The opinion of one longtime member echoed that of many others: "The fact that Holly was in the entertainment business for so long [is great], and she puts that fun aspect into the church." She added, "Philip and Holly both are so entertaining, but yet their heart is on fire for God."

Until the late 1990s, attenders could still see Holly on TV talk shows, commercials, or dramatic series. But despite a good income, her expanded involvement in the public ministry of the church (in addition to more time spent with their two young children) led to her dropping her acting career. "There came a time when my desire shifted from wanting to entertain people to wanting to help them," Holly said. "Not that entertaining is bad; I just started pouring more of my heart into the church, and then felt God directing me a different way." Her turn from entertainment to ministry, from drawing attention to herself to serving the needs of others, became paradigmatic for the church as a whole. And since the building itself provided an undeniable connection to the entertainment industry, it was no longer necessary to have a prominent church leader on staff active in the business. Now, the theater provided the legitimacy of the church's intimate connection to the industry. The external transformation of the dilapidated theatre metaphorically points to the attempt to transform the internal world of the actor and the entertainment industry as a whole.

By meeting in a refurbished movie house, Oasis unknowingly manifests the uniquely American transformation of sacred space. Jeanne Halgren Kilde's fascinating book *When Church Became Theatre: The Transformation of Evangelical Architecture and Worship in Nineteenth-Century America* articulates the significance of the development of the church that favors theater auditorium seating over boxlike pews and altars as a radical shift in evangelical Protestant architecture. Associated with the change in architecture, the late nineteenth and early twentieth centuries witnessed a tremendous shift in the nature of evangelical worship services and the rise of new forms of pastor performance in the pulpit. Evangelists accommodated their styles to forms of entertainment to enhance the appeal of the gospel message, borrowing forms and idioms of popular entertainments, commercial emporiums, and master marketers to promote its message (Oberdeck 1999; Winston 1999). As popular entertainment focused on the growing industrialized class of workers, so did evangelical religion. Some churches appropriated movie theaters and replaced vice-promoting godless films with morally uplifting religious ones. As Lindvall notes: "As the churches began adopting theaters, they also began adopting theatrical methods to attract worshipers" (2007, 81). The appeal of evangelical leaders like Billy Sunday, Charles Finney, and Aimee Semple McPherson are decisively situated at the juncture of evangelicalism and popular entertainment culture (Bendroth 2004; Epstein 1993). Inherent to the birth of mass American culture is the mixture of entertainment and evangelistic forms, since both seek appeal to the broad mass of ordinary people (see chapter 4).

Shifts in architecture thus indicated changes in worship style and religious mission. In the past, clergy were physically raised above the audience, which emphasized the authority and the higher nature of the message conveyed from the pulpit. In contrast, the auditorium-style church features a prominent stage and rows of pews radiating up a sloping floor. Although theaters may seem an unusual source for religious architecture, Kilde asserts that both churches and theaters share the goal of bringing together large groups of people to hear a speaker. The upward slope of the auditorium allows the speaker to stand below the audience and the voice to carry up, which is acoustically superior to traditional arrangements. Increasingly clergy were speaking out of and to the audience, so the audience was now raised above the speaker, which made the reactions of the audience inherent to the effectiveness of the performance. In the auditorium church, the entire building proclaims that the message will be accessible and keep one's attention. It promises entertainment. A further connection between church and theater is the increased theatricality of pastoral performances as preachers moved away from pulpits and immovable lecterns. As Kilde points out: "The preacher now has access to the performance authority of the actor" (2002, 34).

In essence, the move toward a consumer-oriented religious participation began with the reconstruction of evangelical Protestant worship buildings. A new relationship between clergy and congregation was forged as clerical power increasingly lay in the dramatic expertise with which a pastor imparted religious messages. In addition, the architecture that encouraged focus toward the speaker and performance on the stage also allowed members of the crowd to see and hear one another more than ever before. This had marvelous effects, increasing responsiveness and heightening personal reactions, as attenders gauged reactions from each other. Increase in audience participation appears to be correlated with the increase in the ability of congregants to observe each other. As worshipers see themselves corporately engaging in the same activity, for example, singing becomes less an act of private devotion and more an act of public participation. In worship, the group enacts itself, and the crowd becomes alive as a corporate body (for more on worship, see chapter 8).

The increased affinity of Protestant church leaders for entertainment is the result of neither a fleeting fad nor a knee-jerk submission to popular culture. Leaders found that duty, loyalty, and familiarity were not sufficient to keep churches filled. Changes in architecture responded to new beliefs about how urban crowds meet together, what modern populations expect in group experiences, and the competing choices city audiences have for their attention. And changes in pastoral style were both encouraged by the new structure of preaching space and necessitated by change in audience demand.

From the standpoint of church architectural history, the notion of worshiping in a theater is therefore not new. Jeanne Halgren Kilde (2002, 28–47) reports that the first recorded instance of a church meeting in a theater was in the spring of 1832, when Lewis Tappan and William Green purchased a ten-year lease on Chatham Theatre in lower Manhattan as a permanent post for the great revivalist Charles Finney. The theater had once been a respectable playhouse for working-class audiences, then a place for illicit sexuality, accommodating prostitutes and attracting a much less presentable clientele. Finney was reluctant to rent the theater because he wanted to appear respectable to his peers and other churches in the city. In that day, evangelicals commonly condemned theaters in sermons, tracts, and newspaper articles, labeling actors' performances and audience activities as immoral. Placing the church in such a space, Finney feared, would connect it with the immoral and potentially advocate immorality (McConachie 1992, 161–197; Shiffler 1953, 159–164). But his advisors convinced him that holding church in the theater would be sensational in a positive way: The strangeness of having church in the theater was to be its strength, as curiosity and excitement would draw people to visit. Moreover, holding church in a place that had been viewed as evil and immoral would demonstrate the triumphant nature of Christianity, for, as Kilde writes, "if Christianity could transform a theater, surely it had the power to transform any degenerate soul" (29). Similar to Finney's church, Oasis boldly contested public entertainment space by turning it into a religious space.

The theater design eventually provoked an energetic response in churches interested in having the same level of passion, excitement, and vitality evident in popular entertainment. Whether seeker oriented or not, auditorium-style churches lessen the difference between the outside world and the church. By integrating forms of theater into church life, worship services become more exciting and attractive. The church becomes more accessible, and therefore the message gains a wider audience. The buildings themselves advertise that churches' focus on the desires and tastes of an expanding middle-class audience.

Philip and Holly resonate with the historic desire of ministers and congregants for compelling services that stir up religious sentiments, and the design of services in new, theaterlike environments increases the active engagement of the congregation. The expertise of pastors to entertain certainly rises as competition for a comfortable place to worship and an interesting pastor to listen to define the marketplace of religion. The expectations of church audiences are growing, and church services are becoming more a commodity as religious patrons pick and choose which services provide the most entertaining way to engage their devotional life. Believing that the draw of a worship service is only the beginning of the cultivation of a fully formed Oasis disciple, Philip and Holly accentuate the possibilities of their physical space to attract guests and potential members.

"Let's Have Some Fun": Feeling Energized in the Spirit

Summarizing the purpose of the church, Holly said, "I think we are supposed to create an environment where people are accepted just as they are and challenged to become better and grow. And we just do that laughing." Over and over again, "fun" is the word used to describe the church. A mature African American woman in television production said, "I laugh. Church is fun. It is not a chore for me to get up on a Sunday morning and come to church because I know that our church is going to be fun. And how many people can say that? . . . I've never heard the words 'fun' and 'God' in the same sentence. Until I got here." A Hispanic in her early twenties said of Holly, "She is fun. She is keeping my attention." Another young Hispanic woman who had left the Roman Catholic Church: "I didn't know church could be fun." A middle-aged African American who recently left acting behind: "You walk in and you just see smiles on people's faces. And they are not forced smiles. They are just people that are happy." A white model-actress: "There's no place you'd rather be. You just lose yourself. You just come in and you're just so happy to be here and it's fun. It's so much fun."

Once people are through the door, the first priority in the services, Philip said, is "to have fun and put fun in the service on purpose." Early in the shifting style of services in the theater, Holly encouraged Philip, saying, "Let's play with each other on the platform. Let's be a little sassy together. Let's heckle each other from the front row." Philip and Holly also committed to being open about their own issues and struggles, and attenders noticed. A regular attendee said, "One thing that's definitely unique is that we see parts of Holly and Philip's relationship, and they joke about each other and whatnot." Their playfulness reduced the distance between the platform and the audience. Partnering together on the platform, they shunned the polish, formality, and gaudy style of many of their heroes to create a more casual and relaxed public style. Philip welcomed guests from the platform, saying, "We like to have fun here and we want you to relax, but I don't want you to be confused that we are not serious about our faith in God." Humorous stories and their speaking styles softened the intensity of conservative moral teachings.

Attenders are impressed by the liveliness of services at Oasis, where energetic worship is a signature of the congregation. Services feature polished and powerful worship music with a conscious rejection of staid liturgy and monotonous ritual. Attenders describe the music as "hot," "lively," "upbeat," "exciting," and "alive." An African American in his early thirties said, "Our style of worship is unique, very celebratory, very bold, and very public." The larger theater space resulted in a louder sound. A Hispanic woman in her early thirties labeled services at Oasis "more vivacious, more energy, more freedom." A longtime female member listed appealing characteristics of the church: "Just the intensity, the worship, the friendliness of the people that were there, the openness, the freshness." Cool visual graphics and a stylized ambiance contribute to "a very MTV vibe." One first-time Hispanic attender was shocked into asking, "Is this a church?" He continued, "The first twenty minutes were a little uncomfortable. These people are just rocking. Look at that!"

The cultivation of fun and the energetic worship services are drawn directly from the congregation's roots in neo-Pentecostalism. John Wesley's second blessing sanctification, Holiness and Keswick movements, and Pentecostalism and its twentieth-century developments—all emphasize the importance of a vital spiritual connection that goes beyond the staid nominalism of Reformed, Calvinist-influenced ecclesial traditions (Synan 1997). The typical narrative among Pentecostal believers is that Pentecostalism represented a vital break in the history of Christianity, revitalized the Christian experience, and delivered it from becoming an empty, formalized set of rituals. Old-style Pentecostals are often considered to be austere and enforcing righteous codes of conduct. But neo-Pentecostals exhibit more flexibility, emphasizing personal freedom and releasing the expectation of puritanical asceticism while keeping an appreciation for divine power and ecstatic experiences.

The experience of joy in the presence of God within the Holiness-Pentecostal tradition is far more important than correctness, doctrinal truth, or proper ritual (Nichol 1966). The movement is more emotive and positively affective. Theology is not systematic but rather an expression of personal testimony. Religious experience is accentuated through emotionally engaging worship like that found routinely at Oasis. The pattern is one of upbeat, high-energy worship at weekend services and more intimate, high-touch midweek gatherings and services that emphasize intimacy and community—also indicative of new paradigm church worship increasingly common not only among West Coast evangelicals but across the country (Miller 1997).[4]

Many of us still remember unsatisfying church experiences as solemn occasions—dry, boring, and drained of emotion. Yet in the *Elementary Forms of Religious Life*, Durkheim is very clear that rejuvenation of personal energy came from active participation in rituals of a community: "Since utilitarian purposes are in general alien to them, they make men forget the real world so as to transport them into another where their imagination is more home; they entertain. Sometimes they even go as far as having the outward appearance of recreation. We see those present laughing and openly having fun" (1995, 384). In Durkheim's understanding, the cult is not merely restrictive but also an occasion for merriment, laughter, and true enjoyment (380–387).

The cultic ceremonies at Oasis do not fulfill merely instrumental purposes. Participation in the worship services of the moral community of Oasis is a fundamental way people are reenergized. The experience of delight described by Oasis attenders in their worship is in direct contrast with the drudgery and disappointment described in their work. After the initial months of excitement of moving to Los Angeles, finding and keeping a steady workflow quickly becomes tedious for Oasis workers. Only occasionally do exciting career events inspire them with a hope that motivates them to continue pursuing the next big thing. In the meantime, Oasis workers routinely find a level of enjoyment through participation in their church that is rarely paralleled in their all too often overglamorized world of work.

Thus, a neglected element of understanding religious life is the element of enjoyment, what Durkheim called the "recreational and aesthetic element" of religion (1995, 383). A religious service is not always a solemn affair that represses individual motion; the activities of the cult during a service are also an opportunity to express joy. Durkheim goes on to point out that "it is well known that games and the principal forms of art seem to have been born in religion and that they long maintained their religious character. We can see why: while pursuing other goals directly, the cult has at the same time been a form of recreation. Religion has not played this role by chance or happy coincidence but as a result of its inherent logic" (385). Some things are done in the midst of religious activity not for particular purposes or to accomplish particular goals: "Religion would not be religion if there was no place in it for free combinations of thought and action, for games, for art, for all that refreshes a spirit worn down by all that is overburdening in day-to-day labor."

Of course, Durkheim is quick to say that religion is not solely entertainment and that rites that only entertain are no longer religious rites, that is, "a rite is something other than a game; it belongs to the serious side of life" (1995, 386). Nevertheless, to miss out on the entertainment aspect of religion is to miss out on one of the most powerful draws of religion in contemporary life. In a world where work is unstable, leisure time has been curtailed, and individuals are more and more often alone, participation in congregational life becomes deeply meaningful as rejuvenation and sustenance for individuals as they move back into the day-to-day drudgery of their economic lives. Again, Durkheim: "Once we have fulfilled our ritual duties, we return to a profane life with more energy and enthusiasm, not only because we've placed ourselves in contact with a higher source of energy but also because our own capacities have been replenished through living, for a few moments, a life that is less tense, more at ease, and freer."

"Let's Make It Relevant": Demystifying Spirituality

In addition to "fun," "relevance" is a key word often heard at Oasis. One longtime member said, "So many people's impression is that the church isn't relevant; therefore, God isn't—but God so is." Church leaders explicitly acknowledge they define relevance as remaining connected to younger generations, and the increased attendance of young singles is typically understood as a mark of their success toward the goal to become relevant to culture. Music and services are designed to connect with the popular culture of younger age groups. Rocco, among others, believes that Oasis "models what the pop culture is about." As attendance grew, longtime members agree, Oasis shifted toward a more youthful focus. Gladys said, "When I arrived, there was more of a nuclear family focus. But the congregation shifted; now the focus is on younger adults." From being a church of thirty- to fifty-year-olds, it is now dominantly a group of twenty- to thirty-year-olds.

Overall, the focus on relevance at Oasis manifests a growing trend among evangelical churches to be seeker sensitive, that is, to make Christian faith and practice readily accessible to those not raised in Christian churches (see Sargeant 2000). Although nearly every attender at Oasis is a committed Christian, every staff member and regular attender defined the congregation as made up of the unchurched. For many, the word "unchurched" is just code for casual dress. For an African American woman in her forties, it means "not being a formal church, not wearing a hat or hose or gloves." The more important use of the word "unchurched" expresses a profound desire among seeker churches to demystify spirituality in order to evangelize more effectively. As Matt said, "Your relationship with God doesn't need to be spooky. We don't get up and say, 'Amen, amen, amen.' We're regular people."

In striving for relevance, people at the church are especially mindful of others' negative judgments of Charismatic and Word of Faith believers. Members who came to the church in the 1980s and early 1990s say Oasis then was "a little more Pentecostal, a little more Word of Faith." All insist Oasis is now more balanced. Santiago said in order to attract people, the church can't be too religious and regular members have to be real. One staff member put emphasis on "being normal, just regular people"—"Let's be normal so we can present something to this world and draw them to Christ."

The earnest attempt to "be normal" is in part reflected in the design of the church's coffeehouse. Adjacent to the worship auditorium, the café at Destiny Theater looks almost exactly like the Starbuck's coffeehouse one block east. It is decorated in contemporary brown and black and features an eye-catching long bar. The price for coffee is the same as Starbuck's; my latte cost $2.50. The coffee comes in the same kind of cup. There are small tables, comfortable chairs, and an area for sugar, cream, stirrers, and napkins similar to Starbuck's. Christian books and other items are available for sale. The café is a place to hang out and is full between services.

Sermons at Oasis are conversational, given in an ordinary, plain-speaking tone. One member said, "Philip, when he preaches, he just knows how to relate to people and make them feel comfortable." Despite the consistent eloquence evident on the platform, Philip and Holly show themselves to be ordinary people who have had their own issues and struggles in their families and in their work lives. This speaking style can be traced back to the earliest preachers in America, according to Nathan Hatch (1989, 57): "The resulting creation, the colloquial sermon, employed daring pulpit storytelling, no-holds-barred appeals, overt humor, strident attack, graphic application, and intimate personal experience." The style connects more immediately with the practice of modern-day preaching pioneers, including Chuck Smith of the Calvary Chapel movement as well as Kenn Gulliksen and John Wimber of the Vineyard movement. For its connection with the history of Pentecostalism in Southern California, we can look to the unforgettable example of Sister Aimee McPherson, who marvelously combined conversational speech with narratives, infusing biblical references with contemporary idiom (Blumhofer 1993; Epstein 1993).

In addition to avoiding religious stigma through ordinary behavior, stylish ambience, and colloquial sermons, there exists, among several longtime members, an explicit reluctance to identify Oasis with the Pentecostal tradition inherent to the church's doctrinal framework. I was surprised when one male staff member said, "I wouldn't identify us with Pentecostalism," until he explained his view of that tradition: "That's like the fervor of the holy fire, the shaking, the carrying on, being slain in the spirit, those kind of things." Oasis members are not encouraged, as one male staff member said, "to leave your mind at the door and just be a bunch of lunatics." A female staff member said that Oasis does not stress spiritual gifts, such as speaking in tongues or prophesying a direct message from God, because "our church is so practical and wants to be so relevant. Even though we completely agree [with other Pentecostals]—I mean foundational issues, we don't disagree with anything like that—but the way we use it in the service would be very different." A male staff member said Pentecostal gifts are "not something that we spend too much time emphasizing."

Such negotiation of religious tradition is particularly interesting in relation to speaking in tongues, or glossolalia. When Oasis began in the 1980s, speaking in tongues was considered part of the normal evangelical Christian experience and a requirement for membership. The membership application as recently as 2000 required potential members to check if they had experienced "spiritual baptism with evidence of speaking in other tongues." And applications to serve in volunteer ministry required a person to mark boxes with respect to such things as smoking, alcohol consumption, drugs, and involvement in the occult, in addition to glossolalia. The gift of tongues, like that of healing, is available to all believers. Pastor Philip routinely gave an invitation in the service to pray for infilling, and longtime members commonly accepted the invitation and were "filled with the Holy Spirit," evidenced by their speaking in tongues. And there are many in the church for whom spirit baptism evidenced by ecstatic utterances is vital to their Christian experience.

Although speaking in tongues is desirable, it is no longer considered essential at Oasis. By the early 1990s, the emphasis on spirit baptism had greatly softened. Pastor Philip said that when someone in the new-member class asked him if Oasis was a charismatic church, he "felt so guilty." A staff member said, "It used to be a part of our services" but it's "not nearly as pronounced as it used to be." Some staff members would like to see spirit baptism emphasized much more, and one longtime member said, "For us personally it is an experience we would point to as being significant in our Christian life, and we want to see other people have that opportunity. It's something we want to share." Another said, "If you're a Christian and not speaking in tongues, you've missed something." A fellow member agreed, to a point: "Speaking in tongues is wonderful, yes. I'm like the apostle Paul [1 Cor. 14]; I speak in tongues a lot and think everybody should. But, does it mean you're not as good of a Christian [if you don't]? No." One member who had been at the church for more than five years said she had never seen ecstatic utterances in the service. Alesha, among others, told me she spoke in tongues, and I asked her about glossolalia in the services

ALESHA: No, I speak in tongues but not in public, never.

GERARDO: Never?

ALESHA: No, I've never been prompted by the Spirit. There is order for that. . . .

GERARDO: Whereas at your former church you were encouraged to—?

ALESHA: You were encouraged to [speak in tongues publicly] there. Here if you do, you do. If you don't, you don't.

At Oasis, tongues have become a private rather than a public experience. As one of the staff explained, "I encourage the team to honestly have those best moments like that in their quiet time with God. It is not something that needs to be showcased up on the platform." Teachings on how to attain spirit baptism are channeled into a seventy-five-minute Wednesday night discipleship class where people are given the opportunity to be filled with the spirit at the end of the session.

What accounts for the shift away from the public manifestation and general expectation of spirit baptism? For Philip, minimizing tongues was tied to letting "the Holy Spirit do what he's going to do in each person's life," as well as deliberate attempting "not to upset people" with unfamiliar practices. A female staff member suggests that the celebration services are "really geared towards the unchurched, who wouldn't have a clue to what that is." Tongues would lead people to see the church as weird or crazy rather than mainstream and normalized. Although occasional praise and worship nights allow people more "liberty" and "freedom" (code words for allowing people to speak in tongues without stigma), otherworldly utterances are out of place in a congregation that aspires to connect with people in the circumstances of their everyday life.

Today, neo-Pentecostals across the United States, predominantly middle class, downplay any display of obvious ecstatic behavior. Evidence of the Spirit no longer demands that a person be seen losing control over their body; it is up to the believer who speaks in tongues where and when to do it. One frequent attender echoed others: "I do [speak in tongues] every now and again, but it's not like I'm there all the time doing it." Robert Mapes Anderson (1975) compellingly argued that as the standard of living among the Pentecostal movement has gone up, the respectability of its members affects their ecstatic manifestations. It is the desire to appeal to a mass audience that compels changes in the practice of ecstatic utterances, and the pressures of maintaining one's economic status beyond church services put a conscious limit on ecstatic behavior. These believers at Oasis are still pursuing celebrity status as above-the-line industry workers, and tongue-speaking believers want to avoid marginalizing themselves as religious persons among colleagues, coworkers, and family who do not share their convictions. The softened focus on otherworldly behavior also reinforces the concept that an intense commitment to the Christian faith does not need to be segregated in church services but rather to be integrated into life, as it makes a practical difference in everyday experiences.

"Let's Keep It Practical": Applying Faith Monday through Saturday

Hollywood workers arrive at the door of Oasis with economic, relational, and emotional needs. They come with a desire to pay their bills, cultivate intimacy, and sustain their constantly threatened self-esteem. So alongside fun and relevance, the Wagners accentuate the practicality of their teachings. "Real," "sincere," and "practical" are the words most commonly used to describe their messages. A black man entering his forties said, "Bible teaching from both Philip and Holly announces, 'Hey, this is what's up and this is how it applies to your life today.'" A recent white attender in his twenties said both "are very practical in their approach." In comparing the two, a young Hispanic woman in her early twenties said, "They have different styles of teaching, but they both have the same spirit of teaching that says, 'We want to communicate relevance to you, we want to be practical, we want you to be able to apply the Word, we want you to be committed to that, we want you to be champions, we want you to succeed in life, we want you to enjoy what you are doing.'" A black woman in her fifties said, "They are there to help us and show us how to know of God in a real way. Not in a religious way—a real way." A longtime white member in her forties described Philip's teachings as "relatable," "brought down on my level." Another white woman in her thirties said, "He teaches the Bible in a way that's applicable to the things you're going through." An Asian woman said, "I can actually take that message after I walk out that door and apply it to my life." Similarly, a black woman in her forties said, "Pastor teaches more on how you can deal with it in your day-to-day life." Another white longtime member in her forties said, "He is so down to earth," and "it applies to everyone on a personal level." Hearing Holly speak at church, a female staff member commented, "I can actually apply this, like, Monday through Saturday."

Much of our understanding of how evangelical churches become practical stems from the example of Willow Creek Community Church (Sargeant 2000). Founded by Bill Hybels, the church focuses on the needs and desires of its target group. Questions that arise normally in daily life are addressed openly, and the Bible is expected to provide answers to everyday problems. Another outstanding model is Saddleback Community Church, whose founding pastor, Rick Warren, explicitly offers practical messages in simple and straightforward ways to address the common questions and everyday desires of an upwardly mobile middle class.

It is striking to note that Durkheim views religion much as the leaders of Oasis do. "The real function of religion is not to make us think, to enrich our knowledge, . . . but rather it is to make us act, to aid us to live," he wrote in *Elementary Forms* (1995, 463–464). What Durkheim seems to refer to as the latent function of religion—the empowerment for action—is for Oasis the manifest function. Religion is not intended to be merely book knowledge. We are not to simply busy ourselves with arcane study and endless exegetical disputes. The true function of religious life promoted through the church is to provide practical assistance in living our lives.

While practical, the teachings can be confrontational. A white woman in her thirties said about Philip, "He doesn't sugarcoat anything. I mean, he puts it out there. We know what we're supposed to do. We know what's wrong. We know what's right. But he puts it out there in a very loving way. I always feel like he's there loving you but telling you, 'Go this way.'" The church's teaching on tithing is an especially important example of the fearlessness with which its leaders handle tricky subjects.

Tithing is regularly addressed from the platform. Every service includes a five- to ten-minute exhortation before the offering to give people a biblical understanding of their relation to their money. A longtime white female attender said, "I love the way we talk about it. We break it down." Many people cringe at churches asking for money (and services at Oasis regularly include a statement that the church expects nothing from guests or visitors), but the expectation of giving is a regular aspect of teaching integrated into the overall discipleship of the believer. More than introducing the offering, it is always a teaching message with a theme such as, "We are the trustees of God's money." One member said, "When I give money, I'm thinking, 'Oh, this is making the church so much more comfortable and so much more beautiful to bring more people in so they learn about God.'" Through giving, individuals are encouraged to willfully act and express themselves and thus assert their agency in the world. She added, "I love to tithe. I love to serve here. I love to see how people's lives change." The act of tithing is always connected to helping people. It's interesting to note that the pink-colored giving envelopes at Oasis feature several portraits under the caption, "Investing in the lives of people."

Neither Philip nor Holly apologize in stating that giving is an essential aspect of the Christian life, and that the local church is the place in which the riches of God's people are redistributed for the work of the kingdom. In pragmatic terms, giving to the local church is important "both as a prerequisite for receiving financial blessing and as the natural response to it" (Perriman 2003, 19). In gaining a grasp of this, I found the practicality of Oasis's messages is tied to the church's distinctive accommodation to Word of Faith teaching on giving and its attendant prosperity message developed in the latter twentieth century.[5] Oasis is not part of an established denomination and does not receive financial support from other organizations. The pragmatic attention to raising funds is an essential aspect of successful ministry for any independent church. The Word of Faith orientation gives leaders a discourse for raising money without apologizing or begging, as teaching on giving is couched within a broader message of encouragement and hope about one's spiritual life.

Some might suspect that prosperity teaching motivates people to give more, thus serving the interests of leaders who want to make sure the church sustains itself and further consolidates their base of power. But this view underestimates the pastoral concern of the leaders of a church like Oasis, which attempts to acculturate in members an orientation to think not about themselves but altruistically. Any provision or prosperity that God may grant is not for the comfort of the believer, but to stir the believer to be generous to others.

One night when Holly came up to speak, the first thing she said was, "Hold up your Bible." As those with Scriptures held them up over their heads, she quoted Joshua 1:8: "Do not let this Book of the Law depart from your mouth; meditate on it day and night, so that you may be careful to do everything written in it.

Then you will be prosperous and successful." She admitted she wanted success—everybody wants that—and then looked intently into the crowd. "Do you want to prosper? Then this is what it says, 'Don't let this book get away from you.'" She moved to the New Testament book of Galatians, chapter 5, and talked about sowing and reaping. She emphatically stated, "I determine my harvest." She repeated it several times: "I determine my harvest." Good investments yield good results not just financially but in all arenas of life. She talked about finances and then about healthy marriages. She connected being successful, prosperous, and ambitious with marriage, relationships, intimacy, and companionship.

On hearing teachings like this when I first arrived at Oasis, I began to think the church was guaranteeing success to people of faith in the church. God wants you to have influence and power so wherever you are now, if you keep being faithful you are going to have increase. God's intention for people is that they increase in influence and in power. Today you may be a movie extra, but tomorrow God wants you to be a star. But was this really the teaching of Oasis?

Several members called Oasis a faith church and the leaders faith teachers. Many had been part of other faith churches as well. While there is no single, uniform dogma among these believers, it is helpful to note a family resemblance uniting this loosely affiliated fellowship.[6] The Word of Faith movement is a uniquely American contribution to revivalism that goes under various names, including positive confession, the prosperity gospel, and the health and wealth gospel.[7] There's no formal hierarchy but rather a loose relational network based on an understanding—most often referred to as the faith message—that believers are entitled not only to salvation and the indwelling of the Holy Spirit but also to health and prosperity. Despite severe critiques of the Word of Faith movement, it is increasingly respectable and widespread both in the United States and the world.[8] In the face of critics who assert its doctrine goes against the teaching of the Bible, believers cite many scriptural passages that indicate prosperity as a condition of life to be sought, enjoyed, and even expected, a message particularly appealing in large urban areas among the middle class. Sociologist Milmon Harrison (2005) speculates that the Word of Faith movement will continue to grow in popularity and influence because of changed national and global economic circumstances that lead individuals to be much more concerned about the practicality of religion in an environment almost completely centered around individual achievement and choice.

Most significant, as an outgrowth of the nineteenth-century Holiness movement, the Word of Faith movement stresses that the Christian life is practical and achievable in this life, and arises out of the concrete activity of believers (Dieter 1996; Anthony Pinn 2002, chap. 3). Godly living is oriented less toward pietistic introspection and more toward pragmatic Christian activity. Religious faith is not routine or ritualized but vital and dynamic. The oscillation between the heavenly and the earthly, the divine and the human, making the tangible the transcendent and sacralizing the mundane, characterizes the dynamic tension continually evident in the movement. Faith is lived out in practical terms in everyday life.

Three names conspicuously appeared over and over again in interviews with Oasis leaders—Kenneth Hagin, Kenneth Copeland, and Fred Price—all prominent leaders of the Word of Faith movement.[9] However, when I directly asked leaders and members about prosperity teachings or connections with the Word of Faith movement, they distance themselves from the movement as a whole. They are uncomfortable with "faith churches" that are "all hype and no substance." After my extended time in the congregation, I understand why. I agree with Joel Edwards that teaching in the Word of Faith movement is "far from monolithic" and "not only controversial and sensitive, but theologically, sociologically and historically complex" (qtd. in Perriman 2003, vii, xi). Oasis does not display the most egregious aspects of what is labeled the "health and wealth gospel." One African American member said that at his previous church, "it seemed more to me like you give, and then you will receive back," and "when I do this, I expect that." Oasis does not peddle the crass form of prosperity theology that is so often criticized. Never in my interactions at the congregation did I hear any form of positive confession—the practice of vocalizing a promise of Scripture with faith so as to have it materialized in one's life. "There's no name it and claim it at the church," a longtime female leader in the congregation said. "If you tithe, you're not going to get money back or anything."

Oasis exists with the Word of Faith movement in its background, but it does not offer empty promises to potential converts.[10] The Word of Faith movement provides a way for Oasis leaders to affirm a Christian identity within secular workplaces and a set of doctrinal beliefs that encourages believers to remain vitally connected with the Spirit of God through all challenges and temptations. Rather than believers being saints in exile (see Sanders 1996), living as aliens and strangers in the world, Oasis places believers firmly within the day-to-day machinery of the modern world. A white male member in his twenties said, "When they talk about being prosperous and successful, it may not be what you expect. There is a lot more to it, your relationships with other people, your job, and issues you may be struggling with." Similar to other "progressive Pentecostals," the focus is on an overall orientation for one's life (Miller and Yamamori 2007).[11]

Essentially, Word of Faith teaching has been distilled in the context of Oasis to a focus on obedience to Christ and a trust in God's ability to work out one's circumstances as one remains diligent in one's work. Oasis draws from the Word of Faith movement an affirmation that salvation is not just an internal transformation that waits a heavenly revealing; it is also an earthly reality that affects the life circumstances of faithful believers. Rather than challenging Christians to move toward asceticism and retreat from the world, Oasis embraces aspects of the Word of Faith message that challenge believers to take responsibility for their lives as an extension of their stewardship to God. As the prosperity gospel emerged as a means of revitalizing spirituality among those who were apathetic in their workaday lives, so Oasis seeks to energize weary and frustrated workers with a sense of mission and purpose.

In Oasis's belief system, prosperity is less a result of God's provision and more the result of a person's hard work. A staff member of the church told me, "The Word is filled with simple principles that work whether you are saved or unsaved about frugality and about being focused and the diligent hand will be made rich." Positive confession at Oasis is affirming one's identity as a champion of life, taking on productive roles, and understanding a believer's responsibility to expand the kingdom of God on earth. At Oasis, the teaching involves less a promise of prosperity than an expectation that diligent work that exercises one's talents brings success in one's secular career. A longtime member and small-group leader said, "If you get in line with what God wants you to do, you will be blessed and that will give you the desires of your heart." The church provides ongoing classes and workshops to provide practical help toward this goal (see chapter 7). Similarly, Miller and Yamamori note in their observations of Pentecostal churches across the globe that "some of these Prosperity Gospel preachers actually offer sound advice regarding lifestyle change, budgeting, family planning, and business investment" (2007, 176).

The Oasis Christian Center does not believe that the attainment of wealth is an end in and of itself, nor do leaders say that wealth is promised. The promotion of wealth "is linked to the promotion of not only personal growth, but also a sense of projecting a mobile and inspired self into the world" (Coleman 2000, 188). The self is interjected into the world in order to transform it. Frequently drawing on images of God as king, Oasis believers are to consider themselves heirs to divine royalty. They are not to squander their abilities and the potential wealth available to them. They are to be wise in their investments and to use all personal and professional resources to expand their personal influence, thereby expanding the living presence of the spirit of God. A staff member said, "We emphasize a lot more discovering your purpose, understanding why you are on the planet, what were you created to do, what are your unique gifts, those kind of things." Further, "we primarily believe you should love God with all your heart but also that he has you here for a purpose, so we want to help you understand how God has wired you up, what are the gifts he has put in you, what are the things that you love to do—that way we can help you do what you are placed here to do." Another member who is part of the Oasis worship band said, "It really isn't about living abundantly and financially. It's about being happy because you understand God's will for you and you're doing it or accomplishing it."

In his comprehensive assessment of Word of Faith teaching, *Faith: Health and Prosperity*, Andrew Perriman states that "Word of Faith teaching promotes a fundamentally positive outlook on life" and notes that "the focus on prosperity can be construed in very humanistic and self-centered terms and at times hardly differs from secular self-help ideology. But the optimism is also quite consistent with the belief that our Father in heaven will 'give good things to those who ask him' (Matthew 7:11)" (2003, 219). Such teaching

> may easily be confused with American feel-good ism and self-assertiveness, but we ought to be able to differentiate between such culturally determined attitudes and the profoundly hopeful trust in a loving and creative and generous God that we find in Scripture. If Word of Faith teaching overstates the dynamic of fullness and abundance and victory in the Christian life, this is largely as a corrective to the apathy and negativism that dominates the Christian mindset in the West. The Word of Faith movement sees many Christians as cowed by the forces of secularism anti-supernaturalism and has sought to reinforce the Christian self-perception as children of the King, heirs of divine promise.

In addition, "by stressing the intrinsic goodness of material things, the comprehensiveness of divine blessing, the requirement of righteousness, and the godly dynamic of giving and receiving, Word of Faith teaching has sought to shift prosperity from the kingdom of mammon to the kingdom of God so the believer may produce and enjoy wealth without being enslaved to it" (221).

Reflecting on Word of Faith teachings, a staff member explained that Oasis rejects "a very self-indulgent, 'God's my butler' faith" and that "the principles in the word of God that shape our faith are for me and my advancement." The orientation of being about the Father's business is critical to understanding the orientation at Oasis of how believers are to be responsible not only with finances but in every aspect of life. The staff member illustrates this with a story:

> It's like a farmer who says to his farmhand, "Take my cell phone. I need you to go out to the corner of the property and fix that broken-down fence so the horses don't get out. And whatever you need, just call me." So, he drives out there in his pickup truck, works on the fence, calls the farmer, and says, "I was thinking, and I would like a new suit and two tickets to Hawaii and a nice dinner for me and my wife." The farmer did say, "Whatever you need, just let me know," but he was saying it in relation to getting the job done, which is obviously very different. We believe in the part of prosperity that says while you are about your Father's business, he is meeting needs and giving people favor, not for the sake of promoting people but for the sake of—What's that Scripture in Psalms? "Let those who favor my righteous cause say continually, 'The Lord has pleasure in the prosperity of His servants.'"

This staff member said, "We believe that our commission as believers is similar to that of Jesus when he said, 'I must be about my Father's business.' . . . His mission really is our mission." Another member said, "He gives you so many gifts, so many things to do in life, and it's just a matter of how many things are you going to accomplish with God's will for your life. So that when you come home to God in heaven, he will be able to say, 'Well done, good and faithful servant.'"

Churches, Innovation, and Social Change

The Oasis Christian Center blends the motivation of the founding leaders with current Christian leadership philosophies, recent congregational innovations, and theological developments from the past century to accommodate the life conditions of below-the-line Hollywood workers. At Oasis, the incarnation prompted by Pastors Philip and Holly is not only embodied in the unique use of Church Growth leadership principles but also in negotiating the centurylong development of Protestant church architecture, Pentecostalism, the seeker church movement, and the Word of Faith movement. The pursuit of entertainment, fun, relevance, and practicality together yielded the most spectacular growth in Oasis's history. Attendance grew from five hundred to over two thousand in the two years from 2001 to 2003.

Can we describe the growth of Oasis as due simply to incorporating contemporary culture into religion? Is Oasis placating consumer-driven popular culture? Is Oasis a secularized, Spirit-filled church? I believe such a bland pronouncement is insufficient. Any time new forms of religious vibrancy clearly manifest social change, critics attribute their success to crass appeals to popular tastes and lament the compromise of religion. Stephen Ellingson, for example, reminds us that some historians see churches on the West Coast as more prone to innovation because "geographic distance and pervasive individualism and pragmatism in the West have produced congregations less interested in following or reproducing the doctrine, theology, and ethics emanating from denominational centers and more interested in creating church life to fit the local context" (2007, 35). But such observers overstate the exceptionalism of "crazy churches from California." Broad societal changes are prompting a reframing of religious traditions not just in California but across the country.

Ellingson is entirely correct in saying that "the underlying codes and logics of pietism—namely, individualism and experience, consumption and choice, pragmatism and efficiency—increasingly are shaping life inside [mainline] congregations and, in so doing, pushing many of the congregations to minimize the historic . . . tradition" (179). For Ellingson: "The genius of pietism is that it borrowed and sacralized the more general cultural codes, values, and logic of the market and American individualism in order to sell God and Christianity to nonbelievers" (180). I agree with Ellingson that "the boundaries between old mainline Protestantism and evangelical Protestantism are weakening" because the tone of instrumentalism and consumerism reigns in contemporary society and church leaders are forced to come to terms with it (183).

Ellingson concludes: "By freeing themselves from an overly tight adherence to and preservation of one tradition, congregations may gain the flexibility to tailor the tradition to fit the religious interests and needs of people within particular markets. In doing so, they may be able to expand the boundaries of the tradition so that [denominational traditions] can remain relevant and competitive in an increasingly nondenominational religious world" (192). In other words, the strain of pietism characteristic of contemporary evangelicalism and nondenominationalism resonates with the life circumstances of parishioners, and leaders draw on these cultural currents to cast the widest net possible to draw people into a common worship and common mission.

The rapid pace of social change is prompting focused investigations of the negotiation of religious tradition (see Ellingson 2007; Marti 2005).[12] Rather than lament such developments, it is critical that as sociologists we recognize that religion does not fall from heaven to manifest itself untainted in the world. Religion must always be incarnated, since "the Spirit" always manifests itself through "the flesh." No religious tradition exists which was not forged through historical processes of accommodation and acculturation. A sober look at church history reveals that in every era ecclesial structures, sacred music, and interaction among believers use available elements from the surrounding culture to create and carry on congregational life.

Even new sites of worship are prompting important changes. At Oasis, having church in a movie theater alone may help prompt innovation, as it has been noted that the more the physical site of worship differs from previous experiences with religious ritual, the more likely innovation is to be stimulated (Chaves 2004, 153). If other church experiences (whatever their location) somehow appear more religious than secular, it is only because later generations fail to see the secular elements that have been selectively incorporated into the persistent religious structures of today. Religious structures may appear to freeze time, in the naive belief that they may hold at bay the inexorable processes of social change. This does not stop the process of familiar elements in worship being recombined or reincarnated to give established traditional elements a new spin. Mark Chaves (2004) and Roger Finke (2004) both indicate the importance of keeping familiar elements in order to establish the religion as legitimate. Familiar elements are routinely given fresh interpretations that stimulate a revitalization of religious commitment and a renewed connection to the sacred. In the end, innovation will always include familiar elements, but it is still innovation.

Fade to Black

RODRIGO: It doesn't matter if you're black, white, purple, or green. Just come on in, and let's do life together.

Oasis conducts its ministries with the intent of resolving the tensions inherent in the world of work for those in the entertainment industry in much the same way the black church historically has resolved the tensions inherent in the world of work for African Americans (see Frazier 1974; Myrdal 1944; Anthony Pinn 2002; Pinn and Pinn 2002). Indeed, it conducts its ministry in a way that connects with African Americans who grew up in the black church.

Racial Diversity at Oasis Christian Center

At 45 percent, African Americans comprise the largest proportion of Oasis's 2,200 members. Whites represent the next largest at 40 percent, followed by Hispanics at 10 percent, Asians at 3 percent, and others including Middle Eastern and non-native blacks at 2 percent. This diversity, especially the outstanding presence of African Americans at Oasis, is astonishing in a city historically characterized by segregation and racial tension and disharmony. Across the United States, churches like Oasis are equally rare: Churches remain the most segregated social institution in our society.[1] Michael Emerson and Christian Smith (2000) established that only 5 percent of Protestant churches in the country (and only 7 percent of congregations overall) show any significant racial or ethnic diversity. Among these few, only one-third have significant percentages of whites and blacks in the same congregation (Emerson 2006, chap. 6). In short, only 2.5 percent of the nation's churches achieve a significant black-white composition. And racial segregation is highest among conservative Protestant churches like Oasis, Emerson reports in *People of the Dream* (2006, 42), where he also affirms the scholarly consensus that black and white in America are oppositional cultures, which explains the difficulty of uniting these races, with their distinctive styles and preferences, within congregations.

If racial diversity is so rare (and if black/white diversity is especially difficult), how does a church filled with highly ambitious fame- and profit-seeking attenders become one of the largest, most racially diverse in the United States? Certainly, the answer lies partly in the congregation's commitment to racial and ethnic diversity. Leaders and attenders universally agree that Oasis is committed to diversity and that racial equity is fundamental to the mission of the church. Messages, ministries, and counseling sessions regularly deal with prejudicial attitudes. I often heard direct confrontation of interpersonal discrimination. Holly said, "We talk about bigotry. We don't just talk about it on Martin Luther King Jr. Day either. We talk about it all the time. We try to deal with it straight on." Stacie said, "Philip brings it up and keeps it in front of our faces." And Philip concurred: "No matter what topic I'm teaching on, that usually comes into play. We will use an example because it affects so much of our lives." The church regularly gives away CDs with Pastor Philip's message on racial harmony. I found especially significant an Application for Ministry form dating from the late 1980s and filled out by those who wish to volunteer and lead in the church. The form inquires about drugs, sex outside of marriage, and other behaviors typical of such applications but also asks, "Are you racially prejudiced or do you have struggles in that area?" With this question, the church boldly acknowledges racism as a sin for which one must be accountable. Yet sincere commitment to diversity is not sufficient.

Believers at Oasis share a deep purpose: becoming champions of life, pursuing their God-given potential, and becoming able to withstand disappointment and heartache. In the pursuit of their mission to empower believers with an awareness of their significance in the world, the congregation cultivates a new identity centered on this purpose, which encompasses a commitment to racial equity. Overarching the commitment to racial equity, Oasis builds a distinctive religious community based on shared struggles, goals, and ambitions.

At one worship service as the vibrant worship music subsided and people sat down, an associate pastor jumped onto the platform. Holding a brightly colored card in his hand, he shouted, "John Smith, you rock the house!" Everyone enthusiastically whooped and cheered as the crowd turned to spot John, who looked a little embarrassed. The pastor read from the card and talked about John, telling the congregation that he worked "faithfully" every week in the church, "serving with love." The crowd nodded with appreciation, with several "hmms" and "yeahs." The pastor finished his public bragging, stretching out his arm and saying, "John, *you* rock the house." The congregation laughed and clapped their approval as the service moved on. Later I found a stack of sturdy, graphic-designed cards in the lobby. Below the letters UROCKTHEHOUSE, a bordered region indicates, "_____ is a champion of [check boxes] friendliness, hospitality, encouragement, creativity, kindness, faithfulness," and at the bottom, another box says, "recognized by: _____." The other side reads UROCKTHEHOUSE with a set of lines to write comments. Members are encouraged to submit these cards year-round, and surprise announcements routinely recognize admirable members.

UROCKTHEHOUSE cards are an example of Oasis's constant attempt to provide members opportunities to feel successful and appreciated, experiencing affirmation by earning the esteem of their peers. Through ministries that offer both public recognition and private comfort, Oasis intentionally strives for relevance to those in the entertainment industry who routinely experience disappointment, giving them hope of fulfilling not only their personal dreams but also a God-sanctioned purpose in a heartless world. The experience of work in the entertainment industry is often harsh, but in the context of energetic worship and practical messages the congregation pushes believers toward perseverance and purpose.

I recall one key conversation with an African American member. She said, "There is pain being black in our society, but there is a certain type of pain in being a Christian actor trying to make it in the industry." She spoke at length of this shared pain between blacks and workers in the entertainment industry, especially if they were Christians. "There's something that a person who is African American understands and a person who is a Christian actor understands that *they both can meet in that place* trying to make it" (emphasis mine). For her, "the connection is that it's a struggle."

To understand what makes this connection work requires an understanding of generational shifts among African Americans. Oasis is not a black church, but it does present an interesting compromise between the historic functions of the African American church to advance the dignity and rights of African Americans as a racial group and the encouragement to pursue individual social mobility among younger African Americans integrating into the white-dominant world. Indeed, research indicates blacks of middle age who are raising families and younger black professionals are returning to the black church, but they are returning to black churches of a different orientation. What Shayne Lee calls "the new black church" emphasizes individual upward mobility rather than collective corporate advancement. According to Lee, these black, neo-Pentecostal churches appeal to the growing number of educated, middle-class African Americans. "As a result, almost every city nationwide has at least one black neo-Pentecostal megachurch where middle-class and wealthy African-Americans worship, network, and put their skills and talents to use. Prosperity teachings allow them to enjoy their wealth and consumerism as their rightful inheritance as God's faithful children" (Lee 2005, 102).

These churches are more highly individualized and privatized, affirming wealth and ambition in mainstream culture (Anthony Pinn 2002; Lee 2005, 100). In particular, young and upwardly mobile African Americans at Oasis do not blame racism for whatever difficulty they may have in achieving career success. Instead, they look to the same kinds of explanations nonblack aspirants reference about the difficulty of achieving success. Racism, then, is not acknowledged as a vital force in the lives of these younger African Americans. Consequently, they do not attribute their frustration from lack of opportunities or failure to advance as far as they desire in their work lives to societal forces beyond their control—institutionalized racism—but rather to broader labor circumstances or the particular difficulties of succeeding within a particular career path. These younger, middle-class, and upwardly mobile African Americans are less likely to point to racial distinctions as reasons for their lack of economic success than are older African Americans in the congregation. In the midst of their experience of frustration in advancing economically, these younger blacks instead pick up on other complaints or other explanations for their difficulty and find an affinity with those who are not African American who share similar frustrations at their lack of success.

Generational Shifts in African American Religious Orientation

Several black members told me their black family and friends ask, "How could you go to church with a white pastor?" Charlene added, "People hate the fact that I come here. [They refuse] to come because the pastor is not a black man. They say, 'There is no way those two people understand anything about us. They have no clue. They could not really empathize or sympathize with an African American.'" Charlene was dating a black man who would not come to the church. He said to her, "Never. I'll never sit through his preaching and pastoring me." Damion explained, "It's sad but true. It has to do with 'There's this white man up there. He can't really relate to the struggles that I've been through.'"

Older Blacks' Rejection of White Spiritual Authority

It appears from speaking with African Americans in the congregation (including the few older males) that their discriminatory experience before and during the civil rights movement radically affected their willingness to associate with whites in authority. Gabriel said, "When I grew up, they had white and black bathrooms, and you had to go in or out the back door." He was told in school to avoid professional careers and pursue a practical trade like being a carpenter or a welder. "People had a mindset that blacks were limited academically." He joined the militant black movement as a young man. "I was rebellious, pretty violent, because I had a chip on my shoulder." He asked himself, "What worked better, Martin Luther King and my aunt and cousin on their knees praying and asking for God's divine intervention? Or me and H. Rap Brown and Huey Newton with guns and bandoleers and shotguns?"

Rocco, in his thirties, talked about "very old-school people," in particular, "fifty- and sixty-year-olds who still might have issues with something as superficial as taking advice or listening to the word of a white pastor. I've actually heard that quite a good number of times over the years. 'I just can't be under a white pastor.'" He mused, "If they grew up with the idea of 'black' within their identity, . . . they came from a very different place from where Oasis is right now." Indeed, the records of the church and systematic observation show only a few black men between the ages of fifty and eighty. When I mentioned this to one mature and single African American woman, she laughed and said, "I've been checking that out too, Gerardo." Research generally suggests that church attendance is greater among black women than among black men. But older black men fail to commit to Oasis not for religious reasons but for explicitly racial reasons. Black men over the age of forty-five refuse to sit before a white pastor.

All the African Americans I encountered at Oasis had immersive experiences in the black church. Historically, much of the black church's ministry has been in political mobilization and corporate empowerment, since the oppression of blacks in U.S. society is what prompted the development of the black church (Harris 1999; Patillo-McCoy 1998). Although we should not assume that black churches are homogeneous, scholars of African American religious history have long argued these churches have a shared tradition within Christianity and are fundamental to the collective experience of African Americans in the United States (see Lincoln and Mamiya 1990, 45; Anthony Pinn 2002, xii). Further, I affirm with Lawrence N. Jones that "there is a sense in which all black congregations and denominations respond to identical external circumstances and share common internal strengths, pressures, and tensions" (1999, 582).

The experience of racism led African Americans to a collective solidarity and obligation to support one another. With its emphasis on corporate problems, the black church often viewed individual achievement as conflicting with communal responsibility. It did not encourage the successes of its most wealthy members because individual well-being and personal materialism were seen as unwittingly reinforcing class structures inherent to U.S. culture. However, young and upwardly mobile (what some would call privileged) blacks see themselves as responsible for their own destiny and able to control their circumstances. In the end, according to Dale Andrews, younger and upwardly mobile members of the African American middle class are being isolated from the black church due to the perception that successful African Americans have overly accommodated to the white culture in pursuit of personal success, and members of "the black middle class feel the church has become irrelevant to their daily struggles" (2002, 68).

Younger and Upwardly Mobile Blacks Embrace Mainstream Culture

It turns out that Oasis captures a sea change in the religious orientation of African Americans. The successes of the civil rights movement unintentionally created a cultural gap between older and younger African Americans. Civil rights legislation resulted in a broader participation of African Americans in American social life. And the black church failed to deal with emerging moral and theological issues in ways that satisfied younger and upwardly mobile cohorts. The salience of the black church declined. African Americans at Oasis are among the many who moved away from the black church in an attempt to enter what they understand to be mainstream culture. Younger blacks like Damion said they immerse themselves at Oasis because "they see the big picture that it's not about just being black. We no longer live in this bubble. We've got to get out and mingle."

Andrews asserts that middle-class blacks seek opportunities and gain confidence on the basis of "their individual strengths and personal identity" (2002, 79). They relate to the world based on a deep confidence in their ability to control their own lives. Younger and upwardly mobile blacks are more optimistic about their willful agency and their ability to participate in whatever social realms they wish regardless of race. They believe their personal and professional networks are based on their chosen affiliations. And when they succeed in the workplace, they attribute their success to their own abilities.

The optimism of believing in freedom from racial dynamics is reflected in a conversation with Rocco, who told me black is an attitude. Rocco believes younger blacks are self-aware and independent. "What defines a person who is black is completely independent from the observer and the observed. *The observed decides what they are going to be*" (emphasis mine). When I asked, "Would you say you are black?" he answered:

> I wouldn't mind somebody making a physical description of me as a long-haired, two-hundred-ten-pound black man. Because that is an appropriate description of my physical characteristics. But, I don't necessarily embody black exclusively. . . . When you say "black folk," what exactly does that mean? There aren't necessarily any rules on how to be black. There aren't necessarily any guidelines for being black. But there are plenty of people who would like to tell you in the context of certain situations how it makes them feel. I never blend into that. I've always been, "Here I am. What are you coming with?" And if you are coming with, "I'm black and we're going to relate as a black man to a black man," I have the ability to adapt to just about what anybody is, but I'm going to tell you that now you have limited your ability to relate to me. We are going to relate on a very narrow band now. Because you have a very narrow perspective. I have a much broader perspective.

By avoiding a racial identity, Rocco and others are not attempting to "become white" but to avoid being just black.

Younger blacks at Oasis are more concerned with elevating their own status than with pursuing a broad social agenda that would empower all African Americans. This distinction among blacks is similar to patterns described by E. Franklin Frazier's controversial 1965 analysis of the black middle class, *Black Bourgeoisie,* in which he maintains that "the single factor that has dominated the mental outlook of the black bourgeoisie has been its obsession with the struggle for status" (194). Frazier believes African Americans moving into the middle class reject identification with being black and move away from their folk heritage, which includes leaving the black church: "A measure of success leads them away from a focus on the larger political and economic issues of all African Americans and motivates them to attempt to live 'normal' American lives not confined to focusing on racial issues" (193). That is, "the middle class rejects identification with Africa and wants above all to be accepted as 'just Americans'" (78; for a current and wide-ranging assessment of Frazier's ideas, see Teele 2002).

Andrews (2002) points to 1975 research by James Blackwell indicating that middle-class African Americans not only see themselves as distant from lower-class African Americans but also stigmatize them as stuck in poverty due to their own fault. Upwardly mobile African Americans distance themselves from urban poor blacks because the associated stigma affects their chances to succeed in the dominant society. A critical distinction emerges in the use of racism as an explanatory tool among African Americans for understanding the less than desired economic circumstances of black middle-class workers. The individualistic and decidedly nonracist explanations for economic success at the Oasis Christian Center sidestep beliefs that could potentially disrupt a feeling of unity between racial groups.

Ellis Cose (1993) emphasizes that white Americans do not give credence to the pervasiveness of racism in their society and are likely to dismiss experiences of racial prejudice even among successful African Americans. For Frazier, members of the black middle class cultivate a delusional world that pretends racism does not affect their economic lives: "Their 'wealth' and 'social' position cannot erase the fact that they are generally segregated or rejected by the white world. Their incomes and occupations may enable them to escape the cruder manifestations of racial prejudice, but they cannot insulate themselves against the more subtle forms of racial discrimination" (1965, 181). Frustration mounts among middle-class blacks because they cannot avoid their identification with other African Americans due to their ascriptive status within a racialized society. Continuing Frazier's argument, Cose in *The Rage of a Privileged Class* forcefully argues that the accumulated frustrations of small racial incidents over the lifetime of black professionals result in an outstanding sense of outrage (see also Benjamin 2005).

Since upwardly mobile African Americans want to avoid the racial stigma associated with the black urban poor, they are not likely to name racism as an explanation for lack of success. Since racial injustice is not an explanation in which they find comfort or refuge, they are able to construct a form of solidarity with nonblack workers in the common sense of frustration and common explanations as to why a particular path of career success has not been fulfilled. Here lies the reason why older African Americans are not as likely to participate at the Oasis Christian Center. As racism rises in importance in one's understanding of one's personal experiences, the likelihood of finding solidarity with those who have not experienced similar racial obstacles diminishes. However, to the extent that African Americans minimize expressing their experiences and belief in racial discrimination, they decrease their distance from whites who see such statements as unsubstantiated complaints.

In short, African American believers at Oasis navigate their lives based on frameworks for explaining failure that do not rest on the historic issues of U.S. racism. Rather than addressing a collective group assumed to be united politically, economically, and historically, this voluntary community of individuals at the church offers mutual support. At the same time, the congregation's affinities to the black church bring them to a place that affirms their African American heritage.

Reproducing the Historic Functions of the Black Church

By intentionally seeking to relate to those in the entertainment industry, Oasis unintentionally captures the historic functions of the black church in a manner that appeals to African Americans—especially younger and upwardly mobile African Americans—who are seeking to overcome pain, frustration, and oppressive systems. Oasis attributes difficulties of attaining economic success to the generally difficult circumstances of the Hollywood labor market (see chapter 5). Through a variety of mechanisms to support and encourage members, Oasis builds familylike intimate bonds to strengthen racially diverse strangers as they struggle to make it in risky careers and forge a common identity together.

Messages and Mistake Stories

The oppressive experience of African Americans did not allow them to ignore the conditions of the world around them. Instead, the black church historically maintained a concrete connection to the activities and necessities of everyday life. The black church emphasized a necessary intermingling between the earthly and the transcendent. The exigencies of work life and financial management were not considered activities separate from the holy life. And historically the churches' embrace of the social gospel, the concern for the concrete financial and social needs of individuals and not merely their otherworldly, afterlife need for eternal salvation, fit the very real conditions of their lives. Of course, from the days of slavery through today, preaching in the black church also supported the attempt of African Americans to live their day-to-day lives connecting the Scripture to the experience of the world of work.

Within the black church, concerns focus on the racial experience of African Americans, but at Oasis, concerns focus on the people of urban Los Angeles who struggle to fulfill their economic ambitions despite setbacks and disappointments. In the black church, according to Anthony Pinn: "From the beginnings of the sermonic tradition to the present, the basic purpose of the sermon has been two-fold: (1) to glorify God and bring people into the church; and (2) to provide information, drawn from scripture, relevant for daily living" (2002, 59). At Oasis too, the emphasis is on evangelism and relevance to practical living while at the same time putting a high value on the transcendent, awesome nature of a holy, loving God. The messages delivered at Oasis in every worship service consistently express compassion and resonance with shared hurt. Messages at Oasis are based on "the principles of Scripture" but are not necessarily exegetical or doctrinal. Stories from the Scriptures are connected to the concerns present within the congregation and in the larger community. Personal stories take up at least 50 percent of the talking time, the rest of the time being used for the reading of Scripture or the articulation of take-away truths. The Oasis Christian Center does not attempt to shape public policy, and it shuns any explicit political discourse. Discussion of current events is largely limited to anecdotal happenings in popular culture. The emphasis of the preaching at Oasis is on using Scripture to help people live their everyday lives.

The public ministry of Oasis is oriented around working through disappointment, abuse, suffering, and hardship. Indeed, one of the most important ways communities of affinity are formed is by expressing one's mistakes and inviting others to be in relationship on the basis of the rapport built from sharing how one worked through these failures. Are you an actor having difficulty finding work? Are you a single mom struggling with parenting? Are you divorced and unsure where life will take you next? Come to this ministry and you'll find many who are experiencing the same. Are you an entrepreneur trying to keep your business in the black? Come to this ministry where you can be with others who are in the same situation and pick up a few tips on how to succeed. All these groups have as a base that people who experience failures don't have to feel like losers but see their ongoing efforts as part of learning and growing, making it through life today.

Messages continually advertise brokenness as a normal state of being among believers, but one that can be healed and overcome. The use of life experience is not unique to the black church, but a noted quality nevertheless, and speakers at the Oasis routinely use their life experiences as illustrations (Anthony Pinn 2002, 61). In one message, Pastor Philip connected some of his experiences with the apostle Peter: "I relate to Peter not because he messed up, but because he messed up and God still used him. I messed up and I hope God still uses me." Santiago said, "In their teaching the pastors use their experiences. It's just cool because sometimes you look at them and say, 'Do they make mistakes?' They tell you what their mistakes are. You know, like we all make mistakes." Gladys said the leaders are genuine. "When they make mistakes, they acknowledge it and try to make amends to the extent possible. They are transparent about their processes as Christians. They don't hold themselves as faultless paragons of Christian virtue but acknowledge that there are struggles and they are growing and not necessarily all knowing."

The distinctive aspect of the sharing of life experiences at the Oasis is their departure from many such stories in other religious contexts, which involve a radical reversal of fortune. Elsewhere, stories recount terrible circumstances when things looked dark and grave followed by a miraculous event. In other words, most churches use miracle stories, but at the Oasis Christian Center, I do not hear miracle stories, I hear mistake stories. Certainly miracles are said to occur in the congregation, but these occupy a surprisingly small proportion of the overall discourse of the church. The dominant discourse is one of human experience lived in a very day-to-day fashion. And rather than securing a miracle, messages reinforce that it is in working through the disappointing events of one's life that the lessons of godly living are found.

For example, Pastor Philip freely admits from the pulpit the failure of his first, three-month marriage after which his wife left him. His parents had divorced, and although he never wanted that in his own life, disappointment is evident in his voice that it did indeed happen. The admission of Pastor Philip's failed marriage is a good example of a mistake story. Another is a message by Pastor Philip called "I Blew It, I Knew It, and What I Learned Through It." One member described this message as classic Philip—"just being real, like he is all the time, sharing personal examples in his marriage and his life and even ministry of blowing it and having the wrong idea and it's a great message."

A mistake story is a form of testimony, a public declaration that involves a person telling their life story in the context of church service (Anthony Pinn 2002, 64–65). What is expressed in a mistake story is a sharing of a particular type of spiritual experience. There is no pretension in telling a mistake story. A person is not attempting to show their best side. "Of more importance than form or style of presentation is a basic sincerity, an indication to listeners that the experience is true" (66). At the Oasis, a "true story" is authentic, real, everyday, and accessible. It is a story with which one can easily relate and a processing of an experience every person can follow.

Through mistakes, the image of speakers is brought down to earth, and they become everyday people. Public conversations like this serve "as a way of humanizing preachers who are often thought of as 'larger than life'" (Anthony Pinn 2002, 61). In the context of the black church, "sharing a personal experience in this way allows ministers to create a sense of commonality, of solidarity, and allows congregants to think of their struggles as communal challenges. It provides a form of vulnerability that many preachers argue creates a stronger connection between the preached word and the congregation" (61–62). What is important here is the emphasis on struggles as communal challenges. I heard an associate pastor in one talk repeat, "Anybody else relate to that mistake?" Individual mistakes can become shared mistakes that indicate a source of our common, broken humanity before God. Although we strive and we try, we don't always make it. Through such stories, narratives are made publicly accessible for others, who make use of them to work through issues in their own lives (see Smilde 2007).[2]

How does one's mistake become a model for godly living? It turns out that the lessons that are learned include: (1) how to avoid future mistakes (this happened to me, and it doesn't have to happen to you); and, more important, (2) how to work through failure (this happened to me, and here's how you can work through your own failure). Mistake stories are testimonies that not only share what happens in one's own life but also provide a model for living out one's faith. Luther, an African American, said, "The whole vibe of what Oasis is all about is relationships and not religion. It's about, 'Hey I can do things.' It gave me an idea that Christianity is like riding a bike. If you fall down, get up, dust yourself off, and ride again." He added, "I may fall down, I may have my mistakes, but Oasis gives you the idea it is about relationships and Jesus is just like your bigger brother and God is like your father. He says, 'Hey, good brother, get up,' and doesn't allow you to be a victim, doesn't allow you to feel sorry for yourself." One woman talked about how the teachings of Philip and Holly rescued her marriage: "They have got such a gift in their honesty, their openness. . . . If they have gone through problems, I'm not alone. This isn't wrong for me to feel like this. I'm not abnormal." The comfort of others' mistakes gave her the confidence to stay in her marriage and work through problems.

By walking through the mistakes of others everyone experiences cathartic satisfaction. And seeing the frustration of another person result in a blending of their devotion to God with an attempt to make it in the world, every person experiences a greater sense that knowing God and serving him makes a difference in how one lives. Charlene:

> I have such a hunger and thirst and I know it's coming from a ministry like this and making myself understand that it's okay if I don't do it all perfectly. I remember I was listening to a radio preacher and when he finished telling me all of the things I needed to do as a Christian, I started to cry because I thought, "I'll never measure up. I can't." I felt so hopeless for a moment. And I come here and I realize, "Yes I can. I can do this if I take it step by step. If I just understand that God's got the big picture. All I need to do is just on a daily basis come to him, trust him. I can do this."

Bridgette said, "Nobody's perfect. . . . It's so human. But you get back up. What does God say? You've got to get up." Mistakes are okay and that gives members hope. Pastor Holly once preached, "The only person God can't use is a quitter." Even amidst talking about a sense of failure in their work lives, members often assure each other, "Don't give up," and "God has something better for you. We just have to find out what that better is."

Encouragement and Social Support

On a broad level, the historic black church provided hope amidst despair. Studies of black churches consistently emphasize the consolation and emotional strength that can be found within these congregations, for example: "The main responsibility of the black preacher was to speak a word of divine hope to the oppressed that would inspire them in the same way as the slave spirituals" (Bridges 2001, 74). The black church is recognized as providing a place where blacks have found safety and security (Paris 1982).

Although Oasis clearly addresses the problem of racism in its ministry, it defines its ministry of hope as more abstractly aimed toward any person who experiences despair and frustration. When I asked an African American woman who fits best at Oasis, she proudly said, "People who have been hurt and are looking for acceptance and love." Repeatedly, acceptance, love, and social support were viewed as core functions of the ministry. One person said the starting point of all of Pastor Philip's messages is "God loves us and is on our side." Tyler said he's "found that everyone is really willing to help you with your own situation and wants to help you. And that's awesome." Stacie asked me in our interview, "Where else can you go where you see a girl sitting and crying and you can just go up and tell her it's okay?" And she started to cry herself.

One afternoon, I came into the Oasis offices to talk and hang out. One of the staff came out of the staff kitchen looking a bit tired. When I asked how he was doing, he said he had just come out of a "coaching session" and explained that "coaching" is the word used for counseling at Oasis. The church staff does not consist of licensed counselors, but they freely provide encouragement and spiritual guidance. So the church has a coaching rather than a counseling ministry, a concept that reinforces the thematic ministry of the church to train members to become champions of life. Champions need coaches, and this sports metaphor accentuates the goal.

Small groups, which have proliferated as programs of care and support in churches across the country in the last two decades, are part of the coaching ministries at Oasis (Wuthnow 2001). Groups at Oasis use sanctified self-help materials to help people through addictions, marriage troubles, and emotional turmoil. An African American woman said, "I needed to find out that I'm loved and worthy and that a merciful, benevolent God has my best interest at heart rather than I must have messed up some place and didn't say the wrong Scripture and didn't have enough faith." The church even has a special group called Extra Love specially designed for people going through emotionally difficult times.

Talking about these and other ministries, a staff member emphasized that the focus at Oasis is "relationship, relationship, relationship." When I asked one staff member about the theological distinctiveness of the church, the first answer was "relationships." Another said, "Everything about this church is about relationships." Luther said that when he came to Oasis, "It was about relationships and not religion." Santiago said the core of the church is to "love people for where they are" and confirmed that "it all boils down to relationships. It all boils down to someone just saying, 'Hey, how are you doing? Come on over. I want to introduce you to somebody.'"

Many spoke of the church as a place that shows the love of God, "a place where you can learn that you're valuable," as Gladys said. Danielle said, "No matter what your life is, you are welcome here." Another staff member said, "Here what we emphasize is much more relationships, understanding forgiveness, how to heal relationships, how to work together, how to live the second greatest commandment, 'Love your neighbor as yourself,' and how to really effectively do that." Many talked about feelings of warmth, love, and acceptance. At her first service, Gladys said, "I cried during the whole service. There was just a warmth and love. . . . I mean I was just sobbing, sobbing, sobbing." Charlene too "was literally overwhelmed. I was overwhelmed at the warmth that the people extended." Donna has found "such a feeling of love and acceptance and what Jesus should be about. I have goosebumps up the back of my head right now." Rodrigo said, "People are willing to come here because they feel important when they come. They are not just a number, they are recognized immediately," and "if you get connected, that means that you are going to meet someone that is going to encourage you, someone who is going to be praying with you, someone that is going to be loving on you and making you feel good."

Many consider the culture of acceptance the factor that successfully cultivates the racial diversity at Oasis. "We don't care what race you are," Rodrigo said. "We'll love on you if you let us. So it doesn't matter if you are black, white, purple, or green. Just come on in and let's do life together." Lynn insists, "People are people and we love you and just like I said before, you kind of forget—'Oh, we're diverse. We forgot.'" An African American man said "I've got tattoos, as you can see, and I'm used to the Northwest where it's a sea of white people who look at you like, 'What are you going to steal?' But you don't get that here. Here you get, 'Come on in. Let's praise God together.'"

Energetic Worship through Music

The most fundamental experience of worshipers at Oasis is the reenergizing and revitalization of a person's spirituality in connection with the divine. A woman who worked on the Oasis praise album released in 2003 said the core song is the first track, "Are You Ready." She said, "It's not a passive song at all. And we're not a passive church. It's like, 'Are you ready?' because we're ready. It's time for us to take the city, it's time for us to take things for Christ, take back what the enemy has taken from us and stolen from us." Together, worshipers experience the Spirit anew by expressing gratitude to God and reestablishing their commitment to God. Worship is a time when God is felt. While music is used as a way of expressing faith and devotion—an affective connection to God—worship is also a force of regeneration and a way of building up one's spiritual strength. Similarly, C. Eric Lincoln and Lawrence H. Mamiya write that in the black church, "the weekly worship service gives the strength to go back to their jobs to survive another day, another week" (1990, 272). This is true even for the many professional musicians I spoke with at the church.

Church services at the Oasis Christian Center are not opportunities for administering sacraments or accomplishing high-church liturgy. Worship is a source of spiritual renewal. Like many nondenominational, evangelical churches, services are celebrations characterized by verve and spontaneity. Worship is a time of happiness, encouragement, and gaining a sense of being alive. The sounds that move attenders to dance are not the presexual rituals of a dance club but rather a shared sacred devotion, as the people of God express their joy and commitment to their God. This involves a dynamic tension between dance music and church music which has an interesting affinity for young singles who channel their energy into spiritual concerns and for all who benefit from the hopefulness, energy, and vitality involved in this music (Sanders 1996, 82).

Worship music is also one of the distinctive markers of the black church experience that grew out of the collective experience of African Americans, from the historical oppression of institutionalized slavery to the modern discrimination of institutional racism (Anthony Pinn 2002, 56; see also Lincoln and Mamiya 1990, chap. 12).[3] Since every African American at Oasis had extensive experience in the black church, connections to the music of the black church is important to them. For example, Rocco explained how the structure and style of music at Oasis is reminiscent of black church music: "Every now and then we can do one of those little double-time things with the band, and they will do it just for fun because it brings back some memories for people, and people will remember something they don't normally get in our church. And that makes them feel more connected."

People of all races emphasize that the worship music at Oasis is a form of black music. In accounting for its sound, I was frequently reminded that Pastor Philip is a musician with a deep love for black gospel music. In a conversation with him and Holly, Holly said to Philip, "Even from before you knew me, you liked the black gospel music, so you were even into the culture that way." Philip replied, "I embraced and loved the gospel culture." An African American man said Philip likes soul music; "he grew up on some serious Motown cats." In addition, it is interesting that almost all of Oasis's regular musicians (both black and nonblack) have had long experience playing what was often called "straight gospel music" in black churches.

The R&B-funk-gospel music at Oasis is a form of soul music and reminiscent of singers like James Brown, Aretha Franklin, and Wilson Pickett. Brent explained how the music that is central to black gospel churches has had a significant impact on the sound of music played at Oasis, and he struggled to define that sound: "It's the music, the feeling, the soul. The soul of the music.

The soul rhythm. I really believe rhythm has a lot to do with soul in music. It's coming from the heart. There's this backbone or foundation or rhythm." He said Oasis music mixed "jazz and gospel and funk and R&B and world beat music, lots of reggae, and lots of Caribbean music," and that "it's all about rhythm." Brent reflected that musically "there's a very, very strong foundation that has been laid years ago in [black] churches that is now coming into a place like Oasis and is really heavily influencing Oasis in great ways." Although 80 percent of the music played at Oasis is original, it strives for a consistent sound. "I don't know how else to describe it except music that has more soul to it, meaning elements of gospel," Brent said. "There is a back beat to it, a lot heavier or more intense, stronger back beat to it."

Although gospel music developed as a byproduct of Christian worship, the genre was much in demand by the broader public. The popularity of gospel music created a connection between the black church and mainstream white culture. Soul music has been performed by white artists and popular among white audiences since the 1950s. In the 1960s, soul music incorporated gospel to reengage the black experience of pain, suffering and, hope amidst exploitation. According to Cornel West, soul music affirms black identity outside the church in a celebratory atmosphere (1999, 478–479). Similarly, Cheryl Sanders notes: "What is clear is that the primary context of this new genre was not the Church but the house party" (1996, 82).

At Oasis, that middle ground between energetic, expressive music and more reverential, calming music that often distinguishes black Baptist from black Pentecostal churches is the locus for high-energy, deep-bass R&B rhythms and funk that encourage people to clap and move in their seats without encouraging them to spill into the aisles. The fact that soul music emerged to affirm a party atmosphere has a deep resonance with the energetic, new paradigm church worship described by Donald Miller (1997), which is both more casual and more energetic than traditional church music. The music challenges those from more conservative backgrounds to be looser and have fun while satisfying the demands of believers who see worship as a time of utter abandonment. Oasis also reflects developments in contemporary worship music among neo-Pentecostal black churches that intentionally incorporate innovations in secular music. High-tech instruments are reclaimed for sacred use to mix in the soulful rhythms many African Americans enjoyed as they grew up (Lee 2005, 164–165). (BeBe and CeCe Winans, Fred Hammond, and Kirk Franklin are among those who have most prominently revamped gospel music worldwide.)

What distinguishes neo-Pentecostalism is not its doctrinal teachings as much as the experience of worship, and specifically in black churches, neo-Pentecostalism "tends to draw upon the reservoir of the black folk religious tradition which stressed enthusiastic worship and spirit filled experiences" (Lincoln and Mamiya 1990, 386). While the worship experience is an extension of theological convictions developed in the black church, the neo-Pentecostal style of praise and worship flowed into celebration services nationwide. With praise teams leading worship songs, visible movement in dance, and an energetic updating of gospel rhythms to include funk and R&B, the influences on contemporary worship are so broad that churches across denominational lines and those that claim no denomination have a similar feel, whether located in Los Angeles, Houston, Detroit, Richmond, or New York. Oasis certainly captures and sustains this increasingly global musical phenomenon.

Overall, music at Oasis is not intended for passive entertainment but active involvement. Worship is also a means to be rejuvenated, to rest. Durkheim echoes this dual theme in his understanding of the persistence of religion: "The demands of material life" are centered on "private interest," he writes. "On ordinary days, the mind is chiefly occupied with utilitarian and individualistic affairs" (1995, 352). But this is insufficient for humanity since private, utilitarian concerns alone wither the human spirit, which needs to be recharged for daily living. "They are constantly frustrated and held in check by the opposing tendencies that the requirements of the day-in, day-out struggle produce and perpetuate." He contends that "all forces, even the most spiritual, are worn away with the passage of time if nothing replenishes the energy they lose in the ordinary course of events" (342). Worship is necessary to reenergize humanity. "The individual soul itself is also regenerated, by immersing itself once more in the very wellspring of its life" (353). Moreover, "once we have fulfilled our ritual duties, we return to profane life with more energy and enthusiasm, not only because we have placed ourselves in contact with a higher source of energy but also because our own capacities have been replenished through living, for a few moments, a life that is less tense, more at ease, and freer" (386).

Reflecting Durkheim's insights, a white musician in his late twenties said of Oasis, "I have never been to a church that is so energetically and spiritually uplifting. Every time I leave, I feel recharged."

Social Services for Economic Needs

Alongside professional career workshops, Oasis regularly features ministry activities devoted to financial planning and stewardship. The black church has a long history of serving African Americans with assistance through economic hardships (Billingsley 1999; Frazier 1974; Lincoln and Mamiya 1990; Smith 2005). The black church came into its own when African Americans from the rural South migrated north and west during the Great Migration to the urban metropolis in search of jobs and new lives. World War I stimulated a demand for labor and manufacturing, and the conditions of labor and agriculture became increasingly difficult as environmental and political conditions deflated opportunities to earn a decent living (Baer and Singer 2002, 44–55). Practically speaking, the black church provided a buffer against unemployment, illness, and death (Williams

1974). Today, most black churches still maintain an outreach that focuses on the social and financial needs of African Americans (Billingsley 1999).

Historically, preaching in black churches included not only doctrinal and theological themes about one's relation to God or aspects of the supernatural but also real-life strategies congregants could pursue in order to make it in this world of trouble (Simpson 1970). And because financial resources were not readily available for the establishment and growth of new churches, it became important for leaders not only to preach the gospel but also to possess acute business skills and to be knowledgeable about constructing and maintaining buildings. As Anthony Pinn writes, in many aspects, "black churches are marked by a tentative positioning between two worlds giving attention to both—the secular and sacred" (2002, xiv).

Although Oasis does not define itself as a socially activist congregation, the church is involved in various forms of charitable work and provides practical assistance to those in need. There is evidence to support that conservative theology tends to suppress social activism (McRoberts 2003, 107–108; see also Paris 1982, Williams 1974), and like other neo-Pentecostal churches, Oasis takes an incremental approach to social change (Miller and Yamamori 2007, 213–216). Oasis contributes physically and financially to local and global efforts to alleviate poverty. Also, the Oasis Christian Center provides social and financial assistance to members but moves away from political discourse in favor of personal discourse. Oasis provides many ways to help individuals in economic need, focusing on how individuals can cope with economic hardship rather than on structurally changing the societal order. It is not surprising that Oasis provides social services in the form of workshops, since it insists on the achievement of its members in their chosen professions. This moral imperative obligates the congregation to provide help to its people.

So the emphasis on financial well-being is evident in the Oasis ministry; at the same time, the church affirms that individuals are on their own by providing tools to help them make it. Oasis does not focus on economic difficulties in a collective sense; rather, collective opportunities are provided to encourage and empower individuals to manage their own economic lives. Financial help is given, and workshops of various sorts are offered to help people manage their personal finances. Groups, classes, and workshops both onsite and offsite feature speakers sharing personal experiences, with a pragmatic emphasis on how to have better work lives and personal relationships. Such opportunities for growth and learning are also typical in the black church. Lincoln and Mamiya describe "the black self-help tradition," which consistently helped African Americans learn how to manage their economic lives through long-term, rational planning of saving and spending (1990, chap. 9). In the black church, support groups and self-help spirituality provide free education and nurture personal skills for the workplace (Mays and Nicholson 1999, 429).

Oasis also incorporates therapeutic models and self-help materials in the construction of its ministry (see Hunter 1987). For a time, a twelve-step program was incorporated into the church as a means of helping people move out of unhealthy or disruptive lifestyles and move into wholeness as disciples of Christ. Today, Monday Night Solutions is the only ongoing, and therefore most consistently accessible, class at the church and deals with troublesome emotional issues. For example, Monday Night Solutions spent a month focusing on significance, the message being, if you feel insecure and have low self-esteem, Monday Night is for you. Other themes include abuse, addictions, and personal relationships. As a form of group counseling, the sessions focus very much on "healing the soul" and providing an outreach to "wounded" people.

Job-training programs common in other churches are replaced at Oasis by affinity groups that share common occupational concerns, as well as frequent workshops that help people with career planning and business management. This trend is consistent with recent moves by black megachurches, especially neo-Pentecostal churches with elements of prosperity teachings, as Lee notes: "Many black megachurches offer empowerment seminars in which business strategies are combined with spiritual principles to teach Christians how to attain first-class lifestyles" (2005, 164). The sacred community becomes a resource of experience and encouragement so that individuals, while pushed to take personal responsibility for their financial well-being, don't feel alone as they go about doing it.

Nurturing Artistic Talent and Leadership

Ethnographies of individual churches show that the black church provides a place where individuals can experience a sense of accomplishment, status, and even a deep sense of self-worth, despite a lack of success in the dominant social world (Paris 1982; Williams 1974; Kostarelos 1995). One of the most distinctive aspects of the black church is the manner in which it continually seeks to develop the talent of its people. Benjamin Mays and Joseph Nicholson considered this part of the distinctive genius of the black church: "Certainly the Negro church is the training school that is given the masses of the race opportunity to develop" (1999, 426). Exercising their independence, individuals within the black church implemented opportunities to engage their talents without restriction (Mays and Nicholson 1999, 424). A variety of volunteer roles in the church gave them a chance to exercise leadership in ways that were unavailable to them in the broader society—as elders, deacons, evangelists, missionaries, ushers, choir members, and teachers. The church therefore is not simply a refuge from the world but also a social group that "allocates social status, differentiates roles, resolves conflicts, gives meaning, order, and style to its members' lives, and provides for social mobility and social rewards within its confines" (Williams 1974, 157).

The social services of the black church, then, extended beyond mere survival to the development of the dignity and creative humanity of every person. "Not only did it give birth to new institutions such as schools, banks, insurance companies, and low-income housing, it also provided an academy and an arena for political activities, and it nurtured young talent for musical, dramatic, and artistic development" (Lincoln and Mamiya 1990, 8). Artistic forms such as music, drama, storytelling, and humor were all nurtured within the black church. Consequently, many black singers and musicians receive their first experience and training in public performance through church. As Mays and Nicholson note: "The opportunity found in the Negro church to be recognized, and be 'somebody,' has stimulated the pride and preserved the self-respect of many Negroes who would have been entirely beaten by life, and possibly completely submerged. Everyone wants to receive recognition and feel that he is appreciated. The Negro church has supplied this need" (1999, 426).

Similarly, Oasis provides an opportunity for those in the creative arts to experience recognition regardless of their success outside the church. The 24/7 arts ministry provides ongoing development of creative skills in acting, graphic arts, filmmaking, and dancing. It also organizes performances every six to eight weeks to highlight drama and musical work from the congregation. It is a place of affirmation, as Danielle, a producer, found in talking with one of the pastors, who said, "I see how you work and there are so many great things about you. But I hear that you don't believe that in yourself." Such recognition and appreciation are especially significant for African Americans at Oasis, who told me that difficulty in finding work in entertainment is much greater for African Americans than for whites. One black member said, "It depends on whether we're the flavor of the month. So sometimes black is in. Sometimes Hispanic is in. Do you know what I'm saying? But white folks are always in. And that doesn't mean that I'm speaking from a prejudiced place, it just simply is truth."

Making Church My Other Family

Just as the black church became an institution characterized by familylike bonds of commitment, Oasis establishes a form of spiritual kinship among members and calls itself a family. Matt said, "We are family. We can get in each other's business, and we can challenge one another, and we love one another. We are committed to one another. We are family." One actor said he was single and lonely when he arrived in the church and got involved in the dramatic arts ministry there. "When you are doing a play, you gel with each other. They become your family." Still, he was suspicious that people from the church would reject him if they really knew him. "I figured they liked me as long as I was an actor, but they've got to find out the real me. They would find out that I had issues and find out that I'm not this fun-loving guy all the time." He decided to pursue relationships, soon made friendships, and committed to the church.

Lynn said the church greets first-time guests, making them feel important—"If you come, you're going to be bombarded with people." Church members have an earnest desire to be friendly, "to say hi and have that friendly environment throughout the church because there's no real ulterior motive to that." The church strives to be high touch through the development of its Welcome Teams, Care Teams, and Follow-Up Teams. One staff member said, "We feel that if we are able to connect with you and able to provide you an Oasis experience, the likelihood of you getting planted in our church is much, much higher than us not doing that."

About 75 percent of the congregation is single, and I found that many are disconnected from their family of origin both physically and emotionally. Oasis becomes for them a source of familial life and indeed may be the best family experience they've ever had. Adrian is among many at Oasis with a strained family past. She left her family to move to Los Angeles, partly to pursue a new career in entertainment and partly to leave home. She justified changing her name as an attempt to appeal to talent agents, but she told me changing her name was also a way to break away from her father. Another woman member said, "I started running at a young age. It was like, 'I want out.'" Another member told me how his father left the house when he was little. "There was a lot of physical abuse toward my mom and my siblings, including myself. There was a lot of mental abuse. It was a very abusive environment. . . . It was a painful experience," and he remembers "as a kid always telling myself, 'When I grow up, I'm going to be completely different from my father.'"

Kilde compares the Protestantism and homes of today to those of a century ago in terms of sanctuary:

> There are, of course, similarities here to the nineteenth century situation in which churches drew upon the ideology of the sanctified home in defining themselves as places of sanctuary, as spiritual armories, in a turbulent Society. The family home at the time, however, actually vied with the church in offering the most attractive respite from the world. In the late twentieth century, the church locates itself on a separate plane of respite outside of the stresses of everyday life by identifying with other contemporary places of peace, places where people spend their leisure hours (hopefully) untroubled by the cares of the world: the shopping mall, the sports arena, the movie theater. The church home is no longer relevant, but the mall provides the feeling of worry-free comfort for which the megachurch strives. (2002, 219)

Today, many of the unmarried (both divorced and never married) no longer see homes as places of respite or refuge. Rest, refreshment, and recreation are sought out in public venues, including larger churches.

Of the experience of alienation in Los Angeles, a staff member said, "We have a city of orphans basically. We have a bunch of people here searching for significance, wanting to get a big break so they can become a big star, and no one is from Los Angeles here. You ask people and they are from all over the place, all over the world, coming here for one reason. But you know what? A lot of those people don't have family. They don't have family here. And that's another reason why they connect with the Oasis. Because this is the place where this becomes your family, it's an extended family." Pastor Holly concurred: "This culture is very familyless. We are without family. People are moving here and leaving theirs. And then we have people here raised in single-parent or no-parent homes, and they don't understand the concept of family." Another staff member said, "We feel like we are in a city with a lot of orphans, people that come here like me and change their name and cut themselves off, just lost, disillusioned, insecure, messed up, whatever, wandering."

A banner prominently displayed in the lobby outside the worship auditorium reads, "Welcome Home." The homey, familylike environment appeals to the disconnected singles moving to Hollywood. Danielle's Hollywood world of high living was filled with "a lot of insincerity. Nobody really cared about anybody. The friendship was over when the job was over." In contrast, the family of Oasis is always there to help, to nurture, to encourage, to pick up after your messes, and to hold you when you need comfort. In the office, one staff member said, "our phone rings constantly. It's not unusual for me to receive thirty to forty phone calls a day from people just asking questions, wanting to pray, wanting to seek counseling, and we are all pretty busy around here."

Indeed, the church home of Oasis does not mirror domesticity but a kind of energetic fraternity/sorority, clublike social atmosphere that allows people to mix and mingle in a freestyle and friendly way. It's a place to make friends. It's a place to be with friends. Yes, some are looking for a spouse, but until that happens the ongoing activity is one of constant opportunity to be around people in a socially safe place. One single woman said, "Most women my age would be losing their mind if they weren't married." She quickly added, pointing upward, "God knows what shape my ovaries are in." Another mature single woman said, "Quite honestly, I'm happy. I'm not lonely. I don't feel like I'm missing anything. Like, my husband is there somewhere if it's supposed to be. If it's supposed to be, he will be there. But I know that this is my church and if he walks up to me in this church, great; and if he walks up to me on the street, great; but this is my church." The atmosphere of spiritual kinship also cultivates a means to bridge racial and ethnic differences in the church. "Family is family and it's at a place where I really do forget, 'Oh, you are black and I am not,'" Lynn said. "Yeah, we are really diverse and so I think that minorities might come in and go, 'Wow! There's people like me and everybody's here.' But that quickly fades because you are just family."

Although Oasis is a large church, the feeling of solidarity and belonging is fundamental to the experience of the congregation. "It's nice to be accepted,"

Damion said. "That's why people go to church, is to find that community, and I've found it." Donna said, "There is family, there is friendships. A lot of people can't count their friends on one hand. You know that old saying that if you have a handful of good friends, you're lucky. That's not true. You should have thirty or forty good friends. There's no limit to how many good friends you have." When I asked one single young man what attracted him to Oasis, he answered in one word: "Intimacy." Singles in the congregation told me they go home to an empty house; even if they have roommates, they're often not there and often uncaring. Home is neither restful nor sacred; rather home is a place to sleep. Home is often viewed as a place of conflict, abuse, loneliness, and pain. The added failure of these individuals being unable to create a home in Los Angeles gives a church like Oasis the chance to cultivate a different type of home.

The black church emphasizes both group solidarity and personal well-being, as Oasis does (Ellison 1991). A staff member talked about the atmosphere: "There is just a much stronger sense of the house, you know, and the calling on the house, which obviously is the calling on their life." For the leaders of Oasis, "house" and "family" are synonymous.[4] When you join the Oasis, you join this "house," and the moral directives of the church apply to every committed member. This is reminiscent of Durkheim (1978), for whom intimate bonds established through a common set of sentiments and ideals characterize the family sphere. The family contrasts with civic society, where solidarity is based on complex interdependent bonds. As Durkheim describes in *The Division of Labor in Society*, people take on various roles and functions in civil society, each providing goods and services. Broad society fosters connections between people on the basis of the necessity of their different contributions to the corporate survival. When family bonds are missing, individuals in modern society are left with formalized relationships built on utility and exchange, where skills are more important than sentiments, not built on care, affection, and shared affective meanings. But in a church family, there is a loyalty, duty, and obligation to do those things that would reflect best on the family.

Durkheim consistently framed the family as the most basic institution of society. Morality begins with the family; it is the place where an individual first learns to displace egoism and make sacrifices for others; it demands individual loyalty and devotion. The emphasis on family as a base of morality is found in the earliest of Durkheim's manuscripts (1884), which describes parents using authority to instill in children habits that prepare them for a future apart from the family; indeed, the morality of parents prepares children to be independent, yet morally responsible, people.

In the familylike aspect of Oasis, the experience of sacrifice is most evident. While religious ceremonies typically exemplify ritual sacrifice in highly symbolic terms, sacrifice is tangible, personal, and concrete. At Oasis sacrifice is rooted in relationships, apparent in the common practice of friends helping friends. The capacity for self-sacrifice for friends and strangers is a consistent demonstration and manifestation of religious practice at Oasis. One single woman found herself incapable of taking care of herself after an illness. She remembered thinking, "I have no family here. I can't drive. How am I going to get groceries? What am I going to do?" But the Oasis family took care of her. Every morning a different person came to her home with bags full of groceries and flowers, took out the garbage, cleaned the kitchen, and washed the dishes. They gave hugs. They provided company. They provided financial help. Such care became a profound religious experience for her: "I had this revelation of how much God loves us." She then said, "That is why I tell people, 'How could you be without a church family?' Because your 'family-family' will occasionally let you down, God love them all."

Not only was her commitment to the church cemented but also a reciprocity of generosity ensued. "I found myself being ridiculously generous with finances because if someone walks by and I hear them at the grocery store and they say they are short on cash, I give it to them. They're like, 'Oh, no.' And I say, 'Trust me, it's been given to me.'" Looking back on her experience, she said it "teaches you to be even more [generous] because there's always enough. You never have to worry about yourself. If you always just worry about others, you're always taken care of. I just let go. I take care of others when I see a need because I know that God will take care of me."

Racial Unity through Shared Struggle and Hope

The Oasis Christian Center does not exhibit a black Christian theology, a distinctive mode of thought focusing on the oppression and suffering of black Americans (see Cone 1990; Thomas 2004). But Oasis does have a theology that has a strong affinity with black Christian theology, tying in themes of oppression and suffering as well as a yearning for liberation and holistic humanity. As Lincoln and Mamiya write: "From the very beginning of the Black experience in America, one critical denotation of freedom has remained constant: freedom has always meant the absence of any restraint which might compromise one's responsibility to God" (1990, 4). With its focus on freedom, the black church in America developed amidst the oppression and exploitation of African Americans, and scholars conclude that this shared experience placed an indelible stamp on this particular religious institution (Lincoln and Mamiya 1990; Wilmore 1998). Similarly, the choice of champion of life as the dominant metaphor of Oasis has enough affinity with the liberation theology of African American churches and prosperity theology that it relates to the experience of black attenders. The cultivation of bonds of spiritual kinship is part of the process of cultivating the champions of life at Oasis.

Oasis nurtures individual achievement in the context of collective frustrations. It is the feeling of frustration in pursuit of status that connects the experience of African Americans with workers in the entertainment industry. At Oasis, the spiritual power available to entertainment workers and African Americans is the same power made available to all who experience loss, frustration, or fatigue and who desire a renewal. Oasis is not revolutionary; there is no attempt to overthrow the basic framework of the current economic system. But, the innovative shift is the radical integration of a profound Christian morality that states that wealth and status may accrue to a successful believer and that those who elevate their social status with attendant privileges, power, and influence should act as a part of a distinctive moral community—that of being a Christian. The successful believer channels wealth and privilege with generosity on behalf of the believing community first, and the world in need next. Egoism would not prevail, since personal ego is subsumed to the corporate initiatives represented in the spiritual mission of the congregation as a whole.

The successful diversification of race-ethnicity in the congregation demonstrates the fluidity of a personal identity that allows racial and ethnic heritage to be obscured while other, valued aspects of the textured self come to the fore as significant bases for affiliation and rapport. This fluidity and reorientation is similar to the process of "ethnic transcendence" I observed at Mosaic (Marti 2005, chap. 7). Ethnic transcendence occurs when individuals take on a new shared identity on the basis of a uniquely congregational understanding of what it means to be "Christian" (Marti, 2008). A new corporate identity overrides the potentially divisive aspects of ethnic identity. Understanding this corporate identity is key to appreciating how the tensions of faith and fame are resolved.

8   Becoming Champions of Life

DONNA: Yes, I'm ambitious. But I let God make my goals.

How can Oasis confidently and aggressively send out ambitious workers to succeed in the materialistic, exploitative, profit-driven, and image-conscious culture of the entertainment industry? The answer lies in understanding that the religious identity formed at Oasis does not thrust forward individuals as autonomous workers but with a corporate identity that radically binds them with a deep sense of commonality and solidarity with other struggling Christians who are trying to make it in a difficult world. "My motives, my everything behind my reasons for being a part of this is not what I was seeking when I was seeking fame and fortune," an Oasis musician said. "It's not about fame and fortune for me. It's more about being a part of a Christian family that is out there impacting the world in different ways." At Oasis, the individual is part of a corporate group. Members come to believe that when they go out into the world they are never truly alone.

Oasis draws the ambitious who have been burned in their ambition. They have dreams and goals but fail to see how they will be fulfilled. Many who are pursuing careers in the entertainment industry are out of work, low on cash, and do not know when the next gig will happen. The teachings at Oasis regularly emphasize God's care for people if they continue to do what is right. For Durkheim, people experience in life a "day-in, day-out struggle" full of "incessant conflict and friction" (1995, 352). In book 3 of *The Elementary Forms of Religious Life,* he analytically describes rituals of integration that bring together a sacred people. Coming together through ritual "refreshes a spirit worn down by all this overburdening and day-to-day labor" (385; see also Jay 1992, 17–19). At Oasis, the consistent, public encouragement is to come, get some love, and get some help so that you can go out there and "do your thing." Oasis is a refuge for people who have been hurt, abused, mistreated, and demoralized. As Durkheim explains, through participation in the congregation, the "individual soul" is "regenerated by immersing itself once more in the very wellspring of its life. As a result, that soul is stronger" (385).

"Champion of life" is the single guiding image of Christian discipleship that centers the thought, motivation, and activity of Oasis believers. "That's the core thing," Bridgette said. "Becoming the champion—who you're supposed to be."

Oasis succeeds in its vision to cultivate "champions in life" by effecting a strategic reorientation of personal identity. Understanding the power of this identity is part of understanding the power of religion as a cultural force within society. Reflecting on many years of research, R. Stephen Warner emphasized that "religion in America is especially important because it provides group identities . . . and helps them act together in the world." Further, "in the most robust cases, religion engenders intense solidarity, courage to face adversity, and inspiration to better the group's lot. Understanding the grounds and the significance of such group-formation functions of religion is a research frontier in sociology of religion that is especially central to the new paradigm as I understand it" (2005, 284). While the image of being a champion of life is not deterministic, it is a rich base of common identity that vitalizes worship at Oasis and repurposes members' work in the broader world (see Marti 2008).

As Oasis negotiates social change by providing this religious identity as champion and overcomer as an anchor in the midst of difficult career choices and failed opportunities, individuals subsume themselves to a religious system that sanctions ambition and provides handles on how to work through failure, cope with challenges from overwhelming social structures, and manage exploitation and injustice. The fully formed disciple at Oasis is an empowered achiever. This person is aware of challenges and struggles that exist in their world. While most Americans have trouble seeing the connection between their own ambitions for achievement and the institutional structures that make them possible (Bellah 1985, 1991), the believers of Oasis readily connect their own economic lives to their involvement in the congregation.

The church is acknowledged as a place that helps them actualize their dreams and build the moral strength to pursue those dreams and enjoy life along the way. And while scholars like Robert Bellah (2006) and Stephen Ellingson (2007) express grave concern over the individualism increasingly characteristic of Protestant religion, Oasis demonstrates a form of individualism bound to collective solidarity and moral duty. The ongoing worship services at the church and personal coaching through various levels of involvement in the congregation cultivate a strong sense of being part of a family that encourages you and your ambitions but will be there if you fall. In short, Oasis achieves a strategic reorientation of personal identity to form a community of ambitious achievers able to withstand the constant disappointments and frustrations of pursuing a career in a difficult industry. And it does so in a manner constrained by an other-oriented Durkheimian morality that curbs purely egoistic behavior.

From Individual to Collective Ambition

In the process of cultivating a collective identity as champions of life, members of Oasis see the church as a place to "get priorities right." Establishing right priorities involves members' "getting a foundation" and "cleaning up their lives" so they can "then move up and do great things." In talking about the church, Damion stressed, "I really want to make sure I'm lined up right, that in any and everything I do I'm not doing it for any other reason but to glorify God." Such explicit, self-monitoring statements occurred over and over again. Getting priorities right begins with regularly attending services. Jennelle avoided attending church with her new friends for months. "I was still trying to become famous. How dare I say, 'I don't have time,' but I felt I didn't have time for church or for God." But beyond regular attendance, getting priorities right ultimately means integrating spiritual concerns with occupational concerns. Tyler is among those who is learning to integrate his faith into his profession as a musician and make it a Christian ministry even though he is the only Christian in his band. "I would really like to be in a position where we are gathering in his name in hopes that he can do something through us." Playing good music is not sufficient. "We don't have the objective of bringing God's kingdom to that club. We are just there to make people feel great, and I feel like I could be manifesting more of God's will than that." At the core, getting priorities right involves experiencing a fundamental reorientation of ambition. Lawrence said, "Before, my ambition was built around myself." Donna said, "I was very driven, very ambitious. Now I am still very driven, but I notice I don't make goals as much as I used to because I had this revelation about goals: Are they my goals or are they God's goals? . . . I still make goals but I don't hold them so tightly. I make them, I let them go, I tell God what I would like but I tell him it's his will. What does he want for my life?" She summarized: "Yes, I'm ambitious. But I let God make my goals."

Kyle moved to L.A. "to be in the industry, to be a successful musician, meaning fame and fortune." Now, after a few years, he said, "seeking the fame and fortune is not what my life is all about"; it "was not God's vision." Kyle resigned himself to marginal status in the industry. "I'm not going to have fame in the way I thought I would have it, but maybe I'm going to have fame in a different way which God intends for me to have." Discovering "God's vision" was not easy, and he continues to be ambitious—"very much so. Just the drive." The challenge was to place the demands of his career within a system of priorities that places church-based spirituality at the top. At Oasis, "I was able to face that discomfort of finding out that God didn't necessarily want that [fame and fortune] for me to have, but he had better things for me that were more beneficial for me as well as others in this world."

Releasing the desire for self-oriented fulfillment as a star, Kyle found fulfillment as a social worker. "Oasis has helped me to grow in that manner." He said, "I was much happier finding out God's will for me was not in a famous role, meaning on a stage, but famous maybe impacting kids and other young adults in different ways than I ever would have imagined." The goal of life, according to him, is "how many things are you going to accomplish which are in God's will for your life so that when you come home to God in heaven, he will be able to say, 'Well done, good and faithful servant.'" Investing in the younger generation has become Kyle's "purpose in life," and he hopes to create a performing arts center for youth.

The common challenge of struggling with finances is what makes the act of tithing (donating at least 10 percent of one's income to the church) among the members of Oasis stand at the center of their redirecting their ambition for personal financial success into charitable work. After one service, Tim told me how much he appreciated the teachings on tithing "because the only voices that are talking to me are saying it's all about the money, it's all about the money, you've got to have it, you've got to be after it." Lisa's experience with tithing connected to what she called a very long lesson in learning "not to be a slave to money anymore." Even when her income was much higher several years ago, she struggled financially and faced enormous debt. "I had a beautiful house in North Hollywood. I had a great car. I was getting massages and facials and everything, going to spas and going out to dinner at really great places. I stayed in the greatest hotels. I had everything on a silver platter. . . . It was this lifestyle I felt I deserved." From being at Oasis, she came to think, "This isn't what I'm about anyway." Overall, "it was freeing because I didn't have to keep up with that image anymore," she said. "I don't need to wear Armani every day. I don't need those labels anymore because I have (not to sound corny) a bigger label." For Donna as well, money has a "place" and is "not the driving force" of her life. Her lessons came "through tithing and through having a giving heart." She provides her formula: "The more you tithe, the more you let go. You live less in fear and more in faith. Your heart gets stronger. The more you serve, your heart gets stronger. The more you love, your heart gets stronger. So to me, it's really about working that heart in every area of your life so that you are always putting God first. It's like science. It's basic. Like making a cake."

Through These Doors Walk Champions of Life

At its core, much of the pastoral work in the church is aimed at getting members to step back from their Hollywood identity and take on a broader, church-based Christian identity. Believers at Oasis tell me the Hollywood industry enforces a moral framework focused on individual profit and ambition. But, a television producer said, "My ambition is more towards being who God wants me to be than it is in terms of what I do," and "while we're in this industry, we don't want the industry to get in us." A staff member said, "I have to remind them not to get wrapped up in the industry and not allow whatever they do—dancer, writer, actor—to make that your identity. That's not who you are." As another staff member explained, "We are constantly challenging and getting in people's business about serving and selling out and putting God first and making him a priority and honoring him." Success is not about being famous. "No, you are representing him and living for him and wanting to honor him no matter what you are doing, if you are waiting tables or auditioning for a movie or sitting in church, teaching kids, or whatever."

Champions of life are fundamentally people who allow God to use their desires to fulfill his overall plan to actualize his purposes in the world. "A lot of people in the entertainment industry find coming here good for them," Charlene said, "because it does help them to understand that it's not just an actor or producer or whatever it is that you do in the entertainment industry, it's that you can still lift Jesus Christ up and live such a lifestyle that people will see him." David Snow and colleagues (1986) insightfully describe how organizations connect the life experiences of members with the purposes of the organization, and Erving Goffman (1974) introduced the notion of "frames" to synthesize theories of such thinkers as William James and Alfred Schutz and reveal how socially derived and socially enforced schemas channel our experiences. Omar McRoberts has applied Goffman's concept of framing to the way congregations help believers understand their world (2003, 65). Frames are necessary to organize the chaotic bundle of experiences and perceptions coming at us at any particular moment. They organize our perceptions of happenings in our personal world, so that we can act in meaningful ways.

A similar point is made by Timothy J. Nelson (2004) who references anthropologist James Fernandez to describe how metaphors of identity provide blueprints for organizational and individual action. For Nelson, one of the most powerful sources of guiding metaphors for our relationship to the divine in everyday life is the local church. By framing the frustrations of members of the church, Oasis helps believers come to see themselves as working in the difficult field of God's orchard. The places they live and work are places in which God is actively attempting to accomplish his will despite obstructive spiritual forces and the inevitable recalcitrance of a fallen world.

Despite their difficulties, believers at Oasis see themselves through immersion in the congregation as moving toward greater spiritual growth, and their personal perception of progress in spiritual growth constitutes their "moral career" (Goffman 1961, 127; see also Allahyari 2000). Moral careers, that is, progressive stages of perceived change and growth in an individual's development, occur within this institutional context. Goffman emphasizes the importance of institutions to the construction of the self:

> Each moral career, and behind this, each self, occurs within the confines of an institutional system, whether a social establishment such as a mental hospital or a complex of personal and professional relationships [like that of a congregation]. The self, then, can be seen as something that resides in the arrangements prevailing in a social system for its members. The self in this sense is not a property of the person to whom it is attributed, but dwells rather in the pattern of social control that is exerted in connection with the

person by himself and those around him. The special kind of institutional arrangement does not so much support the self as constitute it. (168)

The profound implication of Goffman's theoretical perspective is that the champion of life cultivated in the Oasis Christian Center is a characteristic of the congregation itself. It does not exist without the institutional arrangement of the church. Individuals joining Oasis who take on the identity of champion embrace a collective identity supported and sustained by the congregation and defined within the Oasis Christian Center, a powerful, institutionalized role because it persists beyond their participation in the congregation.

The ambitious individual transforms into a sacralized self that is connected to a community that engages in fulfilling the mission of God to extend his kingdom in this world. Thus, for the champion, success in a job is only at extension of the successful work of God in allowing his representative to work in the power of his spirit in gaining influence in nonreligious and irreligious realms. Champions are empowered individuals, empowered by the community to work confidently and independently for God.

Goffman's ideas extend Emile Durkheim's essential framework that stresses the self cannot exist outside of the collectivity, a contested notion today among theorists who view individuals as increasingly distanced from social groups and therefore left to construct their own identity (Aldridge 2000). Tracing the transformation from traditional to postindustrial society, modern individuals are said to be free from a fixed social order, their positions in society fluid. It is certainly true individuals are increasingly on their own to cultivate a sense of identity, yet the structuring of one's own identity without access to social groups is impossible. Even in "modern" society, individuals require social structures to sustain a sense of self (see Seligman 2000). And individuals do not endlessly choose from the "toolbox" of culture (Swidler 1986) but rather seek a stable basis for personal identity. Individuals use whatever freedom they possess to align themselves with selective affinity groups that provide cohesive structures for the self. This is one reason religious affiliation continues to be a persistent and powerful anchor for the self.

Churches like Oasis with a strong collective identity are among the institutions that provide a moral base for understanding one's place in the world. As localized, accessible resources for achieving a continuous sense of self, churches in America are affectively based communities; individuals not only believe but also belong such that individuals assimilate into a congregation by taking on a particular identity. This collective identity is just as freeing and constraining as the tight-knit social groups that existed in the past. The individual who assimilates a church-based identity is able to live more spontaneously by taking advantage of highly ritualized forms of action, a choice that leaves the individual with a number of decisions and negotiations already settled. Moreover, belonging to a church-based social group involves a form of self-discipline that defines standards of right and wrong and appropriateness and offense, guiding people in their overall choices, values, motivations, and goals.

Worship as Letting Go

Worship is one of the most important elements of the church for evoking identity reorientation, emphasizing believers' identity as Christ followers amidst competing identities and distractions. Durkheim (1995) also emphasizes the corporate empowering of individuals through ritual worship, and I found worship to be the most consistent element in all the activities of Oasis. There are many different speakers, there are many different types of activities, and meetings happen throughout the week. Yet the most energetic and consistent experience available at Oasis is participation in musical worship at the beginning of every service.

For the champions of Oasis, high-quality, energizing, foot-stomping, body-swaying, hand-raising worship at the church encourages spirit-filled believers to accomplish great things in the world as sons and daughters of the king. Many emphasized how important the music was to them in coming to the church. A full band, energetic singers, and a beat with a heavy and steady blend of bass, funk, and rhythm played by professional musicians provides an engaging, even enveloping, social experience. To be in the worship service at the Oasis is to stand, clap, sway, and smile as both audience and performers lose themselves in the service.

"Yeah, the music was so powerful," one young musician said. "I mean, that's what I do. I feel like the music is such a gateway into the presence of the Lord. And so I felt like immediately here I could feel that presence." It was through the music, he said, that he "felt God's presence working in my life to get me in the church and to get me working for the kingdom." He now is completely committed: "I'm full force." He concluded, "This is an amazing place and it will change your life. And I personally have never been to a church that is so energetically and spiritually uplifting." The church is energizing, he finds: "Every time I leave, I feel recharged." Empowered achievers fuel themselves up in worship, accept being loved by God, and take the risk of getting themselves out into the world one more time.

For Danielle, learning to worship was the "first hurdle" in becoming a champion of the Oasis. "I kept looking around thinking, 'What are they doing?' People were raising their hands, clapping and singing and smiling and looked happy. What kind of place is this?" She said, "I stood up. I didn't clap my hands. I kept looking around and not understanding why people were raising their hands and I had no idea what that was about." Nevertheless, "the music was a big draw. I loved the music."

Over time, Danielle "learned" to worship. "The first time I actually got into praise and worship and the first time I ever raised my hands, it was kind of like a submission. The first time I just kind of like submitted my heart to God. That was a huge step," she said. "I felt compelled to just kind of raise my hand and let go. I felt self-conscious at first but it was just I closed my eyes and decided, you know what, Pastor always talks about how the praise and worship time is your time to be with God and to worship as a church but also as a very private moment for yourself. So I decided not to think about anybody that was around me." Friends who had introduced her to church had become familiar and safe. "I felt a level of comfort with them. So I felt safe around them to kind of let go. And it was just a feeling of letting go. It was the first step of me believing that I was in God's hands. And there is a way that I have to communicate that back to him. And it was just a really great feeling." In time, worship became so significant for Danielle, it became her essential connection to the spirit of God.

At Oasis, worshipers abandon themselves to a participation in the divine and experience empowerment that is reinforced in the practical, encouraging teaching designed to coach champions as they walk through life. As Miller and Yamamori note: "For Pentecostals, worship provides the opportunity to experience an alternative reality" (2007, 221). The key to good worship is to lose self-consciousness and the concern that other people are in the room. "I had to learn how to worship and the way I had to learn how to worship is to just let go, to let go," Damion said. "To let go and let God." An attitude of surrender is implicit to worship. "Anytime that you're aware of people around you, then I honestly feel that you're not praising God the way that God wants you to praise him." Damion broke down the process: "The music would touch my soul. If it touched me, then it moved me. So at that point, the music touched you, and it got you emotional, and when it got you there, then that was the point that you let go." Oasis for Damion became an important place for the process of "letting go," which means "letting go of my problems and everything else." Worship is "letting go and you don't care." What is most important is "learning to just let go."

Timothy Nelson (2004) rightly emphasizes giving up of control as characteristic of emotional worship. Individuals willingly, voluntarily, and with anticipation yield themselves to the elements of worship for the duration of the service in order to experience God, and by doing so enhance the performance of those on the platform, increasing their intensity, which further accentuates the corporate experience in a circular fashion—leaders to worshipers, and worshipers back to leaders. Again mirroring a historical function of the black church, the Oasis through worship provides strength and empowerment to face the ongoing struggles of day-to-day life.

Through attendees' participating in a corporate orientation to the sacred, the reconstruction of identity happens in the abandonment of self to worship. Corporate worship allows for a process of reshaping one's identity toward a transcendent divinity being worshipped and also constitutes a process of dynamic bonding among worshipers through the shared experience of empowerment. According to Max Scheler: "Nothing unites beings more immediately and intimately . . . than the common worship and adoration of the 'holy'; . . . it lies in the essence of the intention toward the holy to unite and join together" (1973, 94).

Moving from Welcome to Wanted: Getting Connected

"Letting go" in worship is powerful, but it is not enough. At Oasis, "serving the church" is equal to "growing spiritually." And while attenders are actively encouraged to take on ministry roles, members are required to do so. Service is not merely an appeal to an individual's involvement; it is a strategy for corporate formation. Members are encouraged to attend classes, especially the Vision Class, the basic course required for membership, and to invite nonmembers to serve. More than just voluntarism, serving in a church ministry contributes to shaping collective identity.

One day in the Oasis offices, I noticed a group of photographs arranged on a wall. These were the graduates of the previous month's Vision Class. The final session includes discussion with church leaders about class members' skills, talents, and abilities that could be used in ministry. Learning about the variety of service opportunities available, new members indicate their preferences before having their picture taken. The church initially assigns people to ministries based on their individual abilities with the explicit intent of immersing them in a social context. Their pictures are then displayed in the offices with their name and assigned area of ministry so staff can get to know the steady stream of new members.

Assimilation strategies like this are typical in large churches. The intent is for people to move from feeling welcomed in the church to feeling wanted. Lynn is among many who see this push for involvement in ministry as part of the process of spiritual growth at Oasis. "You need to feel needed. You need to make that transition. You need to go from 'Wow, everybody's so friendly, and I'm really getting some good friendships,' to 'You are really great at this area. We need you to serve here. You are part of this team now.' . . . It's like you have got to make people feel like they are essential to the team, even if they are not. But if we make that person feel they take ownership of it, they can make it something huge. They make it something great. And that's what betters this church. . . . That's how you grow people. That's how people develop and grow."

Another staff member stressed how the church assists people to discover their skills and talents, with their discovery followed by the imperative to apply their gifts to spiritual work. "We bring out this gift in you. All right, now serve. Use it for the kingdom." The appeal to the individual's unique contribution—a form of specialized division of labor described by Durkheim as "organic solidarity"—is a means for integrating individuals into the work of the congregation that subsumes individualism into a shared corporate identity sharing a common purpose. Damion said, "This is our church, so you have to put in the time and work. 'Let's make this church a great church and go out and reach a lot of people out there in the world.' It's that type of attitude, teamwork, like, 'Hey, we're a team. This is your church.'" The appeal to the self is therefore a means to integrate attenders into a system of shared moral authority.

Of course, church leaders admit there are "seat warmers" who attend the church "for a year or two and don't serve." But these are people who don't "get it." Gladys said, "People have to make a decision whether we go to church to have our needs met or we go to church to be a blessing for others." Serving in the church is characteristic of people "getting it," meaning that they begin to embrace the norms and ideals of champion and overcomer Oasis seeks to cultivate. Jody was a person I spoke to at length who has trouble "connecting" at Oasis. She feels people are telling her she needs "to get up to speed with God." At the same time, she feels part of the problem is that she doesn't have time to serve with others in the church. Although she has been working backstage helping produce Sunday services, it is solo work and not really part of a team ministry. For Jody, a lack of time to serve in a team ministry is keeping her from connecting relationally to the church and personally "growing" and "changing" to conform to the moral community of Oasis.

Immersion in the congregation through volunteer work reinforces connection to the moral community of the church, sometimes in unexpected ways. After one woman made a commitment to be a follower of Jesus at Oasis, she discovered sex outside of marriage was not acceptable in the theology of the congregation. She called her friend and said, "You've got to be kidding me. This is a deal breaker for me." What changed her mind? She said:

> I started serving in the youth ministry, and I had teenage girls in my small group. They were all struggling with stuff. I remember teaching one night trying to make them believe they were "fearfully and wonderfully made" [Psalms 139:14]. I realized the biggest problem was they had no self-esteem. None of them thought they were worth anything. . . . So, I remember talking to them about responsible dating and not having sex. I went home, and I broke down into a million pieces thinking, "I can't teach this, because I don't believe it." I had a very hard journey that had to happen very quickly. I had to start believing that I was worth it. And I had to start believing what sex really meant. . . . It was one of those things that I couldn't have learned unless I was teaching it.

Although this woman was immersed in a network of social contacts and countless project assignments in the church's ministry, it was active participation in the explicitly moral community of congregational life that reoriented her behavior. Specifically, in her role representing the moral community she in turn applied moral discipline to her own life.

Joining the Team under Spiritual Authority

In short, the work of discipleship or moral reorientation happens in the course of doing ministry. Central to the process of collective identity formation is learning to follow directions and work as a team under spiritual authority. One staff member said, "We are interested in seeing people grow. We are interested in seeing people demonstrate that they are willing to do sometimes even things that are not reasonable. Things that don't always make you feel comfortable." Another staff member gave an example:

> If somebody is in the creative arts and they are doing great and they are serving and we are loving it, but all of a sudden we ask them to do something one way and they're like, "No, no, no, this is my thing. You gave it to me." It's become an issue now. That heart issue has come up, and so we need to address that. We are not saying, "Okay, now you're gone." But we're saying, "Okay, we need you to do this. You need to submit. We need to work through this. What's going on in your heart? Why is this a problem for you?" And sometimes they are not able to make that transition. They say, "No. We're either doing it my way or [I'm] going to leave."

Although self-promotion is required to attain a level of work success in the entertainment industry (see chapter 5), self-promoting ambition and self-oriented activity are redefined as pastoral needs at Oasis that are corrected by learning to serve others under shared authority. "There are a lot of people that will come in with their careers and their choices, they can come in very self-seeking, self-promoting," Lynn said. "That's just part of L.A. 'Hey, here's my card. Hey, let's see if I can hook up with you and get this connection and this connection.' We get that; but if you're here long enough, one of the first things [you learn is] that this atmosphere here is you serve other people, you love people."

This delicate balance of promoting the mission identity of the church without promoting the self is ambiguous and problematic. When I arrived at the church to begin my interviews, there had been a recent conflict involving ministry leaders who had left the church. According to those who stayed, the leaders had placed their own ambition in front of the ambition for the church as a whole: "They wanted to be stars, and we are not into building stars. We are into building servants." The church is not to be a vehicle for self-proclaiming celebrity, but rather a community of servants who share life together. The desire of Philip and Holly is that the church not be a springboard for the gifts of a few highly talented leaders but rather an expansive accelerator of creative talent among attenders over a long period of time.

The care and concern evident among ministry leaders for their team members cultivates loyalty that is channeled into service. One staff member recalled, "The leaders of this church had invested so much time and poured so much into us, our lives have changed because of this Oasis experience we have had. . . . I've been able to grow this much because of people like [several pastors and staff members]. Those guys are family; they are friends. We are doing life together." And when leaders like these make requests, many members I spoke with expressed the sentiment, "I can't say 'No' to a person who's taken that much time to invest in me." The gratitude and immense satisfaction of experiencing care and satisfying relationships create exuberance for duplicating the experience for others. "We have had the experience, and we know how much it has changed our lives." Charlene said, "You can actually feel like God really loves you and cares about you and has something for you to do, and this is the place to come and discover that."

Connecting to Moral Agents

Identity reorientation is greatly accelerated when people participate in a ministry team, because team ministry is the point of application for moral discipline in the church. Serving on a team puts people under relationships of spiritual authority and in communities dedicated to the moral refinement of believers. The general messages addressed to everyone from the platform are personalized to attenders through interpersonal encounters with "true believers" of Oasis. Connecting with moral agents from the congregation is usually phrased as "building relationships" and "establishing a connection." For example, in explaining why people leave, Lynn said, "They didn't successfully feel wanted and needed." Rodrigo said, "They don't have any ties, there are no roots there. So it's easy, you know. I couldn't leave this place because I would be leaving my family. I would leave everything that I have. So there is an investment here." Further, "if you get connected, that means that you are going to meet someone that is going to encourage you, someone who is going to be praying with you, someone that is going to be loving on you and making you feel good." A more recent member said, "The way this church works is the more ministries you're involved in, the more people you know." Being connected means having relationships of encouragement and care, and when people "turn to God," they turn to a congregation of God's people.

"The mission of our church is to see people's lives change," Donna said. "I know how much my life changed." Moral reorientation of believers occurs by connecting with moral agents within the congregation. "Everything about this ministry is to get people into relationships with each other," a staff member said. "This is the cornerstone of your faith: You will not make it alone." In the process of meeting other members and doing ministry, members are spending time mostly around others who have made explicit commitments to the beliefs and purposes of the congregation. On this point, although Durkheim has been criticized for asserting in *Elementary Forms* that God was nothing more than the effervescence of human interaction through cultic worship, he is right, in that "God" often means in practice the community of people within a congregation. For instance, when people say, "God will work it out," it is God through the community of the church, the assembly, the congregation that remains vital and necessary for resolving problems and issues. When people say, "God will work it out," it means the believing self commits to engaging with the believing community. People are instruments of God to shape each other. Indeed, within church-based social networks where members share little else in common, there arise frequent opportunities to interact on the challenges and dilemmas of living "spiritual" lives.

Ministry leaders and dedicated members are encouraged to take on a pastoral function to help other members "spiritually grow" by applying moral discipline. God becomes manifest through the disciplined action of members in the church. One staff member described the work of leaders as serving the church and, in the same sentence, noted that "they are holding people accountable." Bridgette said that once members are involved in ministry, "they are confronted. We are a very accountable church. If you want to serve on a ministry, we're going to be all in your face. And it's not just the heads of the ministry that make them accountable. It's the friends that they choose and the church. We keep each other accountable. I love that about our church." She equated the application of discipline in people's lives so that they conform to expectations of discipleship with the "aliveness" of God. For Bridgette, members become champions "by submitting to God and little by little chipping away at things and going to classes and talking with people and praying. It's a whole thing."

Leaders in the church, especially those who are forty and over, are encouraged to interact not only by praying with and encouraging young adults but also by "instructing" them in godly ways. A woman in her early thirties told me about women who come to church "dressed like they're going to a club" and are a "stumbling block to the men." She said she told one woman in the bathroom, "You should pull your shirt up because your cleavage is showing." An African American woman, a longtime member in her forties, said, "Sometimes in the ladies room, I say, 'That's a really pretty top. But you may want to think about wearing it.'" Comments are made "in love" and to people already committed to the congregation. "After seeing someone here faithfully for two months, there's an understanding this person is now committed to this ministry and hopefully to Christ. Then, you know—I have taken ladies out to lunch and just talked about life and living and offered some guidance sometimes." Another mature African American woman who tries to be "a blessing to younger women" described "investing in the next generation" by transforming what she considered her former mistakes into points of advice. "God has given me some wisdom because

I've made so many mistakes and I've done it so wrong, that I can turn it around. When I see somebody moving in a direction that I think [is wrong], I just need to share some thoughts with them."

Manageable Spirituality: Mistakes amidst Purpose

Encouragement and accountability are necessary because a life consistent with the morality of this conservative congregation is hard. Even the ambition for success can be daunting. One staff member defined champions as "people who succeed" in every area of their lives: "People who have a positive outlook on life. People who enjoy their faith. People who are able to lead, who are able to affect the community around them in a positive way. People who are able to be successful in their marriages, to be successful in their finances, to be successful in their careers, to be successful in their social life and in their friendships. . . . So that the world can look at these people and go, 'They've got something going on.' That's our mission here in L.A. To build those champions that people can look at and go, 'That's what we want.'"

Fortunately, Oasis avoids perfectionism in its promotion of faith. Bridgette began defining a champion as "someone who serves, someone who tithes," and then added, "someone who's not afraid to make a mistake. Somebody who's able to say they are wrong when they are wrong—that's a big one. Somebody who makes mistakes. Somebody who has good friends, accountable friends. Someone who keeps striving to be better." Oasis strives to provide a relational community characterized by warmth, love, and acceptance that holds people to moral standards alongside an assurance that a person does not need to be perfect. Rodrigo said the church provides an atmosphere "not feeling like, 'Oh, man, these areas in my life are not in order. I'd better keep those under wraps.' From top to bottom, all this is a journey and we are in this journey together. So we support each other and we know the areas that are difficult for us that we need to work on," that is, "you don't have to be perfect because it's a work in process."

As a historic extension of the Holiness-Pentecostal movement, the Oasis Christian Center contains an anthropology of sin that is critical to its theological framework. The theological framework contains a profound model of God willing to intimately commune with human imperfection as the believer pursues personal holiness and extends the kingdom of God through Spirit-empowered action. Holiness and Pentecostal churches historically separated conversion and moral perfection. A fully perfected, sanctified life is not a prerequisite for the indwelling of the Spirit. Rather, the distinctive emphasis among Holiness-Pentecostal churches from the mid–nineteenth century onward is that the Spirit of God aids fleshly weak believers by empowering them to live acceptable lives before God. The separation between the baptism of Holy Spirit and perfectionism allows the empowerment of service in the midst of personal imperfections. God does not shun the imperfect person, but rather the spiritual empowerment of corrupted and less-than-perfect human beings is a normal and necessary part of God's plan. Struggling Christians who are trying to live spiritual lives can be empowered for success in their personal and professional lives, while still continuing struggle with moral issues. R. A. Torrey in his important 1895 book *The Baptism with the Holy Spirit* wrote persuasively that the infusion of the Holy Spirit into the believer's life did not remove the sinful nature of a person nor did it simply cleanse a person from sin. The single and most important purpose of the Holy Spirit is "empowering for service."

Combining a therapeutic concern for personal hurt with the Holiness-Pentecostal theological framework of Spirit empowerment, a conservative Christian morality at Oasis becomes a manageable form of spirituality. As Maureen said, at Oasis "it's okay if I don't do it all perfectly," while in other churches she felt a conservative Christian life was unattainable. "There were times I felt I would never be what that preacher was saying because I just couldn't do all of that. . . . Philip and Holly are saying the same thing, but the difference is that they make it so that I know I could live this in a way that is real and practical." Before coming to Oasis, she never had "a desire to serve God and to honor him with my body." She said, "When I came to the Oasis, I was still jiving a little bit, you know? After being here and watching, listening, I made a decision: 'Lord, I am going to be celibate. I am going to behave myself. I'm going to do it your way,' because what they presented to me was something I felt like I could do with God. And it made we want to do that." She explained further that Holly and Philip

> say it in a way I can actually digest as opposed to feeling "I can't win this battle. There's no way I can measure up." The truth is we cannot measure up, okay? But when you break it down to me, it's like saying, "Go build a city." And just the thought of that is overwhelming. But if I said, "Let's start by paving that dirt road," that's much more acceptable, that's much more digestible. And that's what I get from Holly and Pastor. Yes, we do have a major purpose and a destiny to live for God, but let's go one step at a time. . . . So in this ministry, I learn to do things a step at a time. I learn to bring things in a practical everyday sort of way. . . . I can do this. Just take it day by day. "Oh, I didn't do too good today. But you give me tomorrow and I promise I'll try to do better." And sometimes I do better and sometimes I don't. And I say, "Okay, could you just give me one more day."

Another woman also talked about coming to embrace the conservative morality of the church. "When my walk was not so straight," she said, "I would come to church but I didn't so much want to fellowship because I didn't want people to notice or point those things out. I didn't want to be held accountable." But the manageable spirituality cultivated at the church creates an atmosphere in which people welcome moral discipline. "Those same people that I would avoid before, now I run to and I only want to be around because I always want to be where I'm at now. I love being around those people because I know I won't fall when I'm constantly surrounded by those people, and I'm living the way I'm living now. There's no way to fall."

For Maureen: "The Oasis is helping me to process, to realize the ambition of wanting to be everything God wants me to be." Internalizing the demands of "holy living" raises anxiety but living in a supportive and forgiving community eases it. "I'm encouraged, I am strengthened, I'm edified," Maureen said. The church is "an oasis. You can find the rest, the water, whatever it is you need in the desert to help you to get to that place where you know that you can say at the end of the day, 'I'm doing what God wants me to.' Because to me there's so much joy in that." Although spiritual life as a champion involves continued application of moral discipline, members achieve great satisfaction through immersion in the community. The new church family encourages and protects their religious identity even when choices and lifestyles fail to measure up.

The exercise of personal discipline and moral restraint among members of Oasis is as evident as it is among members of any moral community. Such disciplined behavior, for Durkheim, is critical to the happiness of human beings. The channeling of ambition at Oasis contributes to personal enjoyment in a Durkheimian framework, since happiness is a function of morality. By shifting their desires toward things that can actually be accomplished, people are happy. Reflecting on Durkheim's (1897, 1951) discussion of anomie, Robert Alun Jones writes: "For happiness to be achieved, therefore, the passions must be constrained; and since the individual has no internal means of constraint, the passions must be restricted by some force external to the individual" (1999, 293). Morality is a regulative force not only for the good of a group and society as a whole, but also for the good of each individual to be maximally fulfilled.

Oasis does not promise wealth and fame but the ability to serve in ministry and exercise Christian virtues. In the transformation of objectives, happiness is therefore attainable through the morality cultivated at the Oasis. Denny said, "That's what Oasis is, a resting place. And when you begin to rest in God, he begins to speak to your heart. He begins to reveal things that you probably have never thought about before." The continual affirmation of moral imperatives in community both highlights and actualizes the religious identity of a champion of life.

Who Do You Really Work For?

Pastor Philip's teachings continually push for a realignment of priorities that challenges the seeking of fame and fortune in the entertainment industry. "Those of you who want to be an actor, that's fine. Remember that God is number one in your life. So when you are accepting the roles, remember to accept a role that you think would honor God. Choose your roles carefully. Always have the thought in mind that we are living for God, and we are representing him." His teachings continually prompt the question, "Who are you really working for?"

The emphasis on Christian spirituality at Oasis stresses "honoring God" and "seeking God's will" regardless of where—or if—one is employed. One staff member said, "You can be a champion housewife and that's incredible to have influence with your kids and in your community possibly, so it doesn't mean you are the pinnacle in the world's eyes of success and all that stuff." Similarly, Charlene said, "Regardless of my work, my real work is working for God." In this emphasis, believers are provided with a beginning moral framework of what to do with their time and their money. Charlene's desire is to see God pleased with her choices in the midst of all her difficulties: "I really would like to have God say every day, 'You did good, girl. I know you really were down today because you lost this job, but I've been watching you, Charlene, and even though circumstances are tough, you're still praising me. I'm proud of you, girl.'" She went on, "At the end of the day, you go, 'Did I do what God wanted me to do today?'"

In the life experience of attenders like Charlene, the shift from personal to collective ambition builds directly on the disappointment and heartache experienced in the entertainment industry. "It's very easy to have joy when you have all the money, when you are 'it,' when everyone is pampering you, everyone is all about you, you always get your way," Donna said. "It is very easy to have joy. The real test is do you have joy when you have nothing? When everything that the world validated you with is now taken away?" As Donna became more involved actively serving in the ministries of the church, she started changing her professional ethics. "I went from making thousands of dollars a year to eating peanut butter five days a week. I have no income. I could have made several thousand dollars in a movie if I just wanted to have just a little less integrity," she said. "I book these big roles and am supposed to make a lot of money and then they throw in something that I can't do. Then I turn it down, and I lose an agent over it. This has happened to me so many times." Finding work became difficult not because she was not wanted but because of new "convictions" about roles she no longer wanted to play. "I just got a new agent again, and they started sending me on auditions for women's underwear again. Now I've got to pick up the phone and tell them I don't do lingerie." Despite her financial difficulties, she expressed utter confidence: "I know that by putting God first, God has a plan for my life."

In the process of such career reorientation, congregants move away from disparate statuses inherent to their race, their professional successes, and their familial frustrations. Instead, sharing a common kinship based on being sons and daughters of the king, they share the status and privilege of their father, God. The status is religiously cultivated and exists in the invisible spiritual realm cultivated and reinforced in the church. Even though outside the church people in their work, school, or home may not recognize their true status, Oasis continually reinforces this altered understanding of themselves. As this reality cannot be denied in the physical realm, it attains a power impossible for the observer to ignore.

A new, privileged self is constructed that wards off low self-esteem, disappointment, and loneliness. Believers at Oasis achieve a great sense of personal purpose. "What has kept me coming back is understanding I do have a purpose," Gladys said, "that there really is a destiny, and that God created me because he has something that he wants me to do." Every person is significant. For Gladys and others, Oasis is a place where believers come to discover their unique role in life. The self becomes an extension of what they can become through God. Bridgette said:

> The biggest thing that's changed in me is I realize that I don't have to prove myself to anybody but God. And I learned that at the Oasis. And it was a very hard lesson for me, and I've spent my entire life being a people pleaser. It was because of the teaching at the Oasis I've realized that I don't have to please anybody but God. That gave me a lot more sleep at night, seriously, because you're so worried about what people think. I don't have to do that anymore. So I am able to be who I am, who God has created me to be, and to do the things that he wants me to do. And I no longer have to please people and be who they want me to be. If I have learned anything at the Oasis, that's it.

By emphasizing morality and character, it is possible to "be yourself" regardless of the variability of work roles occupied over time.

This twist on being yourself forges a new connection between work and identity. Ambitions move from merely working for success in one's occupation to working with the explicit goal of encouraging and stimulating people toward a Christian spirituality. One's talents are dedicated to God's work. Jennelle talked about a CD project among the church musicians, emphasizing, "It's not about us." In such a project "egos can get in the way, and you can lose sight of what it's about." Her conscious negotiation of fame and ministry among the musicians is constant: "It's not about me getting that deal or me being on this new series. If we get that, that's a reward. Great. But what are we going to do with it, how are we going to glorify God if we do get it?"

Constructing a Corporate Morality

The need to give people cohesive moral order in the midst of a complex society where individuals participate in multiple locations was a core concern for Durkheim in all of his theoretical work. Durkheim's theoretical problem is a practical problem for all pastors seeking to build a morally cohesive community in densely populated, metropolitan settings with people from widely differing social backgrounds and with multiple obligations. Santiago said, "This is a purpose-destiny-fulfilled church. We are all supposed to have a purpose and someplace we are going. How do we get there? Do we compromise whatever we do? How do we accomplish it? Then we have to weigh those things with family, church, everything. And keeping everything in balance." Oasis cultivates a public morality, that is, a set of standards for how to conduct oneself with success in the world. And for Durkheim (1961), morality and discipline are interconnected. To cultivate a morality is to cultivate a base of personal discipline and a public concern for other people. Although experienced as external and coming from outside us, morality guides and structures our actions internally in a way that allows us to watch out for other people and avoid being pulled in multiple and contradictory directions. This socially crafted morality also keeps people from egoistically fulfilling their own desires without regard to the needs and concerns of others or society as a whole.

Another example is Damion, an African American, who said his earlier sacrifices for the entertainment industry no longer seem appropriate. He now thinks to himself, "What's important?" For him, family is supremely important. He now turns down career opportunities to protect time with his family. Although he still enjoys acting, "that's my heart," he believes God told him. "Let go. It's time for you to put God first." Serving his church and his family became paramount. "Now for the rest of my life my ambition goes towards that. I think of God, and then I think of family. Anything after that is gravy." Damion channels the majority of his interest in acting, writing, and directing through the congregation. "It's just wherever God wants me to be right now." His new ambition is to create a music workshop for kids in the city.

In Durkheim's discussion of morality, he distinguishes between the anomic, individual self-interested will and the collectively disciplined constraint of duty toward social good. Oasis conflates these two dynamics by saying that it is in our self-interest to accept moral self-discipline that works for the good. In the economy of God, disciplined pursuit results in fulfilling the desires of the individual self-will. The separation Durkheim assumes between corporate and self-interest is ignored by Oasis. God certainly wants each person to be meaningfully fulfilled through visible and socially approved measures of wealth, status, prestige, and success. However, success in one's personal life is redefined around new standards that incorporate conservative moral values continually reinforced through involvement in the congregation. As the congregation promises personal empowerment and self-esteem, it can appear quite authoritarian (albeit using benign and friendly means) in how it exerts social and moral control in the lives of members. Yet accepting the moral self-discipline promoted and highlighted in the congregation is, according to Oasis, the most efficient path toward success.

Since changes in self-perception prompt members to move away from identifying with occupational roles, they have been known to give up lucrative career opportunities to remain close to Oasis as their church. One staff member told me, "People are turning down jobs that are offered for many more thousands of dollars than what they are making right now. They say, 'No, Oasis is where God has called me to be, so this is where I'm going to be.'" Thus Oasis promotes ambition and success in the entertainment industry while at the same time leading members to actually turn down movie roles on moral grounds—roles that might allow a member to move above the line in the Hollywood status hierarchy. One member said she had declined opportunities to work because she had to be at church, "which is not the smartest thing," yet she appeared to be completely fulfilled in her sacrifices on behalf of the congregation.

The realignment of priorities also results in attenders turning down work or even walking away completely from seeking a career in Hollywood. Although one film producer's work has not been steady, his commitment to the church was very great, and he volunteered his time and talents to the creation of new ministries with the pastoral staff. He said, "I was here so much that I actually lost work because of it. I turned work down saying, 'No, I've got to be here.'" Another member who told me that she left her career in the entertainment industry to work for Oasis said, "I'm doing something that's life-changing. I'm actually doing something that is going to be eternal."

Embracing a New Collective Identity

Despite their involvement in congregational ministry, champions are not intended to live their lives solely at church. Oasis seeks to change the world by staffing influential positions in the city with devoted Christians on the assumption that the "privileged role of the church" is "to be an incubator of saved souls and sane psyches, ready to face the world" (McRoberts 2003, 102). These churches, almost entirely Holiness-Pentecostal churches, set out "to equip members to function in and perhaps transform social worlds beyond church walls." In the same way, for those seeking to make it in the Hollywood industry, Oasis helps members work through the difficulties of living in this "spiritually foreign" culture. Similar to the churches observed by Miller and Yamamori, "Progressive Pentecostals are more inclined to create alternative institutions than they are to overturn existing ones. Thus, they are committed to *growing* a new generation of leaders—a rather organic metaphor—by first seeing to it that these potential leaders have a life-changing conversion experience and then nurturing them through communal support systems that build character and develop leadership skills" (2007, 214–115). Oasis members' new identities are to be embodied in the day-to-day world, energized by a corporate purpose.

Among the believers at Oasis, the place in which they actualize their identity is as workers in the entertainment industry. Believers consider the industry "a dark place," but as Christian workers they are "lights." One producer said, "What I've learned is that the entertainment industry needs my light. They need the light in me. That's what I've learned here. They have helped me to constantly remember that I can be a light in a dark place. . . . I can do that even working where I'm surrounded by people who use God's name as the preface to a curse word." And he reiterated, "My part is to be a light in this world that I work in."

While workers in the entertainment industry have no confidence in the stability of their occupations, workers at Oasis have supreme confidence in the sense of purpose they achieve through the church regardless of their level of celebrity. Charlene said, "What has kept me coming back is to understand that I do have a purpose, that there really is a destiny, that God created me because he has something that he wants me to do. Now, that something could be a major thing where everybody gets to see my face or it could be a minor thing. But I do have a role in the body of Christ." She said, "When you come to the Oasis, you find out there is something for you to do. And everybody has a place, everybody has a role. Get it and do what you have to do and just watch God move." The champions of Oasis substitute public fame for personal influence, enacting their ideals through their work. Jarrell drew on imagery from Jesus' Sermon on the Mount (Matt. 5:13–16) to say that in his work on studio lots, "the motive is show-ing the world God's love, being the salt and the light in the world."

Sandra is a producer who began to question her career through her involve-ment at Oasis. "I love the film business. I love what I do. But I tried to get out of it because I thought maybe this was the wrong place for me." She was not suc-cessful in her attempt to find a sustainable career outside Hollywood. "It didn't work. And it was made very clear to me God doesn't want me in a completely Christian environment in my work. . . . I know that 90 percent of the time I'm the only Christian on the set." The church gave her a changed perspective on how to approach her job. "The way I believe in God and the way I believe in me and what my place is has changed dramatically from feeling useless and suicidal to thinking that I have a real important purpose in life." In her overall assess-ment, Sandra told me that "Hollywood in its truest form is a dark place," but she felt she had an opportunity to be "a light" in Hollywood, especially to young women working on the set.

With Sandra and others, a moral quality is attributed to a secular calling, an emphasis that is everywhere evident among believers of the Oasis Christian fel-lowship. In his analysis of Max Weber's Protestant thesis, Donald Nielsen states: "It was Luther's achievement to have valorized work in a calling in this world, while at the same time destroying the legitimacy previously attached to monas-tic life and, thus, shattering the church's integrated medieval dualism of virtuosi and laity" (2005, 60). He quotes Weber: "It is indeed beyond doubt . . . that this moral quality ascribed to life in a secular calling . . . was one of the momen-tous achievements of the Reformation, and it was Luther's own contribution." Nielsen reminds us that Weber emphasized the transition accomplished through the Reformation from the monastic ethic of life to an everyday religious ethic of life. The attendant uncertainty of an emerging free-market economy allowed an affinity to a new, religious orientation leading to new economic conduct. Similarly, the workers of Oasis see themselves as spiritually responsible believers who work outside religious institutions to effect God-inspired initiatives.

The new collective identity as champion culminates in a renegotiation of ambition. Gladys said, "I'm ambitious but perhaps not in ways many people would think of ambitious. I'm passionate about people and helping them be and do the best they can be." Her "ambition has changed because it became more other-focused." Similarly, Sandra: "My ambition isn't for me anymore. I will benefit from it, and I absolutely know that I will benefit from it. But it isn't for me alone." Ambition changes from being solely oriented toward personal career success to faithfully enacting an evangelical morality that avoids immorality and inspires a charitable stance of helping others.

Spirit-Guided Morality in a Secular Calling

Every church has a theodicy, a way of explaining the evil found in the world, of coping with the imperfection of life. At Oasis, evil is not directly confronted. Instead, the theodicy of Oasis is found in a failure to align ourselves with God's purpose for our lives and for the world. Religion at the Oasis does not emerge out of a fear of death but out of a desire for personal fulfillment. Everyone at Oasis assumes that work is a natural and inevitable fact of life. Any hope of fulfillment then must involve our work lives—happiness will involve the rewards of status, pay, and enjoyment found through work. The sense of personal fulfillment through work is inherent to the concept of prosperity promoted in the theology of the congregation. Prosperity that comes from God is not like winning the lottery, where an abundance of unearned cash is showered on the expectant believer. Instead, prosperity is defined at Oasis as the faithful exercise of gifts and talents for God's purposes. Morality structures behavior in a secular vocation, as the individual is a tool of God. Being a tool for God and working in a calling eases the anxiety of salvation because one feels connected to God.

Drawing on Durkheim (1995), Oasis is a moral community crafted through corporate activities of congregational worship and involvement, which guide individual behavior even when the congregation is dispersed. As the believers of Oasis see themselves ambitiously pursuing celebrity and economic success, they draw on the empowerment and normative standards accessible to them in the church. The religious identity as overcomer and champion anchors difficult career choices and failed opportunities. Believers receive moral guidance in a form of spiritual kinship that applies discipline at the same time it affirms encouragement and care. Individuals subsume themselves to a religious system that sanctions ambition while providing handles for dealing with the world's disappointments.

The dignity of the individual, the honoring of mistakes through correction and repentance, the confidence of spiritual empowerment by the kinship connection with the Holy Spirit are all elements of the moral community found at Oasis that channels and energizes believers' individual activity. Their membership in this moral community creates momentum for the moral guidance of the self, which continues to channel and inspire believers' behavior even when they are away from church gatherings. The pursuit of external fame and fortune is viewed as a veneer for the real self who, in concert with the moral community, is seeking to reshape social values to be congruent with that of their religious beliefs. As urbanites that regularly participate in multiple, overlapping social groups, these believers find a stable sense of purpose and life orientation through their religious identity as champions of life.

Conclusion

RELIGION IN THE ERA OF
IDENTITY COMMODIFICATION

LUTHER: This is a place that brings Jesus to the
twenty-first century.

Oasis is a church that celebrates achievement and autonomy in the workforce, one that matches the popular ideal of literate, more educated, capitalistically inspired workers who wish to throw off concerns of structural inequality in the belief that ultimately, with the help of God, their effort and talent will pay off. These workers believe in a God-empowered meritocracy. Yet the goal for a Christian at Oasis is not just to succeed but to be part of transforming the world in partnership with God. Individual-level ambition makes way for a grand, cosmic ambition that encompasses the greater world and the flow of world history. "God's plan is always better than what we think our plan is," Donna said. They stop seeing the entertainment industry as an avenue for personal success and see greater potential for their lives and their work.

This transformation from self-orientation to other orientation, from self-promotion to missional engagement, lies at the core of the identity reorientation evident in this congregation. Individualism coexists with the general call for generosity and self-sacrifice because the individual is seen as the conduit by which God will accomplish his purposes on the earth. The emphasis on the individual is not about individual self-promotion but about creating a platform as an ambassador of the kingdom of God to engage in activities that allow God to work in the world at large. Hope for personal success is transformed through immersion in the church into an overall mission to change the world.[1]

Religion and the Emerging Creative Class

The need for such individual-affirming faith is necessary because our society is one of "identity commodification" where the "branding of the self" is imperative for workplace survival. The moral reorientation of the self toward the ambitious religious identity found at Oasis is not so much the accommodation of an individual to succeed within a particular congregation as a distinctly religious construction of the self that allows believers to press forward within a particular structure of occupations. These occupations mainly comprise artistic, technical, and professional career paths, which are increasingly structured in a looser, more nomadic fashion in relation to projects or firms than the traditional permanent positions of long-term employment.

Entertainment industry workers at Oasis reflect the situation of the broader workforce now referred to as the "creative class," a relatively new and growing stratum comprising as much as 30 percent of the U.S. workforce (about forty million people). Furthermore, Robert Reich (1991) describes U.S. workers caught up in an information economy dominated by the management and manipulation of symbols as "symbolic analysts" who produce and problem solve using information in verbal, numerical, musical, or visual forms. The theology and structure of Oasis connect with the stories, achievements, and dilemmas of this emerging creative class, increasingly clustered in metropolitan areas across the country.

In an age where identity is commodified and people promote themselves to thrive economically, we need to be less critical of fame-promoting faith and look more at the changing structure of society to account for the rise of obsession with celebrity and better understand the dynamic that allows this imperative to exist in a religious context. According to Karl Mannheim: "A social stratum takes on a new structure when it encounters a new situation and evolves a new way of life" (1956, 48). The religion at Oasis is situated for occupational nomads who continually sell themselves as "perfect fits" in a variety of contexts as they pursue multiple opportunities. Similarly, as Thomas Tweed observes: "The religious are migrants as much as settlers, and religions make sense of the nomadic as well as the sedentary in human life" (2006, 75). And the uncertain movement of their lives finds its purpose—being seen—as a progressive revelation of God's activity. Success and failure in one's work communicate to a person God's messages for his or her life. Oasis provides a sense of orientation for lives that would otherwise be considered random or chaotic.

Karl Mannheim in his provocative essay "On Economic Ambition" astutely understood seeking fame as essentially a quest for economic security (1952, 239). Ambition is only for people who believe they have some control over their own destiny. Ambition, then, expresses in some way a desire to shape the path of one's own life. Moreover, the actively ambitious person continually orients toward a goal (however elusive) that

> brings a certain continuity into his life to which he can always cling and towards which he can always turn. Even when the occasional inevitable failure occurs, and the plan temporarily miscarries, so that disintegration and despair threaten, the man with a goal rapidly recovers his equilibrium and determination not to be beaten. Thrown back on his own resources, he will always search for some way of restoring the vanished plan, and with continually renewed energy, radically reorganizes his life stage by stage towards the desired goal. (251)

Although Mannheim was overly optimistic about the ability of ambitious people to maintain their ambition amidst the overwhelming challenges faced by workers today, the inspiration of religious orientations like that of Oasis fuels an ambition that provides a cohesive sense of self and a cohesive life trajectory or life plan (Berger, Berger, and Kellner 1973, 72–77). This is all the more true when ambition is tied less to the precariousness of occupational success and more to an abstract moral orientation of success, such as developing one's religious identity, with its attendant disciplines and duties.

The ambition observed among the people of Oasis as members of the creative class is primarily aimed at achieving a sense of security, at keeping at bay dangers that would threaten one's economic well-being. What is distinctive about the ambition found at Oasis is that it includes the promotion of a set of religious ideals intended for the whole world. The base evangelistic impulse of spreading the gospel globally is at the heart of the broader, collective ambition embraced by believers in this church. Rather than quiet, unobtrusive lives, their professions force them into lives of constant networking and actively engaging with people in the world. And there is a ready affinity between spreading the fame for themselves based on their personal skills and abilities and spreading the fame for their God based on communal values and beliefs. In other words, the occupational circumstances of workers at Oasis force them into a constant stream of self-promotion, and once they have the vision of using their influence to spread ideas and beliefs that they hold dear, they can use the same set of skills to promote the fame of Jesus Christ and his church.

Religion for Occupational Nomads

Capitalism, self-invention and reinvention, individualism, and ambition all have connections to the general U.S. ethos. That religion would reflect these things is neither new nor distinctive. What is new is how the Oasis Christian Center indicates the extent to which religion in the United States might shift toward a faith that requires unprecedented individual self-promotion. Today, it is not merely people who are in show business or sales or politics who must sell their identities, but a great number of Americans. The question to explore is if individualism is contrary to religious devotion or if the value of individualism can be negotiated within a satisfactory religious framework that propels believers to accentuate their duty toward God and others.

Because self-deprecating humility and self-effacement have been so characteristic of authentic religion, it seems incompatible that people can promote themselves and still be pious. Books like *Exporting the American Gospel* are critical of prosperity theology in its accommodation to a highly individualistic, therapeutic orientation: "The new theology is devoted to a form of hyperindividualism, a transformation of one's personal relationship with Jesus into regular concentration on one's own piety, one's own feelings, one's own health, and one's own financial security" (Brouwer, Gifford, and Rose 1996, 241). Focus on the individual is viewed as inappropriate when religion is supposed to inspire humility and generosity rather than self-orientation and self-promotion. Much of the analysis in a recent book on the controversial ministry of the celebrity preacher T. D. Jakes revolves around a continual critique of "need-based ministry" and "aggressive entrepreneurialism" (Lee 2005).

However, the circumstances of the current economic climate of advanced capitalism in the United States (particularly in metropolitan areas like Los Angeles) make an emphasis on the individual inevitable. The care and management of the self is absolutely essential for economic survival. For good or ill, branding is a phenomenon of modern work life, and individuals increasingly become entrepreneurs regarding their own public selves. The steady stream of self-help guides to branding began with Tom Peters's *The Brand You 50* (1999), followed by a rash of similar titles advocating similar strategies.[2] These books emerged from career development guides struggling to give workers a new vocabulary for summarizing the skills and training that they brought to employers (or, in the case of consultants and contract workers, to potential clients) in a changing economy.

For example, William Bridges (1998) emphasizes the tremendous pace of social change and the uncertainty of workers in the new economy. His book does not encourage workers to submit themselves to a corporate hierarchy; indeed, successful businesspersons of the future will carefully navigate among opportunities by seeing themselves as the owners of their own business, the business of "Brand You." Bridges encourages workers to think of themselves as their own CEOs. Workers must now "make a name" for themselves (Roffer 2002), become recognized as "experts" (Eldridge and Eldridge 2004) and "authorities" (Bly 2001). All creative-class workers are marketers who manage the information flow of their own images, presenting themselves as the appropriate geniuses for hire (Silber 2001). To be successful requires one to put a personal PR campaign into high gear, especially women who may be reluctant to blatantly promote themselves (Harrow 2002; Ross and Killorn 2000). There are even tips on how to brag (Klaus 2004). Following the advice of these books, becoming famous is not difficult; in fact, if you believe the hype in the title of one book, it can be accomplished in two weeks or less (De La Cruz and Robinovitz 2003).

Unstable Labor Markets and Uncertain Work

"Nothing is more American than Hollywood," writes Lary May (2000, 1), and not only is Hollywood uniquely American, it is a harbinger of what America is coming to be—especially as it relates to the transformation of work. This modern development of obsession with celebrity was anticipated in the structural changes of Hollywood in the mid–twentieth century. Hollywood is a pioneer because flexible work arrangements based on project assignments and a broad pool of creative, available talent were first developed in the vast network of activities within the entertainment industry, "a dramatic vanguard case of the flexibilization of work arrangements that was later to spread much more widely throughout the United States" (Scott 2005, 121). In anticipation of what is often called "the new economy," the motion picture industry reorganized itself in the 1950s and 1960s, reconfiguring into small and medium-sized firms in shifting coalitions of networks with flexible production schedules. Employment in Hollywood was reshaped into project-to-project contract work, which meant individuals had to keep themselves attractive to employers as they struggled to construct a cohesive series of projects into a "career."

Labor markets like that found in Hollywood are increasingly common. Large segments of the U.S. economy simply accept that this is the new form of work in the world today, particularly for those involved in artistic and creative professions (Blair 2001; Menger 1999; Peck 1996). The award-winning book *Divergent Paths* conclusively shows that the labor market since the 1960s and 1970s is more volatile (Bernhardt, Morris, Handcock, and Scott 2001). Jobs are less stable, and the top of the job pyramid consists of nomadic workers. Highly credentialed, well-connected occupational nomads use short-term projects as springboards to even better opportunities. A new division of labor distinguishes successful nomads from retail workers, data entry clerks, and telemarketers stuck in a succession of low-paying, dead-end jobs. The standard for the Hollywood industry is becoming the standard for all creative and information-centered industries, with contractual obligations entered into on an ad hoc basis (see Caves 2000).[3]

In what is now known as post-Fordism, flexible organizational arrangements (where high degrees of specialization are utilized on an ad hoc basis) cut corporate labor costs while giving companies maximum flexibility over hiring and firing (see Grabher 2001; Hirst and Zeitlin 1992; Piore and Sabel 1984). Since the 1980s, corporations have reduced middle management, creating flatter, leaner organizations. Outsourcing saves direct ongoing expenses and adds a layer of flexibility by allowing companies to expand numbers of contractual workers as needed. Project teams are becoming a model for organizing all forms of production in modern organizations. Workers with concentrations of specialized expertise are recruited around particular projects, and workers may apply a particular skill to a variety of projects in limited periods of time.

According to Richard Florida: "In the view of many evangelists of the new world of work, much of the economy is coming to operate on the same principles as the Hollywood movie industry, with the fundamental shifts reflecting what has happened in Hollywood itself" (2002, 28). Daniel Pink for example, claims that "the individual, not the organization, has become the economy's fundamental unit. Put more simply, we're all going Hollywood" (2001, 17). The Hollywood model is a free-agent model, according to Pink, and organizations are dependent on talented people. (Florida cautions against accepting all the claims that contemporary businesses operate only through small, highly mobile, and highly flexible firms, and reminds us that larger organizations still dominate the business landscape. Also, Hollywood is clearly a highly risky business with low rates of return and inefficiencies resulting from a constant turnover of labor.) Although the "individual" may be more important, it is a result of particular organizational structures surviving in the changing economic climate and not simply big business's conversion to the value for individual people. Pink's over-blown assessment that there has been a "broad shift in power from the organiza-tion to the individual" is a drastic misunderstanding of sociological truths (18). When organizations release individuals to manage their own careers it is not out of a lack of power but rather a redistribution of the power structure itself. Pink emphasizes that Americans would rather be self-employed; what analysis shows is that an increasing number of Americans may have no other choice than to be essentially self-employed. And although Pink claims this is a better way of life, there's conflicting evidence that the advantage of contingent work in so-called freedom and flexibility has considerable downsides in risk and insecurity for workers (Beck 2000).

Hollywood workers and creative workers are therefore part of a growing contingent of the U.S. workforce that operates much like independent contrac-tors (Barley and Kunda 2004). While temporary work promotes an entrepre-neurial attitude and aggressive self-promotion, according to Richard Sennett (2005, 50), Stephen Barley and Gideon Kunda describe independent contractors similarly in *Gurus, Hired Guns, and Warm Bodies: Itinerant Experts in a Knowledge Economy*: "They [independent contractors] were no longer salaried professionals viewed by firms as 'human resources' to be acquired, maintained, nurtured, and profitably deployed. Rather, they became commodities to be bought, used, and discarded as any other resource. Nor did contractors see themselves as human resources. They came to view themselves as independent owners of their own human capital, as entrepreneurs who relied on their own skills to navigate between success and failure. This change of orientation had far-reaching conse-quences for how contractors' lives unfolded" (2004, 289).

As capitalistic structures continue to shift long-term economic responsibility from the corporation to the worker, more workers will pursue individual suc-cess. Within particular industries, especially when there is a need to complete short-term projects in an efficient and error-free manner, workers will be consumed with the effort to become celebrities in their own right. Since mis-takes are rarely tolerated from contract workers in comparison with long-term workers who are intended to learn from their mistakes for an endless stream of future projects, workers seek to establish themselves in the minds of executives and to present themselves as the perfect person for the job. Popularity becomes an indispensable quality for successful economic achievement and for attaining a steady flow of income through a seamless succession of projects.

Accompanying these occupational changes is the change in the structure of work. The greatest expansion of white-collar employment has occurred in craft-oriented, professional, and technical occupations, not low-skilled service jobs as was popularly believed, with about 20 percent of Americans expected to take up these occupations by 2010 (Barley and Kunda 2004, 304–306; see also Hecker 2001). Moreover, there is a breakdown of the one-career pattern of life in postindustrial society as workers become more mobile and firms interact more creatively with each other over time (Block 1990; Szafran 1996). "The traditional career progressing step-by-step through the corridors of one or two institutions is withering. . . . Today, a young American with at least two years of college can expect to change jobs at least 11 times in the course of working, and change his or her skill base at least three times during those 40 years of labor" (Sennett 1998, 22). "Corporations have also farmed out many of the tasks they once did permanently in-house to small firms and individuals employed on short-term contracts." Thus "a change in modern institutional structure has accompanied short term, contract, or episodic labor. Corporations sought to remove layers of bureaucracy, to become flatter and more flexible organizations. In place of organizations as pyramids, management wants now to think of organizations as networks" (23).

The focus among workers is less on being employed and more on "employability," a business term emphasizing the conglomerate of attitudes, experiences, and job skills that will keep a person able to gain employment (see Bridges 1994; Caulkin 1997). Navigating the new market for employment requires a considerable amount of effort and talent, in terms not only of technical skills but also of the social skills of networking, bargaining, and diplomacy. Barley and Kunda (2004) found such workers take time to build a relational community supporting their occupational efforts and providing other types of support that do not directly involve work. Sources of support also included online, virtual communities and face-to-face interactions that provide job-market and technical tips, new skills, and friendship. The rhythm of such itinerant work involves a back-and-forth moving from the market to jobs and then back to the market. Although Barley and Kunda make no mention of religion, since it was not a focus of their study, finding that itinerant workers seek stable face-to-face communities apart from their work lives is significant, and such communities informally enhance their success in the workplace.

Religion in the Age of Identity Commodification

Fame is recognition. Yet the recognition of fame has fundamental consequences to the individual. In particular, the desire for fame is the desire for status and power that encompasses the satisfaction of experiencing the appreciation of others as well as personal security. "In great part the history of fame is the history of the changing ways by which individuals have sought to bring themselves to the attention of others and, not incidentally, have thereby gained power over them" (Braudy 1986, 3). For contemporary urbanites, the striving for fame is a strategy not only for gaining attention and admiration but more importantly for gaining power over the uncertainties of life. The risks of the marketplace and the lack of long-term work threaten a stable structure of identity; in other words, if my understanding of myself is based on the market fluctuations that control my opportunities to gain income based on the commodification of my identity, ultimately I become confused and lose myself in the process of earning a living. In contrast, the religious community of Oasis persists regardless of my interactions outside the religious community and cultivates a coherent and ongoing identity based on my moral obligations and moral commitments to this religious community.

Fame can be a commodity in itself. *High Visibility* (Rein, Kotler, and Stoller 1997), a cookbook for achieving celebrity status, shows that creating celebrity means making people into brand-name products. According to Gamson (1994), celebrity is produced much like any other commodity. In his narrative of the organization of industrialized celebrity production, he makes an important distinction between the aspirant or performer *worker* versus the *celebrity*. The worker is able to play a role or to perform a particular kind of work, but the celebrity has the capacity to command attention (Rojek 2001). It is a quality of being known, different from actual work. Achievement of celebrity is so important and so lucrative that celebrities can pay publicists up to 50 percent of their income (Gamson, 1994, 61). "Notoriety becomes a type of capital. . . . The perceived ability to attract attention, regardless of what the attention is for, can be literally cashed in" (62).

The ambitious life promoted by Oasis is a religious accommodation to a society that demands self-promotion. Since Christianity's historic opposition to the pursuit of fame springs from the belief that fame is a surrogate for wild egotism, the challenge to the congregation is to provide a means by which fame can be pursued within a moral community. At Oasis, self-advancement becomes a form of community advancement, pushing forward sacred, moral imperatives. The pursuit of fame and fortune is not wild egotism but a faithful fulfillment of a moral imperative—to successfully integrate oneself into the mainstream culture through influential positions so that the message and reputation of Christianity is extended and enhanced to the utmost degree.

The history of fame corresponds to the history of power (see Braudy 1986). In striving for fame, the ambitious person attempts to accrue a greater degree of power over others. This power includes that of influence and persuasion based on one's personal attributes. The achievement of fame is the achievement of power that helps to secure a person against personal and economic dangers and to advance agendas that represent a set of ideals intended to be embraced by all. Fame grants one access to the minds of people through the doorway of fascination; individuals so accessed may yield up the orientation of their own belief systems. It is in the development of Christianity that we see a more expansive understanding of the individual and a redefinition of greatness away from self-aggrandizement to a promotion of God and his will for humanity. In Jesus we find a new base for personal nobility, one that is based not on service to the Roman Empire but in service to God, his people, and the world. Whereas the Roman view of fame was intertwined with the power of the state, and individuals supported and reflected the glory of the state, now individuals support God and reflect his glory.

Due to inequality and a structured hierarchy, great achievements in the Roman Empire could be accomplished only by a select few. But in the economy of Christianity, greatness could be achieved by every person regardless of economic or political circumstances. In particular, it is the fame of Christ that is spread through the faithful discipleship of his followers. The retelling of the story of Jesus, whether by word or through the written Gospel accounts, is an act of faith. The fame of an individual Christian becomes nothing more than the reflected fame of Jesus. Jesus taught that to parade one's piety through the streets was a betrayal of true religious faith. The sacrificial acts of faith are not to be done to win the admiration of others but rather to faithfully carry out one's obligation as a righteous person redeemed by God (for example, see Jesus' teachings in Matt. 23:1–33, Mark 12:41–44, and Luke 18:9–14). Because no one but God sees the heart, it is only God who is able to convey praise (Matt. 6:5–6). The call for humility is one that stresses each individual's having an audience of only one person, the person of God himself. In the model of Jesus, there's always an implicit permission to withdraw from public life and the standards of one's culture as a whole. The inner life becomes more important than the outer life. If one pursues greatness and acknowledgment solely among human beings and neglects God, then one accomplishes nothing. Here is where the conflict between fame and Christian faith is most clear. The New Testament repeatedly affirms that attaining fame without the proper orientation of an inner life focused on sacrificial love of God and humanity is empty and meaningless (Matt. 16:26; Mark 8:36; 1 Cor. 13:1–3).

Although fame classically had been related to wealth, in the New World fame became a characteristic of an individual unrelated to one's background or family history. Geographic mobility and new forms of technology introduced in the eighteenth century freed people from the confines of one type of labor spent in one region of the world for their entire life. Freed from any encumbrances of social circumstance, individuals could reshape themselves in any way they desired. From that historic moment forward, individuals have become increasingly self-conscious, seeking to sell themselves in the growing global labor market, and reshaping their lives in light of what may be valuable to others, adapting to whatever social circumstances allow them greater financial success.

The increased ability to reshape the self has consequences for the stability of moral orientation in everyday life. Karl Marx famously warned that under capitalism, all human relationships would become essentially market relationships where everything has a price and personal values are oriented around the maximization of profit. Work stops being an outlet for creativity and, because it is merely a means to make money, becomes dehumanizing. Durkheim argues similarly regarding the structural conditions of anomie, which literally means normlessness, that is, a loss of standards of conduct. According to Trevor Noble: "As the division of labor progresses further, the increased individualism—not only with its growing sense of the uniqueness of every person, but also with the growing convergence of values and of everyday experience—meant that the collective conscience could be severely eroded" (2000, 155). Modern society as a whole loses a shared base of standards, and consequently individuals lose direction as to who they are and what they are to commit themselves to.

Durkheim thought the problem of modern individualism would be resolved as modern workers eventually bonded through professional associations, that is, individuals would find their identity through their specialized work in community with other specialists. In the modern world, this has not proven true. Workers in ever-increasingly specialized occupations are so scattered that they have little opportunity to operate in the kind of intimate community Durkheim envisioned. Also, these workers remain in competition with one another and therefore do not always meet each other on the basis of mutual assistance. The failure of the professions to provide satisfying community is one of the most important reasons religion remains vital in the modern world.

Religion at Oasis challenges laborers to reconsider their self-identity and their self-worth. Fulfilling Durkheim's ideal, relationships are based not on their market value but on a common moral orientation. While the society "out there" outside the congregation demands a market orientation, the moral community "in here" inside the congregation does not, and by pursuing authenticity, vulnerability, and unpretentiousness Oasis provides a place where human beings can find their skills, talents, and personality valued regardless of their relative economic value in the marketplace. This becomes valuable for those who most intentionally and continually commodified themselves in order to survive in society. Certainly it is possible to anchor one's identity within one's work, but the vitality of congregational life in the United States can in part be explained by the opportunity congregations give individuals to base their identities in noninstrumental organizations where neither market valuation nor economic competition rules.

These insights connect with a 2007 study by Robert Wuthnow that describes how the younger adults of the post-baby-boom generation dedicate most of their lives between the ages of twenty and forty to the cultivation of their careers, prompting greater attention to the preparation and crafting of their own selves. As a result, they are developing a more individualistic, improvised approach to spirituality. Although Wuthnow shows how such self-cultivating activity generally keeps these younger adults from commitment to congregations, youthful congregations like Oasis are able to harness these changes into vibrancy in their churches.

Charismata and the Future of Work: Religion and Economics

A growing consensus affirms that the charismatic/Pentecostal form of religion is superbly adapted to our increasingly postmodern, differentiated society. It views the individual as an empowered extension of the divine, yet expects individual action. Workers must be motivated to assemble right relationships and resources to economically survive. At the same time, individual ambition must be managed in a culture where possibilities seem endless and all levels of status appear attainable.

In a remarkable essay in which Bernice Martin relates the growth of Pentecostalism in Latin America to economic changes, she recounts a familiar story of individuals increasingly atomized both socially and economically.

> The current transformation of capitalism in Latin America involves a postindustrial, Post Fordist labor force for whom assembly-line facility, deference to hierarchical authority, or the clock time disciplines of the factory would be anachronistic. What this postmodern economy requires from them is micro entrepreneurial initiative, an individualized and more feminist psyche, a high level of self-motivation, and the flexibility with which to face insecure employment in self-employment, mobility, and the twenty-four hour working day. (1998, 129)

In Martin's view: "Pentecostalism is uniquely poised to affect this cultural transition, not least because its fundamental conception of the human person is as a unique, individual soul, named and claimed by God. Its business *is* the business of selfhood" (130). Premodern religious orientations are repackaged in Pentecostalism with "postmodern individualism, autonomy, mobility and self-determination." And although Martin sees Pentecostalism as a transitional form of religion accompanying dramatic social changes, it may hold sway well into the future because of

> the paradoxical combination of these contradictory elements. The new Protestantism offers converts a novel experience of *spiritual* autonomy which also makes for a deeper sense of the individualizing tendencies in the wider world; it energizes the irreducible human motivation to survive even the most unpropitious circumstances, by harnessing that motivation to transcendent ends. At the same time it roots and supports the individual within a face-to-face, voluntary community of believers: the old ascribed solidarities may help provide the template but it is the *voluntary* nature of

belonging which is new. Within this voluntary community there have grown up practices of mutual help, the encouragement of education and modes of participation in the practical organization, in the pastoral work and in the evangelism of the church which serve to spread widely among the mass of believers the actual experience of individual responsibility and leadership. *Individualization* and the *voluntaristic, collective* creation of a new social capital thus occur in tandem.

In this era of advanced capitalism, the champions of Oasis are indeed isolated as individuals through their work, yet the Pentecostal framework of the church provides a powerful basis for each individual to see himself or herself as an individual who belongs to God and is claimed for his sacred purposes. Their voluntarily participation in Oasis motivates them despite the precariousness of their occupations to work even harder, because their theological beliefs constantly reinforce the idea that their work is the most concrete expression of their God-given purpose in life.

Robert Mapes Anderson in 1975 observed that Pentecostalism emerged during important transitions in the economy of the United States. For Anderson, Pentecostalism may appear to counter modern culture, but it actually serves to perpetuate and extend modernity. He insists that it is the working poor who were predisposed to the Pentecostal movement, and not all working poor but only those who were "predisposed to the movement by some personal crisis which they could not resolve, such as the death of a relative or friend, illness, marital and career failures" (227). Such deterministic language is insufficient for the kind of analysis social scientists engage in today. What endures from Anderson's analysis is his indication of the remarkable adaptability of Pentecostal belief systems to modern economic demands. His orientation is similar to that developed from the sociology of knowledge tradition of Karl Marx and Karl Mannheim in which forms of social life, particularly the ideational aspects of life, are formed in relation to the concrete circumstances of human life. By seeing religion as an "adaptive mechanism" in his study of Pentecostalism, Anderson argues that religion is a reactive rather than proactive dynamic in social life. The development of religion at the Oasis Christian Center further demonstrates the adaptability of religion, which emerges as a response to social change rather than its instigator.

Grant Wacker contributes much to an adequate understanding of the affinity between Pentecostalism and advanced capitalism by insightfully demonstrating the inherent pragmatism in Pentecostal life and thought. As Pentecostals rejected "the world," they simultaneously encouraged believers to adapt to the dominant processes of industrialization and urbanization. It is true that the primitivism of Pentecostalism seeks to throw off the apathy and mediocrity of the established church and to recover the enthusiasm and excitement recorded in the New Testament in Acts, chapter 2. Yet as Wacker points out: "Conversion, sanctification, and Holy Spirit baptism started with the individual, skirted the institutional church, downplayed the ordinances, and ended with the individual" (2001, 29). He quotes historian Joel Carpenter: "Pentecostals can be unblushingly self-interested in their worldly dealings because they know that God wants them to prosper here" (268). While many Pentecostal leaders and scholars see a clear connection between conversion and upward mobility, Wacker finds that "at the end of the day Pentecostals proved remarkably willing to work within the social and cultural expectations of the age. Again and again we see them holding their proverbial finger to the wind, calculating where they were, where they want to go and, above all, how to get there" (14).

According to Simon Coleman, another scholar who asserts that charismatic belief and practice accommodates well to overwhelming economic pressures in the current climate of globalization, neo-Pentecostalism allows believers to transcend parochial circumstances as they adjust their day-to-day lives to global demands in whatever context they find themselves (see also E. Kramer 2002). Similarly, in the African American context, Hans Baer and Merrill Singer observe: "Black Holiness Pentecostal sects tend to facilitate the adjustment or commendation of their members to the values and behavior patterns considered appropriate in a capitalist society" (2002, 174). As David Martin sums up this view: "Pentecostalism works by constant adjustment on the ground" (2002, 170). For him, Pentecostalism "embodies the release of Spirit in harness with the discipline that work in the market demands, above all where life is precarious" (171). Further, the new structure of work "requires a mobile self and indeed a powerful persona constantly redeployed to meet constantly changing situations and exigencies" (17). Arguing an affinity between neo-Pentecostalism and postmodernity, Martin states that Pentecostalism "fits well enough with the elements identified as belonging to postmodernity: the rapid alternation of environments, and the passage across what were the conventional frontiers of culture and ethnic identity. Charismatics who embrace this particular style are effectively laying down their own specific tracks across the shifting sands, creating their own mutually recognizable style of transnational, nondenominational identity, and expanding the self to complement an expanding globe." Pentecostalism involves "a transition from the alternation of work and release to use of expressive modalities within the disciplines of work itself (including God's work)." In this way, Martin asserts, societal circumstances and religious developments are inevitably intertwined, particularly new forms of Pentecostalism and the emerging structure of the global economy.

Religion for Living in This World

Oasis demonstrates a religious accommodation to a particular organization of society. In their day-to-day lives, most workers of the Oasis pursue celebrity as a part of managing their own career paths. This does not mean a worship of oneself but rather a sacralization of action as individuals conduct themselves in the modern world. Here we have a transformed millennialism; instead of waiting for the coming of Christ to transform the world, individual believers can be a part of making the kingdom of God real through their concrete, everyday, intentional actions. The pursuit of fame does not of itself mean believers fail to sincerely pursue their faith. Instead, the people of Oasis come to see the pursuit of fame as a means of dutifully fulfilling their deepest beliefs and values.

The this-world sociohistorical environment contributes to the cultivation of particular otherworldly theological beliefs. Acknowledging the inherently social nature of religious belief (i.e., that all beliefs are crafted in community, that beliefs "exist" before we believe in them as we are "taught" them from others, and that, therefore, there is no such thing as private religious belief) does not necessarily negate the existence of a transcendent truth. Yet, it is important to acknowledge that all theological beliefs contain and express aspects of social structure. The social embeddedness of religious belief is betrayed by any historical or cultural comparison of religious traditions, and especially by the surprising changes in belief within a specific religious tradition. The "clothing" of religious belief does not of itself negate such beliefs; rather, it accentuates that all beliefs are articulated in and through culture using elements available in the immediate social structure in the formulation and crafting of those beliefs for clarity, relevancy, and legitimacy to the intended audience. Theological beliefs respond to culture; ironically and problematically, theologians must use cultural elements in crafting those responses. Theology is always "incarnated," which leaves it subject to the forces common to all systems of thought. The church can neither escape nor ignore the society around it. It is inevitable that the relentless processes of social change will force revision in the religious life of this country. The more rigidly church leaders hold to traditions, the more painful and explosive the changes will be.

Religion in the Twenty-First Century

It is the power of religious institutions like the Oasis Christian Center to build a corporate identity on the basis of shared experiences so that individuals are not left on their own but rather live in a community providing beliefs, symbols, images, and practices that explicitly sustain them in their particular life experiences. It is insufficient to see religion as only an adaptive mechanism negotiating social change. Religion is a creative resource that human beings use in the construction of their lives overall (Smilde 2007). I believe Shayne Lee is perfectly correct in stating that "those churches that adjust to a changing American worldview will flourish, while those that lag behind may lose many of their followers" (2005, 177). What other option is there? As individuals negotiate the many ambiguous and complex demands of modern everyday life, religious beliefs provide moral sensitivities to orient and guide them in particular ways. Churches that connect with modern issues and dilemmas will thrive. The strength of churches is that they offer people ongoing orientation, assistance, and examples through a relational community to "work out their salvation." Relational networks based in religious communities allow access to what David Smilde calls "cultural agency as a process of imaginative rationality," by which he means "humans' ability to get things done by creating concepts" (2007, 215, 13). "People act in the world, get things done, in part by creating concepts that remake, refigure, and reimagine the world in a way that makes it more amenable to their action" (181). In particular, images and metaphors among religious believers allow them "to conceptualize or imagine their social context, the problems that afflict them, and the means for overcoming them" (56).[4]

Religious believers in general seek affinities between their beliefs and their occupational concerns. Although work and faith might be seen as separate spheres, their separation is not possible within modern Christianity. True evangelical believers are especially pressed to find points of integration around worship and service to God in all aspects of life lest they find themselves straying from the faith. At Oasis, the pursuit of fame is a practical occupational concern in the quest for sustenance and security. The work of achieving fame is therefore not merely an egotistical desire for attention and self-worship but a means to successfully accomplish work in the entertainment industry. That God would be seen at Oasis as promoting and providing continual sustenance for such pursuit is critical in order for believers at the church to see themselves as authentically spiritual persons.

By using the notion of ambition as well as acknowledging the increased pressures for self-promotion and self-management of one's career in contemporary U.S. society, the version of religion found at the Oasis steadily empowers the believer experiencing frustration and obstacles along the way to achieving more success. Thus it is possible for persons of faith to be quite well off financially and to seem to have a fair degree of success in their career, yet desire to achieve even more and to move higher on the status ladder and achieve a measure of fame as a way of establishing job security. It is no longer necessary to be poor or destitute to turn to religion for its empowering aspects. Those desiring to move up in any socioeconomic bracket can usefully take advantage of the resources available in this religious orientation and the community established around it.

As persistence and diligent work were important values for an economy structured around mechanical, routinized work, individual creativity and purposeful, goal-oriented achievement are becoming the fundamental values for work. The religious expression at Oasis is not the only form such beliefs can take, but it is one that well fits the current and growing context of work in this country. Further, religious structures that allow for and promote individual "greatness" will be increasingly embraced by workers, who will find ways to be personally inspired and to search for resources for answering the larger questions of the meaning of life and the place of each person in the universe. Values oriented around individual achievement will take on greater importance in comparison with values oriented around loyalty to a company or duty to support one's place of business, since corporations are less and less emphasizing such commitment within themselves. Religious organizations with the imperative of evangelism and church growth will find messages and construct values that maximize relevance to these new economic realities.

The development of religion at the Oasis Christian Center demonstrates the vitality of religion in the contemporary world when it affirms the individual who is striving in a profane world. Religion takes on significant power in people's lives when it legitimizes their everyday and otherwise "worldly" ambitions as a sacred calling. The power of religious commitment is especially evident in the life of a believer when it is seen as an extension of duty to a particular moral community of which one remains a member whether in the immediate presence of the congregation or alone out in the world. The power of congregation is found not so much in the transformations that occur in the meetings but rather in the continued identification and allegiance members take with them beyond the meetings that stimulate self-sacrificial, self-effacing, and self-motivating conduct. The believers view themselves as extensions of the moral community—in the vernacular of the Oasis Christian Center, "champions of life."

Appendix: Research Methodology

I began this study in late 2002 and collected data through participant observation, in-depth interviewing, and examination of archived sources. While the emphasis of this analysis is on those who remain at Oasis, the implications about those who fail to stay are addressed as well. I tried to stay very close to the lived experience of the participants in this organization rather than impose my understanding of the world onto Oasis. I interviewed fifty people currently attending Oasis, including those who made commitments to become dedicated followers of Jesus Christ at Oasis and those who had made such commitments elsewhere, longtime members and recent attendees, men and women, young adults and senior citizens, single and married people, as well as people of different racial and ethnic backgrounds. To preserve the anonymity of respondents and significant figures in the history of the congregation, all have been given pseudonyms except for founding pastors Philip and Holly Wagner. I examined Oasis's twenty-year history based on the memories of long-term participants as they correlated with each other and with the few print resources available. Archived sources consisted of selected books, tapes given away or available for purchase, and pamphlets publicly distributed by the church. I continued to collect data and provisionally interpret them until a general picture emerged and was reaffirmed over and over again.

The general goal of my research corresponds to the goal of social scientific research as stated by Lewis Minkin:

> Primarily, I aim to construct a coherent and adequate conceptual framework grounded in the repeated occurrences found in my empirical investigations. This framework is always analytical in the attempt to establish a pattern which makes sense in describing and categorizing relationships and developments across time, but it also aspires to be explanatory, organising the material in such a way as to indicate solutions to the core problem (or problems) and related questions under investigation, seeking to account for all cases within a particular historical and cultural setting. (1997, 173)

Eventually, a conceptual framework is constructed "not only in terms of its novelty but also in terms of its capacity to order the data" (181). This is "an analytical patterning which provided an arrangement of repeated occurrences" (188). I have made an effort to become aware of my own biases, assumptions, perceptions stemming from my training, social location, and past experiences. I have also made an attempt to be both descriptive and theoretical in the attempt to generate theory regarding congregational processes.

The resulting book represents the experiences of the particular people and staff members I met and the process of their religious involvement with this diverse congregation. It does not claim to represent the views of all charismatic churches nor all churches in Los Angeles. Yet case studies of specific churches can help uncover and articulate distinctive processes in contemporary U.S. religion. My goal is to present a vivid understanding of the life of members in this congregation. I locate this understanding in the context of broader patterns of the religious streams in which they (knowingly or unknowingly) participate, as well as the secular world in which they operate. I allow the attenders of Oasis to speak for themselves as clearly as possible. As a sociologist, I developed a particular interpretation of these findings and the data I present are those that serve to illustrate and substantiate my analysis. I employed several types of checks and attempted to corroborate the data to substantiate my conclusions before writing this account. In that sense, although my account is constructed to portray my understanding of this congregation to the best of my ability and although other researchers may have produced a different account, I am confident that other researchers would not find data that would generally disconfirm my analysis. I tried my ideas out on people as I spoke with them in the field. I shared my ideas with leaders of the church. I shared my ideas with colleagues formally and informally for an initial check on the plausibility of my interpretation and its utility for future social analysis. I examined the scholarly literature to make sure that I was not missing any important themes or that findings from another researcher did not clash with my own. These attempts at good scholarship provide evidence regarding the validity of my findings, giving my scholarly community the opportunity to work with fresh information as we work toward continued analysis and dialogue in understanding the critical dynamics with the congregation as we investigate them together.

Participant Observation

The work of the participant observer is constantly the attempt to see the researched community from an insider's perspective and grasp the subtle nuances in meaning and then situate these meanings in a broader societal context. A core assumption by researchers who use participant observation is that "in the course of daily life, people make sense of the world around them; they give it meaning and they interact on the basis of these meanings" (Jorgensen 1989, 14). "Participant observation, in other words, is a very special strategy and method for gaining access to the interior, seemingly subjective aspects of human existence" (21).

The goal of the participant observer is to make known the meanings people in a given social structure typically have, a world of meaning that is not typically understood or even sought to be understood by outsiders to that group. The concepts of the analysis emerge as much from the participants of the social setting as from the theoretical concepts of the investigators. The social scientist enters the study of a group (whether familiar or strange) to investigate the underlying, institutionalized patterns of social life and thus make a contribution to the general understanding of social life in other social structures.

The key is to seek the "ordinary, usual, typical, routine, or natural environment" of the social group in question (Jorgensen 1989, 15). The benefit of participant observation is that, although at Oasis some were aware of my research agenda, the overall activities and structure of the congregation superseded any concern for my observation. Leaders and attenders sang, swayed, clapped, stood, sat, listened, laughed, and left routinely in their involvement in the congregation. Things happened because this is what it means to "do church" together.

In all instances I remained concerned for the privacy and confidentiality of people and avoided notations that would indicate people by name or other identifying characteristics, with the exception of the lead pastors of the church. I directly quote the founders Philip and Holly Wagner from public statements and personal discussions. I have made an earnest attempt to maintain confidentiality, including that of congregational leaders, unless they were speaking publicly, in print, or on recordings made available either on site for purchase or online. In some cases, I altered identifying characteristics in ways that did not affect the presentation of my analysis.

At Oasis, most people agreed when I asked to interview them. A few openly made themselves available to talk, and a few were suspicious. Overall, people were very willing to tell me about their church experiences before arriving at Oasis, their first encounters with the church, and the nature of their connection with Oasis since then. Throughout the research I clarified for the people of Oasis my own stance toward religion and the church overall. I was open with them that my research goals motivated my presence at the church. When I was asked about my own religious commitment, I explained that I was a member of a large multiethnic Protestant church in Los Angeles. Members and leaders treated me as a curious observer who would never join the church. I did not require conversion as I claimed to already be a Christian; and I did not need a church since I was a member of another one locally. That left a friendly ambivalence about my activities. Those who understood my project were willing to offer helpful information about continuing activities of the church and occasionally asked me how I was enjoying my research. Those aware of my study were glad to have me come to Oasis to learn and share what I learned with others. Although I did not know what the overall findings of my analysis would be, I knew that I was concerned to provide a sociological view on who the people of Oasis were, what they were doing to help (or hinder) the ministry of the church, and attempt to analytically describe it. Even though I was a marginal member of the group, I attempted to strike a balance between interacting with people who were deeply committed to the church and those who were on the fringes. I took field notes, often relying on a tape recorder that I spoke into on the way home from a meeting or worship service and later transcribed. These notes were made computer accessible to NVIVO, one of the latest generation of computer-aided software analysis tools used by social scientists today.

During the twelve months I was around Oasis, I participated in church events regularly attended by members, new guests, and those in the process of joining the church. I went through a guest reception process at the beginning of my attendance. Also, I was readily given permission to attend midweek leadership seminar classes once I found out about them. One of the most interesting experiences was going through the membership process, a four-week activity that introduced people to all the staff members and articulated the core aspects of the church's beliefs and values in a highly compressed form. Comparing the presentation of the church in the membership process with the history of the church, the impressions of recent attenders, and the experience of longtime members was one of the more fruitful opportunities for corroboration of sources regarding the nature of the church, the kinds of people who join, and the typical experiences found as they participate. I always found people at Oasis to be warm, relationally open, and interested in my research project. Numerous conversations occurred with staff members, guests, regular attenders, and longtime members as I was around the church and its services and classes.

My familiarity with Los Angeles as well as church experiences in other churches (both charismatic and noncharismatic) gave me the opportunity to enter the community with an understanding of various subtle rites and rituals, religious lingo used among local believers, and theological distinctions. Some saw me as an outsider; others saw me as inside. Overall I occupied an ambivalent position as a person who was acknowledged to be another "believer" but not necessarily a person who is the same as Christians at the Oasis. The position of researcher definitely set me apart from other people at Oasis. There were a few occasions when a staff member would introduce me to another as a person doing research. On a few occasions early in my fieldwork, a pastoral staff member invited me to come sit in the front row, a place that is held in high honor for visiting guests. I politely declined, partly because my observations were richer from the back of the auditorium versus the front and partly because I feared alienating any nonstaff attenders who might view me as someone important and aligned somehow with the pastoral leadership. Another time I was pointed out to a Bible study class as someone visiting to study the congregation; people turned and clapped as I was introduced. Early pastoral attention did help me gain access and legitimacy because I was recognized as having a permission to be observing and asking questions. Although among a small circle of people, that meant that I lost anonymity, but not for most. The majority of my interactions at church were with strangers and brief acquaintances; a few came to know me by face but not by my research agenda.

In-Depth Interviews

In-depth interviews allow researchers to solicit detailed life stories and life histories that cannot be gained by just observing or hanging out. As Minkin writes in pursuit of getting close to "the real picture" to affirm his growing understanding of a peculiarity, "I interview a lot of people and talk informally to them, often on repeated occasions" (1997, 122). Interviews provide an opportunity to see how people make sense of their own beliefs and practices. This continues a tradition within sociology that includes Max Weber, Alfred Schutz, George Herbert Mead, and Peter Berger that the ways in which people make sense of themselves and their worlds is critical to understanding the dynamics of any social setting.

For this study, I conducted a total of fifty interviews with people of Oasis, twenty-four men and twenty-six women. I oversampled members and attenders who were neither African American nor white, the dominant races in the congregation. Of my interviews, 42 percent were Caucasian, 32 percent African American, 13 percent Hispanic, 5 percent Asian, 2 percent Middle Eastern, and 6 percent mixed heritages who identified themselves as "multiracial." The greater proportion of whites is because the majority of staff and longtime members still in the congregation were white. In terms of educational background, 17 percent had completed high school, 6 percent had master's and Ph.D. degrees, and the rest had bachelor's degrees or some college. Fourteen percent of my respondents were immigrants to America, 10 percent were second and third generation, and the rest had a long ancestral history in the United States. Eighty-four percent of my sample was active in some type of ministry at the church. Although I sought out guests and new attenders, four out of five interviewees were members. Twenty-five percent came from nondenominational Christian backgrounds (often multiple churches), 35 percent from specifically charismatic backgrounds, 15 percent from Roman Catholic backgrounds, and 20 percent from mixed religious backgrounds including no religious background at all. In terms of tenure, 20 percent of my respondents had been attending less than two years, and 40 percent had been at Oasis five years or more. About 12 percent made first-time commitments to become Christians at Oasis. While the average age of my respondents was thirty-eight years, the youngest person interviewed was nineteen and the oldest person who would tell me their age was fifty-seven. In sum, my respondents represented a wide range of social demographic characteristics and came from a variety of lifestyles and life experiences.

My interviews lasted an average of ninety minutes, although one went for almost three hours, and others were less than an hour. (In addition to my formal interviews, I conducted numerous informal interviews with attenders I came to know before, after, and during church functions. This gave me glimpses into the experiences of a wide range of guests and regular attenders and allowed me to contextualize the experiences from those I was able to properly interview.) As the number of my interviews grew, I continued to interview until I approached a saturation of experiences. Themes were repeating and I found patterns that organized the experiences of Oasis attenders, patterns later affirmed in my structured analysis of transcribed interview texts using qualitative analysis software. This number of interviews allowed me to speak to a range of attenders with various levels of tenure and involvement and, as insights began to become repetitious, a reasonable sample of life experiences for my analysis. Most of the interviews were scheduled before or after a midweek meeting or church service; some were in the church offices or at a local restaurant. Overall, scheduling interviews was not difficult. Most at Oasis were eager to share their experiences in a congregation they truly appreciate. Their church involvement was for most a critical aspect of their religious commitments, and such a personally vital topic was worth their time to describe.

I was open to meeting people at their convenience wherever was most comfortable to them. Because the church has a cozy Starbucks-style coffee house right next to the worship auditorium, most people asked to meet there. My discussions were appropriately private, in that even when people were around, the distance between groups and the overall muffling of sound in the room made for an open yet public and safe place for respondents to meet "the guy doing interviews." Elite interviews occurred with pastors and staff members who had been at Oasis for many years, and then I followed up with interviews with attenders with long and short tenure. Overall, my goal was to try to approximate the racial proportion of the congregation in the people I interviewed.

I had prepared an interview guide modified from a previous study (Marti 2005) consisting of several core questions; I then explored experiences, connections, and implications through probes and follow-up questions as I learned more from the respondent within the interview and also, in later interviews, as I learned more about my respondents and the congregation as a whole. I assured each person of confidentiality and anonymity or I explicitly asked permission to use their names and asked for the opportunity to share information gathered with scholars and church leaders interested in congregational dynamics. Every interview began with the question, "How did you get to the Oasis?" With this question, every person had the opportunity to tell me their life history up to the point of their arriving at Oasis in their own terms. In telling me their story, most shared their family backgrounds, religious upbringing, church experiences, relationships both successful and unsuccessful, their schooling and occupational careers and other matters that explained their values and mindset. I asked about their first experiences with Oasis, and then their subsequent involvements. Many shared with me experiences with other members and leaders in the church. Many also shared important changes they've seen in the church throughout their tenure. While my core questions did not change in the course of interviewing people, later interviews included at the end of our time a few summaries of my gut reactions to findings at the Oasis, which served as "member checks" of my initial conclusions. At the end of each interview, I asked whether there was anything else they wanted to share about their experience at the Oasis. Some did; others said they did not think there was anything else they could add. I found most people to be quite open and willing to share.

People emphasized different aspects according to those things they found most relevant to understanding their coming to Oasis. Some talked at great length, while others were asked several follow-up questions for clarification. Although I followed an interview schedule, I changed my mode of exploration, which consisted of dialogue as well as interrogation. These were "conversations with a purpose" (Webb and Webb 1932, 130). Minkin discusses the advantages of interview flexibility:

> Flexibility in response to the conversation . . . allowed me to make the solid information-seeking enquiries on which the creative scholar depends, but also, on occasions to make detours down interesting byways where I saw a connection or a revealing insight. It permitted me to explore an emerging pattern of cases, and to react, there and then, to the sudden appearance of the peculiarities that my nose told me could fruitfully be followed. Thus, I was happy to allow the conversation to take unexpected courses and, at times, to meander along, risking that it would have its creative benefits, providing that I could, periodically and gently, return it towards the priority areas of enquiry. (1997, 149)

While I had several critical topics I needed to understand from the respondents (where they grew up, previous religious experience, racial/ethnic affiliation), a more open-ended interview allowed me to learn about each person's own perceptions of their life experience.

Almost every interview was tape-recorded. A handful of interviews occurred spontaneously as a result of my hanging out around the church that I was unprepared for taping. I still asked explicit permission from each person to share data. I tried to maintain an attitude of being a student of their life experiences, speaking as little as possible. In the process, a handful of people—staff, lay leaders, and regular attenders—were informants who called my attention to aspects of the procedures and settings that I might have otherwise overlooked.

Archived Sources

In addition to observation and interviews, other sources of data included printed and recorded materials available through the church. The leaders of Oasis have published books and maintain tape libraries of sermon series that are for sale. I added to my data selected books and tapes in seeking the "structural corroboration" described by Elliot Eisner as "a means through which multiple types of data are related to each other to support or contradict the interpretation and evaluation of a state of affairs" (1991, 110). The few documentary sources consisted of guest information pamphlets, new member guides, copies of a few notable tape series, and the church's Web site. The small, in-house pamphlets and publications were helpful in understanding the conscious organization and initiatives within the congregation. All the material I used for analysis is publicly accessible. I also asked leaders to indicate books, leaders, and other resources that they considered important to them, and the few that were mentioned revealed certain critical aspects of the congregation's values and beliefs.

Finally, the text shows how frequently and freely I draw on historical materials to account for the development of Hollywood and the place of religion within it. No church exists in a historical vacuum, and this study actively incorporates historical sensibility. I agree with Rebecca Kneale Gould that "it is vital that some scholarly investigations bridge the traditional disciplinary boundaries of history and sociology and work back and forth between them" (2005, 10). Gould and others (Ammerman 1987; Griffith 1997; Orsi 1996) begin with the stories of individuals actively constructing stable social structures, connecting local context to often unintended predecessors and relevant historical occurrences. Although this book leans more heavily on ethnographic fieldwork, I embrace a multidisciplinary approach that "begins with particular people who have devoted themselves to particular places" (Gould 2005, 10). A recent and more expansive discussion on methodological issues involved in such work can be found in *Personal Knowledge and Beyond: Reshaping the Ethnography of Religion*, an edited volume devoted to the study of religion (Spickard, Landres, and McGuire 2002).

Notes

PREFACE AND ACKNOWLEDGMENTS

1. One important theoretical branch in the new paradigm approach to the study of religion is "rational choice theory," which uses an economic model of rational actors maximizing utility in their religious commitments (Stark and Finke 2000; Young 1997). I share with Stephen Warner an unease with the model (2005, 7). Warner concludes that "religion connects too intimately with the emotions for such rational-actor presumptions to be satisfactory."

CHAPTER 1 — INTRODUCTION

1. For more on the rare achievement of congregational diversity, see Emerson and Smith 2000; DeYoung, Emerson, Yancey, and Chai 2003; Marti 2005; Christerson, Emerson, and Edwards 2005; Emerson 2006; and Garces-Foley 2007.

2. The estimate of attenders connected to the Hollywood entertainment industry is based on my overall observations at Oasis. At times, informal surveys of the church related to the industry were taken by a show of hands by speakers during their messages in corporate gatherings; at other times, testimonies of believers sharing life experiences in the entertainment industry produced swells of mm-hmm's, clapping, shouts of "yes" or "that's right," and cheers from the audience. The estimate is consistent with the accumulated estimates from staff and nonstaff attenders I interviewed.

3. Social phenomenologists use the term "life-world" or "social life-world" (from the German *lebenswelt*) to describe the meaningful order of human lives established collectively and maintained by collective consent. The patterns of life and their embedded meanings are socially constructed and socially constrained.

4. While there are various explanations of "creative class," I favor the notion of a group oriented toward artistic and symbolically oriented work.

5. Several histories of Hollywood mention this fact, although it receives little attention in favor of civic, technological, and economic developments leading to the growth of the film industry. See Giovacchini 2001; Torrence 1982; and Zollo 2002.

6. Evangelical sources on the biography of Satan constructed from an exegetical interpretation of Scriptures include Barnhouse 1980; Pentecost 1997; and Lutzer 1996.

7. *Catholic Insider,* a regular podcast, featured in March 2005 episodes entitled "Investigating the Da Vinci Code." The description includes, "Did Dan Brown do his

homework when writing the Da Vinci Code?" and "What is fact and what is fiction in Dan Brown's Da Vinci Code?"

8. Here and elsewhere, I emphasize my understanding of Durkheim's shortcomings as a social theorist. For example, I agree when David Smilde (2007, 125) cautions us to remember "to think of a meaning *system* not as a rigorous structure but as a loosely integrated *repertoire* of meanings that are often multiple and contradictory."

9. See, for example, Allen, Pickering, and Miller 1998; Alexander and Smith 2005; Collins 1990; Emirbayer 1996, 2003; L. Jones 1999; Pickering 2002; Strenski 2006.

CHAPTER 2 — THE MAKING OF A STAR

1. For a brief overview of the sociological analysis of film, see Tudor 2001.

2. The anthropologist Hortense Powdermaker applied her skills to understanding studio production by spending time among filmmakers in the 1940s. See Powdermaker 1950.

CHAPTER 3 — LOVE AND HATE BETWEEN HOLLYWOOD AND CHRISTIANITY

1. Sunday morning Easter services at the Hollywood Bowl remain a major event in Los Angeles. For an early description see Hill and Snyder 1923, 58–64.

2. All quotes in this paragraph are from May 1983; page numbers appear in parentheses in the text.

3. Censorship is dominantly thought of as the removal of offensive material. The original seal of the New York Board of Motion Picture Censorship, which became the National Board of Review of Motion Pictures, consisted of an image of scissors superimposed on a four-pointed star (Sklar 1994, 31).

4. An interesting discussion on nickelodeons drawing on Jurgen Habermas's conception of the public sphere is found in Hansen 1993; see also Lindsey 1996 and Mayne 1990.

5. For an analysis of Willow Creek and the style of seeker-sensitive churches, see Sargeant 2000. The concern for appealing to the unchurched is also evident in the ministry of Mosaic in Los Angeles (Marti 2005).

6. For a more extensive history of the use of films by Protestant churches in the early era of Hollywood history, see Rosini 1998 and Lindvall 2007.

7. William Harrison Hays served as president of MPPDA from 1922 to 1945. His power was drawn in part from his political connections as well as his long tenure as the association's president. For his own perspective on his life and work, see Hays 1955.

8. More on the self-regulation of the motion picture industry can be found in Nizer 1935 and Moley 1945.

CHAPTER 4 — SAVE THE WORLD, STARTING IN HOLLYWOOD

1. Even though such gross exaggerations did not go unchallenged, the overall perception of Hollywood was that it was inhospitable for Christians. See, for example, Davidson 1925.

2. A list of "media-friendly" churches is available from Inter-mission at http://intermission.net/churchlist.html.

3. While Malcolm Boyd believed that Christians should pay attention to the products of popular entertainment and mass communication, he left the entertainment industry to become an Episcopalian priest. Dedicating one's life to a sacred calling through a sacred vocation while keeping an ear to the ground of popular culture is a readily accepted stance within Christianity. What is more controversial is pursuing a sacred calling through work in the Hollywood entertainment industry.

4. Personal communication, February 2002. For more on Erwin McManus and Mosaic's approach to popular culture, see Marti 2005.

5. For exegeses of the spiritual meanings of major films, see, e.g., Anker 2005; Barsotti and Johnston 2004; Godawa 2002; Higgins 2003; Johnston 2000, 2007; Miles 1997; Stone 2000.

6. In looking toward the appeal to conservative Christian audiences, studios occasionally tone down explicit sexuality and include symbols like having Brad Pitt and Angelina Jolie wear "Jesus Rocks" jackets in Twentieth Century Fox's *Mr. and Mrs. Smith* (2005).

7. For more on the Legion of Decency campaign, see Black, Short, Jowett, and Culbert 1996, 149–192, and Maltby 1993.

8. The effort to treat audiences uniformly failed. Studies by sociologists Paul Lazarsfeld and Robert K. Merton (1943) empirically demonstrated that audiences are composed of groups centered on different interests such that a seemingly uniform message is received in diverse ways. The use of "the people" as a trope among filmmakers has unintended consequences, contributing to the unseen inequality between groups on the basis of race, class, and gender in mainstream culture.

9. Peter Lake (2002) provides a fascinating account of how popular media became direct competition for the church in its appeal to mass culture through popular language. The dynamic relationship between the Christian pulpit and the secular pamphlet preceded the now familiar dialogue between sacred and secular media between preachers and blockbuster films.

10. Gibson's anti-Semitic slurs came from an insider who works in an industry with many prominent Jews. Not everyone accepts the sincerity of Gibson's subsequent apologies and rehabilitation process.

11. For reviews of this and other films see www.movies.com (accessed August 15, 2006).

CHAPTER 5 — CELEBRITY, HEARTACHE, AND THE PRESSURE TO MAKE IT

1. Extras in the 1910s and 1920s had to supply their own outfits for contemporary scenes, so they spent strategically to acquire an appropriate wardrobe and explored the industry in both onscreen roles and in off-screen jobs as, for example, dress designers, set decorators, and film cutters. Studios in the 1910s and 1920s gave more opportunities to women than most other industries (Sklar 1994, 75).

2. There is some evidence of decline in the concentration of entertainment industry work in the Los Angeles region as "runaway productions" pursue lower production costs, but historical fluctuations have been the rule and no long-term trend has been established (see Monitor Company 1999).

3. For an overview of the transformation from the studio system to the disaggregate production phase, I draw on industry history described in Bordwell, Staiger, and Thompson 1985; Maltby 1998, 2003; Scott 2005; Sklar 1994; Smith 1998; Torrence 1982; Zierer 1947; and Gomery 2000.

4. While Hollywood initially centered on films, the entertainment industry expanded to include other media, especially music, television, video games, and product merchandizing. Each form blends into the others, and the most successful Hollywood projects build on all of them.

5. Actors as laborers place their work within a network of institutions and power relations. Such a perspective is directly influenced by Marxism and political economy. The Hollywood industry becomes a bounded arena of practical struggle to exercise creative control over one's work and to pursue the craft of acting in a way that is satisfying to the individual but fulfills the production requirements of the controllers of funds that allow the making of the film in the first place. Relations of power produce the "image" that we understand as stars.

6. The broad implications of the notion of "stigma" are more fully explored in Goffman 1963.

CHAPTER 6 — RELIGION

1. For a compelling geographic profile, plot the location of Oasis's building at Wilshire Boulevard between La Brea and Highland on the maps found in Scott 2005, especially figures 1.1, 2.1, 2.2, 3.3, 3.4, 4.3, 5.2, 7.2, 7.3, and 7.4.

2. In the earliest days of motion pictures, exhibiters enhanced the moviegoing experience by copying the styles and tastes of upper-class mansions and high-end hotels, which both appealed to the masses and lent theaters an aura of respectability for the growing numbers of upper-class attendees. Early innovators in theater exhibition included Marcus Loew, Carl Laemmle, William Fox, Samuel Lion Rothafel, A. J. Balaban, and Samual Katz.

3. The most influential architect of the modern theater is Ben Schlanger. For discussion of his work in contrast to previous theater design, see May 2000, chap. 3.

4. A new Mosaic church was launched in Charlotte, North Carolina, not far from my residence, in January 2006 (www.mosaicchurch.tv), aligned with the innovative Mosaic in Los Angeles in its music and worship styles among other things (see Marti 2005). Although new paradigm worship is not unusual for the area, the church's use of colorful graphics, disco lights, and hip music was unusual enough to earn a feature story in both the *Charlotte Observer* and *Charlotte Magazine*.

5. Descriptions of Word of Faith teachings as "practical" also appear among interviews conducted by Milmon Harrison (2005).

6. By calling itself a "Christian center" Oasis is proclaiming that it is affiliated with Christ but in a nontraditional way. One finds Christian centers all across the United States. By and large, these churches affiliate themselves in some way with the Word of Faith movement. At the time of my first acquaintance with Oasis, I was not aware the words signaled a particular framework of belief.

7. In a less complimentary fashion, the Word of Faith movement has also been called "name and claim it" and "blab it and grab it." My understanding of this movement and its most prominent leaders comes from a variety of recent sources on its history and structure, including Anderson 2004; Harrison 2005; Lee 2005; and Perriman 2003, which includes a useful summary of sources (12–14).

8. For critiques of the Word of Faith movement, see Barron 1987; Brandon 1987; Farah 1978; Horton 1990; Hunt and McMahon 1985; McConnell 1988.

9. By referring to Kenneth Hagin, Kenneth Copeland, and Fred Price as major influences on the nature of the Christian faith in the mission of the church, leaders of the Oasis demonstrate that "the Word of Faith movement draws its identity and momentum from the personalities of its leaders" (Perriman 2003, 1). Prominent Word of Faith teachers also include Oral Roberts, Creflo Dollar, John Avanzini, Leroy Thompson, Markus Bishop, TD Jakes, and Joel Olsteen. Books by Kenneth Copeland, Kenneth Hagen, Fred Price, and Oral Roberts have been carried at the church's bookstore in the past. Leaders also acknowledge the influence of Casey and Wendy Treat, Derek Prince, Lester Sumrall, and Norville Hayes, at least at the beginning of the ministry.

10. As a point of comparison, the voices and experiences presented in Harrison's (2005) study of Faith Christian Center are far more pointed and extreme than anything I found at Oasis. Moreover, Harrison asserts that the movement insists on possessing "new revelation" from God that promises material blessings to individual believers and that this knowledge has been held back from believers in other strains of the Christian tradition. In my observation, Oasis makes no claim to special revelation and spends no time insisting on the superiority of its message over those of other Christian Churches.

11. Although the prosperity gospel is widely critiqued as ignoring the structural dynamics of poverty and exploitation that exist in the capitalist system (Lee 2005, 113–122), Miller and Yamamori contend: "Many Prosperity Gospel churches see no con-

tradiction between making claims about God's ability to heal people and bless them financially, and setting up health clinics, developing schools, and the like" (2007, 32). Their observations of "Progressive Pentecostal Churches" reveal intentional (although incremental) approaches to societal transformation of social ills.

12. In his exhaustive study of U.S. clergy, Jackson Carroll (2006, 149) is another scholar who laments "the overwhelming attention given to members' needs and desires, especially if this indicates an accommodation to religious consumerism or a kind of therapeutic ideal at the expense of theological integrity in congregational life." Carroll clearly wishes to see greater attention paid to theological fidelity and believes church leaders who yield to the desires and preferences of members threaten the health of the church. Yet he also recognizes that "given the rapidity of change, no organization, much less the church, can afford to ignore the constant pressure to adapt to new challenges that arise" (150).

CHAPTER 7 — FADE TO BLACK

1. On the segregated nature of churches, see Emerson and Smith 2000; DeYoung, Emerson, Yancey, and Chai 2003; Marti 2005; Christerson, Emerson, and Edwards 2005.

2. In his insightful study of Venezuelan Evangelicals, David Smilde includes an important discussion of the various ways failure can be explained within the evangelical context. "Evangelical men use Evangelical concepts to imagine aspects of their social context and social lives in ways that make them more amenable to their agency" (2007, 150). In short, failure is redefined in a way that enhances the ability of individuals to avoid being overwhelmed by their circumstances and to take control of personal projects to reform their own lives.

3. Sources on the history and analysis of music in the black church are both extensive and fascinating. For a preliminary account see Pinn 2002 (chap. 3); Cone 1992; West 1999; Darden 2004; and Harris 1994. Nathan Hatch notes that experimentation with popular music among white Methodists in the American republic also influenced the development of the black spiritual and is evident in the hymnbook published by the founder of the African Methodist Episcopal Church, Richard Allen (1989, 157).

4. When I asked where the term "house" came from, a staff member told me it came from Hills Christian Life Center in Australia, pastored by Bryan and Bobbie Houston (see Bouma 2007). In a book read together by Oasis staff, Bobbie Houston (2001, 10) quotes Genesis 28: 16–22 in which Jacob established a memorial pillar named Bethel, which translated means "House of God." The word "house" is thus God's church. The term "Bethel" is also commonly used by Christians to signify a house of worship.

CHAPTER 9 — CONCLUSION

1. This final chapter draws together various strands of a theoretical argument about the relationship between Oasis's religious values and practices and the demands of the entertainment labor market. While previously privileging Durkheim's insights, I now

place more of his and Max Weber's theoretical perspectives in dialogue in with each other. In particular, my speculation on the role of religion among the new "creative class" is more Weberian than Durkheimian, since the argument is less concerned with the internal cohesion and moral boundaries of believers at Oasis and more with the intersection of religion, economy, and social class in the current climate of work in the United States.

2. Guides to branding include Andrusia and Haskins 2000; McNally and Speak 2002; Montoya and Vandehey 2003; Montoya, Vandehey, and Viti 2002; Van Yoder 2003.

3. In taking note of this change away from formal integration toward shifting networks of small, flexibly specialized firms, it is important to note that oligopolies have continued to exist and that studios continue to share a great deal of power and influence within the Hollywood industry. A list of critiques can be found in Scott (2005, 37–38).

4. The theoretical sophistication stimulated by David Smilde's (2007) work is accentuated when we recognize its basis in pragmatist philosophy applied to the social understanding of religious practice.

Bibliography

Addams, Jane. [1909] 1989. *The Spirit of Youth and the City Streets*. New York: University of Illinois Press.

Aldridge, Alan. 2000. *Religion in the Contemporary World*. Malden, Mass.: Blackwell.

Alexander, Jeffrey C., ed. 1988. *Durkheimian Sociology: Cultural Studies*. New York: Cambridge University Press.

————. 2003. *The Meanings of Social Life: A Cultural Sociology*. New York: Oxford University Press.

Alexander, Jeffrey C., and Philip Smith, eds. 2005. *The Cambridge Companion to Durkheim*. New York: Cambridge University Press.

Allahyari, Rebecca Anne. 2000. *Visions of Charity: Volunteer Workers and Moral Community*. Berkeley: University of California Press.

Allen, N. J., W.S.F. Pickering, and W. Watts Miller, eds. 1998. *Durkheim's Elementary Forms of Religious Life*. London: Routledge.

Ammerman, Nancy Tatom. 1987. *Bible Believers: Fundamentalists in the Modern World*. New Brunswick: Rutgers University Press.

————. 2005. *Pillars of Faith: American Congregations and Their Partners*. Berkeley: University of California Press.

Ammerman, Nancy Tatom, Jackson W. Carroll, Carl S. Dudley, and William McKinney, eds. 1998. *Studying Congregations: A New Handbook*. Nashville, Tenn.: Abingdon.

Anderson, Allan. 2004. *An Introduction to Pentecostalism: Global Charismatic Christianity*. Cambridge: Cambridge University Press.

Anderson, Robert Mapes. 1975. *Vision of the Disinherited: The Making of American Pentecostalism*. New York: Oxford University Press.

Andrews, Dale P. 2002. *Practical Theology for Black Churches: Bridging Black Theology and African American Folk Religion*. Louisville, Ky.: Westminster John Knox Press.

Andrusia, David, and Rick Haskins. 2000. *Brand Yourself: How to Create an Identity for a Brilliant Career*. New York: Ballantine Books.

Anger, Kenneth. 1973. *Hollywood Babylon*. San Francisco: Straight Arrow Books.

Anker, Roy M. 2005. *Catching Light: Looking for God in the Movies*. Grand Rapids, Mich.: Eerdmans.

Arthur, W. Brian, Yuri M. Ermoliev, and Yuri M. Kaniovsky. 1987. "Path-Dependent Processes and the Emergence of Macrostructure." *European Journal of Operational Research* 30:294–303.

Baehr, Ted. 2005. *So You Want to Be in Pictures? A Christian Resource for "Making It" in Hollywood*. Nashville: Broadman and Holman.

Baer, Hans A., and Merrill Singer. 2002. *African American Religion: Varieties of Protest and Accommodation*. 2nd ed. Knoxville: University of Tennessee Press.

Barley, Stephen R., and Gideon Kunda. 2004. *Gurus, Hired Guns, and Warm Bodies: Itinerant Experts in a Knowledge Economy*. Princeton: Princeton University Press.

Barnhouse, Donald G. 1980. *The Invisible War*. Grand Rapids, Mich.: Zondervan.

Barron, Bruce. 1987. *The Health and Wealth Gospel*. Downers Grove, Ill.: InterVarsity Press.

Barsotti, Catherine M., and Robert K. Johnston. 2004. *Finding God in the Movies: 33 Films of Reel Faith*. Grand Rapids, Mich.: Baker Books.

Batt, Rosemary, Susan Christopherson, Ned Rightor, and Danielle Van Jaarsveld. 2001. *Net Working: Work Patterns and Workforce Policies for the New Media Industry*. Washington, D.C.: Economic Policy Institute.

Beck, Ulrich. 2000. *The Brave New World of Work*. Translated by P. Camiller. Cambridge: Polity Press.

Becker, Howard S., and Blanche Geer. 1982. "Participant Observation: The Analysis of Qualitative Field Data." In *Field Research: A Sourcebook and Field Manual*, ed. R. Burgess. London: Allen and Unwin.

Becker, Penny Edgell. 1997. "Congregational Model and Conflicts: Identifying a Religious logic in Local Congregations." In *Sacred Companies: Organized Aspects of Religion and Religious Aspects of Organization*, ed. Peter Dobkin Hall, N. J. Demerath III, Terry Schmitt, and Rhys H. Williams. New York: Oxford University Press.

Belfrage, Cedric. 1938. *Promised Land*. London: Victor Gollancz.

Bellah, Robert Neelly. 1985. *Habits of the Heart: Individualism and Commitment in American Life*. Berkeley: University of California Press.

———. 1991. *The Good Society*. New York: Knopf.

———. 2003. "The Ritual Roots of Society and Culture." In *Handbook of the Sociology of Religion*, ed. Michelle Dillon. Cambridge: Cambridge University Press.

———. 2006. "Flaws in the Protestant Code: Theological Roots of American Individualism." In *The Robert Bellah Reader*, ed. Robert N. Bellah and Steven. M. Tipton. Durham: Duke University Press.

Bendroth, Margaret Lamberts. 2004. "Why Women Loved Billy Sunday: Urban Revivalism and Popular Entertainment in Early Twentieth-Century American Culture." *Religion and American Culture* 14 (2): 251–271.

Benjamin, Lois. 2005. *The Black Elite: Still Facing the Color Line in the Twenty-First Century.* 2nd ed. Lanham, Md.: Rowman and Littlefield.

Berger, Peter L., Brigitte Berger, and Hansfried Kellner. 1973. *The Homeless Mind: Modernization and Consciousness.* New York: Random House.

Bernhardt, Annette D., Martina Morris, Mark S. Handcock, and Marc A. Scott. 2001. *Divergent Paths: Economic Mobility in the New American Labor Market.* New York: Russell Sage Foundation.

Billingsley, Andrew. 1999. *Mighty Like a River: The Black Church and Social Reform.* New York: Oxford University Press.

Black, Gregory D., Kenneth Short, Garth Jowett, and David Culbert. 1996. *Hollywood Censored: Morality Codes, Catholics, and the Movies.* Cambridge Studies in the History of Mass Communication. Cambridge: Cambridge University Press.

Blackwell, James E. 1975. *The Black Community: Diversity and Unity.* New York: Harper and Row.

Blair, Helen. 2001. You're Only as Good as Your Last Job: The Labor Process and Labor Market in the British Film Industry. *Work, Employment, Society* 15:149–169.

Block, Fred L. 1990. *Postindustrial Possibilities: A Critique of Economic Discourse.* Berkeley: University of California Press.

Blumhofer, Edith L. 1993. *Aimee Semple McPherson: Everybody's Sister.* Grand Rapids, Mich.: Eerdmans.

Bly, Robert W. 2001. *Become a Recognized Authority in Your Field—In 60 Days or Less.* Indianapolis: Alpha Books.

Bordwell, David, Janet Staiger, and Kristin Thompson. 1985. *The Classical Hollywood Cinema: Film Style and Mode of Production to 1960.* New York: Columbia University Press.

Bouma, Gary. 2007. *Australian Soul: Religion and Spirituality in the Twenty-First Century.* Cambridge: Cambridge University Press.

Boyd, Malcolm. 1958. *Christ and Celebrity Gods: The Church in Mass Culture.* Greenwich, Conn.: Seabury Press.

Brandon, Andrew. 1987. *Health and Wealth.* Eastbourne, U.K.: Kingsway.

Brasher, Brenda E. 1998. *Godly Women: Fundamentalism and Female Power.* New Brunswick: Rutgers University Press.

Braudy, Leo. 1986. *The Frenzy of Renown: Fame and Its History.* New York: Oxford University Press.

Bridges, Flora Wilson. 2001. *Resurrection Song: African-American Spirituality.* Maryknoll, N.Y.: Orbis Books.

Bridges, William. 1994. *Job Shift: How to Prosper in a Workplace without Jobs.* Reading, Mass.: Addison-Wesley.

————. 1998. *Creating You and Co: Learn to Think Like the CEO of Your Own Career*. New York: Perseus Books Group.

Briner, Robert. 1993. *Roaring Lambs: A Gentle Plan to Radically Change Our World*. Grand Rapids, Mich.: Zondervan.

————. 1995. *Lambs among Wolves*. Grand Rapids, Mich.: Zondervan.

————. 2000. *The Final Roar*. Nashville: Broadman and Holman.

Brouwer, Steve, Paul Gifford, and Susan D. Rose. 1996. *Exporting the American Gospel: Global Christian Fundamentalism*. New York: Routledge.

Butler, Jon. 1990. *Awash in a Sea of Faith: Christianizing the American People*. Studies in Cultural History. Cambridge, Mass.: Harvard University Press.

Buzzell, Linda. 1996. *How to Make It in Hollywood*. 2nd ed. New York: Harper Collins.

Caillois, Roger. 1959 [1939]. *Man and the Sacred*. New York: Free Press.

Carpenter, Joel. 1997. *Revive Us Again: The Reawakening of American Fundamentalism*. New York: Oxford University Press.

Carroll, Jackson W. 2006. *God's Potters: Pastoral Leadership and the Shaping of Congregations*. Grand Rapids, Mich.: Eerdmans.

Carroll, Jackson W., Carl S. Dudley, and William McKinney. 1986. *Handbook for Congregational Studies*. Nashville: Abingdon.

Caulkin, Simon. 1997. "Skills, Not Loyalty, Now Are Key If You Want Job Security." *San Francisco Sunday Examiner and Chronicle*, September 7, 2.

Caves, Richard E. 2000. *Creative Industries: Contacts between Art and Commerce*. Cambridge, Mass.: Harvard University Press.

Charters, W. W. 1935. *Motion Pictures and Youth: A Summary*. New York: Macmillan.

Chaves, Mark. 2004. *Congregations in America*. Cambridge, Mass.: Harvard University Press.

Christerson, Brad, Michael O. Emerson, and Korie L. Edwards. 2005. *Against All Odds: The Struggle of Racial Integration in Religious Organizations*. New York: New York University Press.

Christopherson, Susan, and Michael Storper. 1986. "The City as Studio, the World as Backlot: The Impact of Vertical Disintegration on the Location of the Motion-Picture Industry." *Environment Planning D: Society and Space* 4:305–320.

Clark, Danae. 1995. *Negotiating Hollywood: The Cultural Politics of Actors' Labor*. Minneapolis: University of Minnesota Press.

Coleman, Simon. 2000. *The Globalization of Charismatic Christianity: Spreading the Gospel of Prosperity*. Cambridge: Cambridge University Press.

————. 2002. "The Faith Movement: A Global Religious Culture?" *Culture and Religion* 3(1): 3–19.

Collins, Randall. 1988. "The Durkheimian Tradition in Conflict Sociology." In *Durkheimian Sociology: Cultural Studies*, ed. J. C. Alexander. New York: Cambridge University Press.

———. 1990. "Stratification, Emotional Energy, and the Transient Emotions." In *Research Agendas in the Sociology of Emotions*, ed. T. D. Kemper. Albany: State University of New York Press.

———. 2004. *Interaction Ritual Chains*. Princeton: Princeton University Press.

Cone, James H. 1990. *A Black Theology of Liberation*. Edited by E. A. Society. Maryknoll, N.Y.: Orbis Books.

———. 1992. *The Spirituals and the Blues: An Interpretation*. Maryknoll, N.Y.: Orbis Books.

Cose, Ellis. 1993. *The Rage of a Privileged Class*. New York: Harper Perennial.

Darden, Bob. 2004. *People Get Ready! A New History of Black Gospel Music*. New York: Continuum International Publishing Group.

David, Paul A. 1985. "Clio and the Economics of QWERTY." *American Economic Review* 75:332–337.

Davidson, Sarah E. 1925. "She Defends Some of the Movies." *Moody Bible Institute Monthly* 25 (June): 460–461, 503.

Davis, Ronald L. 1993. *The Glamour Factory: Inside Hollywood's Big Studio System*. Dallas: Southern Methodist University Press.

De La Cruz, Melissa, and Karen Robinovitz. 2003. *How to Become Famous in Two Weeks or Less*. New York: Ballantine Books.

Denzin, Norman. 1991. *Images of Postmodern Society: Social Theory and Contemporary Cinema*. London: Sage.

DeYoung, Curtiss Paul, Michael O. Emerson, George Yancey, and Karen Chai. 2003. *United by Faith: Multicultural Congregations as a Response to the Problem of Race*. New York: Oxford University Press.

Dieter, Melvin E. 1996. *The Holiness of the Revival of the Nineteenth Century*. 2nd ed. Lanham, Md.: Scarecrow Press.

Durkheim, Emile. 1884. Cours de Philosophie Fait au Lycee de Sens. In *Paris Bibliotheqe de la Sorbonne, Manuscript 2351*.

———. 1887. "La Science positive de la morale en Allemagne." *Revue Philosophique* 24:33–58, 113–142, 275–284.

———. 1897. *Le Suicide; Étude de Sociologie, Bibliothèque de Philosophie Contemporaine*. Paris: F. Alcan.

———. 1951. *Suicide: A Study in Sociology*. Translated by John A. Spaulding and George Simpson. Glencoe, Ill.: Free Press of Glencoe.

————. [1925] 1961. *Moral Education: A Study in the Theory and Application of the Sociology of Education.* Translated by Herman Schnerer and Everett K. Wilson. First Eng. ed. New York: Free Press of Glencoe.

————. 1977. *The Evolution of Educational Thought: Lectures on the Formation and Development of Secondary Education in France.* Translated by Peter Collins. London: Routledge and Kegan Paul.

————. [1888] 1978. "Introduction to the Sociology of the Family." In *Emile Durkheim on Institutional Analysis,* ed. and trans. M. Traugott. Chicago: University of Chicago Press.

————. [1895] 1982. *The Rules of Sociological Method.* Translated by W. D. Halls. First U.S. ed. New York: Free Press.

————. [1912] 1995. *The Elementary Forms of Religious Life.* Translated by Karen E. Fields. New York: Free Press.

————. [1893] 1997. *The Division of Labor in Society.* Translated by W. D. Halls. New York: Free Press.

Ebaugh, Helen Rose Fuchs, and Janet Saltzman Chafetz. 2000. *Religion and the New Immigrants: Continuities and Adaptations in Immigrant Congregations.* Walnut Creek, Calif.: AltaMira Press.

Edmonds, Andy. 1991. *Frame-Up: The Untold Story of Roscoe "Fatty" Arbuckle.* New York: William Morrow.

Eiesland, Nancy L. 2000. *A Particular Place: Urban Restructuring and Religious Ecology in a Southern Exurb.* New Brunswick: Rutgers University Press.

Eisner, Elliot W. 1991. *The Enlightened Eye: Qualitative Inquiry and the Enhancement of Educational Practice.* New York: Macmillan.

Eldridge, Elsom, and Mark Eldridge. 2004. *How to Position Yourself As the Obvious Expert: Turbocharge Your Consulting or Coaching Business Now!* Warren, Mich.: MasterMind.

Eliade, Mircea. 1959. *The Sacred and Profane: The Nature of Religion.* New York: Harcourt, Brace.

Ellingson, Stephen. 2007. *The Megachurch and the Mainline: Remaking Religious Tradition in the Twenty-First Century.* Chicago: University of Chicago Press.

Ellison, Christopher G. 1991. "Identification and Separatism: Religious Involvement and Racial Orientations among Black Americans." *Sociological Quarterly* 31:477–494.

Emerson, Michael O. 2006. *People of the Dream: Multiracial Congregations in the United States.* Princeton: Princeton University Press.

Emerson, Michael O., and Christian Smith. 2000. *Divided by Faith: Evangelical Religion and the Problem of Race in America.* Oxford: Oxford University Press.

Emirbayer, Mustafa. 1996. "Durkheim's Contribution to the Sociological Analysis of History." *Sociological Forum* 11(2): 263–284.

————, ed. 2003. *Emile Durkheim: Sociologist of Modernity*. New York: Blackwell.

Epstein, Daniel Mark. 1993. *Sister Aimee: The Life of Aimee Semple McPherson*. New York: Harcourt Brace Jovanovich.

Epstein, Edward Jay. 2005. *The Big Picture: The New Logic of Money and Power in Hollywood*. New York: Random House.

Farah, Charles. 1978. *From the Pinnacle of the Temple*. Plainfield, N.J.: Logos.

Faulkner, Robert. R. 1983. *Music on Demand: Composers and Careers in the Hollywood Film Industry*. New Brunswick, N.J.: Transaction Books.

Feher, Shoshanah. 1998. *Passing over Easter: Constructing the Boundaries of Messianic Judaism*. Walnut Creek, Calif.: AltaMira Press.

Field, Alex. 2004. *HP The Hollywood Project: A Look into the Minds of the Makers of Spiritually Relevant Films*. Lake Mary, Fla.: Relevant Books.

Finch, Christopher, and Linda Rosenkrantz. 1979. *Gone Hollywood: The Movie Colony in the Golden Age*. London: Weidenfeld and Nicolson.

Finke, Roger. 2004. "Innovative Returns to Tradition: Using Core Teachings as the Foundation for Innovative Accommodation." *Journal for the Scientific Study of Religion* 43(1): 19–34.

Florida, Richard L. 2002. *The Rise of the Creative Class: And How It's Transforming Work, Leisure, Community, and Everyday Life*. New York: Basic Books.

Frazier, Edward Franklin. 1965. *Black Bourgeoisie*. New York: Free Press.

————. 1974. *The Negro Church in America*. New York: Schocken Books.

Friedrich, Otto. 1986. *City of Nets*. Berkeley: University of California Press.

Fulk, Joseph R. 1912. "Effect on Education and Morals of the Motion Picture Shows." *National Educational Association Proceedings* 50:456–461.

Gamson, Joshua. 1994. *Claims to Fame: Celebrity in Contemporary America*. Berkeley: University of California Press.

Garces-Foley, Kathleen. 2007. *Crossing the Ethnic Divide: The Multiethnic Church on a Mission*. New York: Oxford University Press.

Giovacchini, Saverio. 2001. *Hollywood Modernism: Film and Politics in the Age of the New Deal*. Philadelphia: Temple University Press.

Glazer, Nathan. 1958. The American Jew and the Attainment of Middle Class Rank: Some Trends and Explanations. In *The Jews: Social Patterns of an American Group*, ed. M. Sklare. Glencoe, Ill.: Free Press.

Godawa, Brian. 2002. *Hollywood Worldviews: Watching Films with Wisdom and Discernment*. Downers Grove, Ill.: InterVarsity Press.

Goffman, Erving. 1961. *Asylums: Essays on the Social Situation of Mental Patients and Other Inmates*. Garden City, N.Y.: Doubleday.

————. 1963. *Stigma: Notes on the Management of Spoiled Identity*. New York: Simon and Schuster.

————. 1974. *Frame Analysis: An Essay on the Organization of Experience*. Boston: Northeastern University Press.

Goldman, William. 1984. *Adventures in the Screen Trade*. New York: Warner Books.

Gomery, Douglas. 2000. "Hollywood as Industry." In *American Cinema and Hollywood: Critical Approaches*, ed. P. C. Gibson. New York: Oxford University Press.

Goodale, Gloria. 2001. "Will Hollywood Get Religion?" *Christian Science Monitor*, October 12.

Gould, Rebecca Kneale. 2005. *At Home in Nature: Modern Homesteading and Spiritual Practice in America*. Berkeley: University of California Press.

Grabher, G. 2001. "Locating Economic Action: Projects, Networks, Localities, Institutions." *Environment Planning A* 33:1329–1331.

Griffith, R. Marie. 1997. *God's Daughters: Evangelical Women and the Power of Submission*. Berkeley: University of California Press.

Guback, Thomas H. 1969. *The International Film Industry*. Bloomington, Ind.: Indiana University Press.

Halbwachs, Maurice. 1992. *On Collective Memory*. Translated by L. A. Coser. Edited by D. N. Levine. Chicago: University of Chicago Press.

Hampton, Benjamin. 1970 [1931]. *History of the American Film Industry from Its Beginnings to 1931*. New York: Dover.

Hancock, Ralph. 1949. *Fabulous Boulevard*. New York: Funk and Wagnalls.

Hansen, Miriam. 1993. "Early Cinema, Late Cinema: Permutations of the Public Sphere." *Screen* 34(1): 197–210.

Harris, Fredrick C. 1999. *Something Within: Religion in African-American Political Activism*. New York: Oxford University Press.

Harris, Michael W. 1994. *The Rise of Gospel Blues: The Music of Thomas Andrew Dorsey in the Urban Church*. New York: Oxford University Press.

Harrison, Milmon F. 2005. *Righteous Riches*. New York: Oxford University Press.

Harrow, Susan. 2002. *Sell Yourself without Selling Your Soul: A Woman's Guide to Promoting Herself, Her Business, Her Product, or Her Cause with Integrity and Spirit*. New York: HarperCollins.

Hatch, Nathan O. 1989. *The Democratization of American Christianity*. New Haven: Yale University Press.

Hays, Will H. 1955. *The Memoirs of Will H. Hays*. Garden City, N.Y.: Doubleday.

Hecker, Daniel E. 2001. "Occupational Employment Projections to 2010." *Monthly Labor Review* 124(11): 57–84.

Henson, Kevin D. 1996. *Just a Temp*. Women in the Political Economy. Philadelphia: Temple University Press.

Higgins, Gareth. 2003. *How Movies Helped Save My Soul: Finding Spiritual Fingerprints in Culturally Significant Films*. Lake Mary, Fla.: Relevant Books.

Hill, Laurance L., and Silas E. Snyder. 1923. *Can Anything Good Come out of Hollywood?* Hollywood, Calif.: Snyder Publications.

Hirst, Paul, and Jonathan Zeitlin. 1992. Flexible-specialization versus Post-fordism: Theory, Evidence and Policy Implications. In *Pathways to Industrialization and Regional Development*, ed. M. Storper and A. J. Scott. London: Routledge.

Horton, Michael, ed. 1990. *The Agony of Deceit*. Chicago: Moody Press.

Houston, Bobbie. 2001. *Heaven Is in This House*. Sidney, Aus.: Maximised Leadership.

Hughes, Laurence A., ed. 1924. *The Truth about the Movies by the Stars*. Hollywood, Calif.: Hollywood.

Hunt, David, and Tom McMahon. 1985. *The Seduction of Christianity*. Eugene, Ore.: Harvest House.

Hunter, James Davison. 1987. *Evangelicalism: The Coming Generation*. Chicago: University of Chicago Press.

Husserl, Edmund. 1970. *The Crisis of European Sciences and Transcendental Phenomenology: An Introduction to Phenomenological Philosophy*. Northwestern University Studies in Phenomenology and Existential Philosophy. Evanston, Ill.: Northwestern University Press.

Jay, Nancy. 1992. *Throughout Your Generations Forever: Sacrifice, Religion, and Paternity*. Chicago: University of Chicago Press.

Jeung, Russell. 2004. *Faithful Generations: Race and New Asian American Churches*. New Brunswick, N.J.: Rutgers University Press.

Johnston, Robert K. 2000. *Reel Spirituality: Theology and Film in Dialogue*, Grand Rapids, Mich.: Baker Academic.

———. 2007. *Reframing Theology and Film: New Focus for an Emerging Discipline*. Grand Rapids, Mich.: Baker Books.

Jones, Candace. 1996. "Careers in Project Networks: The Case of the Film Industry." In *The Boundaryless Career*, ed. M. B. Arthur and D. M. Rouseau. Oxford: Oxford University Press.

———. 2001. "Co-evolution of Entrepreneurial Careers, Institutional Rules, and Competitive Dynamics in American Film, 1895–1920." *Organization Studies* 22:911–944.

Jones, Lawrence N. 1999. "The Black Churches: A New Agenda." In *African American Religious History: A Documentary Witness*, ed. M. C. Sernett. Durham: Duke University Press.

Jones, Robert Alun. 1999. *The Development of Durkheim's Social Realism.* New York: Cambridge University Press.

Jorgensen, Danny L. 1989. *Participant Observation: A Methodology for Human Studies.* Newbury Park, Calif.: Sage.

Jowett, Garth. 1999. "'A Capacity for Evil': The 1915 Supreme Court Mutual Decision." In *Controlling Hollywood: Censorship and Regulation in the Studio Era,* ed. M. Bernstein. New Brunswick, N.J.: Rutgers University Press.

Kilde, Jeanne Halgren. 2002. *When Church Became Theater: The Transformation of Evangelical Architecture and Worship in Nineteenth-Century America.* New York: Oxford University Press.

King, Barry. 1986. "Stardom as an Occupation." In *The Hollywood Film Industry: A Reader,* ed. P. Kerr. London: Routledge.

Klaus, Peggy. 2004. *Brag! The Art of Tooting Your Own Horn without Blowing It.* New York: Warner Business Books.

Kostarelos, Frances. 1995. *Feeling the Spirit: Faith and Hope in an Evangelical Black Storefront Church.* Columbia: University of South Carolina Press.

Kramer, Eric. 2002. "Making Global Faith Universal: Media and a Brazilian Prosperity Movement." *Culture and Religion* 3(1): 21–47.

Kramer, Peter. 2000. "Post-classical Hollywood." In *American Cinema and Hollywood: Critical Approaches,* ed. J. Hill and P. C. Gibson. New York: Oxford University Press.

Kuznets, Simon. 1976. "Immigration of Russian Jews to the United States: Background and Structure." *Perspectives in American History* 9:35–126.

Lake, Peter. 2002. *The Anti Christ's Lewd Hat: Protestants, Papists, and Players in Post-Reformation England.* New Haven: Yale University Press.

Lazarsfeld, Paul F., and Robert K. Merton. 1943. "Studies in Radio and Film Propaganda." In *Transactions of the New York Academy of Science* 62 (2): 58–75.

Lee, Shayne. 2005. *T. D. Jakes: America's New Preacher.* New York: New York University Press.

Lewerenz, Spender, and Barbara Nicolosi, eds. 2005. *Behind the Screen: Hollywood Insiders on Faith, Film, and Culture.* Grand Rapids, Mich.: Baker Books.

Lichterman, Paul. 2005. *Elusive Togetherness: Church Groups Trying to Bridge America's Divisions.* Princeton: Princeton University Press.

Lincoln, C. Eric, and Lawrence H. Mamiya. 1990. *The Black Church in the African American Experience.* Durham: Duke University Press.

Lindsay, D. Michael. 2006a. "Elite Power: Social Networks within American Evangelicalism." *Sociology of Religion* 67(3): 207–227.

———. 2006b. "From Protest to Patronage: Evangelical Influence in Hollywood, 1976–2006." Paper read at Society for the Scientific Study of Religion, October, Portland, Ore.

———. 2007. *Faith in the Halls of Power: How Evangelicals Joined the American Elite*. New York: Oxford University Press.

Lindsey, Shelley Stamp. 1996. *Ladies' Night: Women and Movie Culture in America during the Transitional Era*. Princeton: Princeton University Press.

Lindvall, Terry. 2001. *The Silents of God: Selected Issues and Documents in Silent American Film and Religion, 1908–1925*. Lanham, Md.: Scarecrow Press.

———. 2007. *Sanctuary Cinema: Origins of the Christian Film Industry*. New York: New York University Press.

Litwack, Mark. 1986. *Reel Power: The Struggle for Influence and Success in the New Hollywood*. New York: Morrow.

Livezey, Lowell W., ed. 2000. *Public Religion and Urban Transformation*. New York: New York University Press.

Lumet, Sidney. 1995. *Making Movies*. New York: Knopf.

Lutzer, Erwin W. 1996. *Serpent of Paradise: The Incredible Story of How Satan's Rebellion Serves God's Purposes*. Chicago: Moody.

Lyden, John C. 2003. *Film as Religion: Myths, Morals, and Rituals*. New York: New York University Press.

Maltby, Richard. 1983. *Harmless Entertainment*. Metuchen, N.J.: Scarecrow Press.

———. 1993. "Production Code and the Hays Office." In *The Grand Design: Hollywood as a Modern Business Enterprise, 1930–1939*, ed. T. Balio. New York: Charles Scribner's Sons.

———. 1998. "'Nobody Knows Everything': Post-classical Historiographies and Consolidated Entertainment." In *Contemporary Hollywood Cinema*, ed. S. Neale and M. Smith. New York: Routledge.

———. 1999. "The King of Kings and the Czar of All the Rushes: The Propriety of the Christ Story." In *Controlling Hollywood: Censorship and Regulation in the Studio Era*, ed. by M. Bernstein. New Brunswick, N.J.: Rutgers University Press.

———. 2003. *Hollywood Cinema*. 2nd ed. New York: Blackwell.

Mannheim, Karl. 1952. *Essays on the Sociology of Knowledge*. New York: Oxford University Press.

———. 1956. *Essays on the Sociology of Culture*. New York: Oxford University Press.

Marshall, Chester C. 1925. "Pictures and the Church: What Shall We Do with the Movies?" *Educational Screen* 4:24–26.

Marti, Gerardo. 2005. *A Mosaic of Believers: Diversity and Innovation in a Multiethnic Church*. Bloomington: Indiana University Press.

———. 2008. "Fluid Ethnicity and Ethnic Transcendence." *Journal for the Scientific Study of Religion* 47 (1): 11–16.

Martin, Bernice. 1998. "From Pre- to Postmodernity in Latin America: The Case of Pentecostalism." In *Religion, Modernity, and Postmodernity*, ed. P. Heelas. Oxford: Blackwell.

Martin, Darnise C. 2005. *Beyond Christianity: African Americans in a New Thought Church.* New York: New York University Press.

Martin, David. 2002. *Pentecostalism: The World, Their Parish.* Malden, Mass.: Blackwell.

Maultsby, Portia. 1992. "The Impact of Gospel Music on the Secular Music Industry." In *Will Understand It Better By and By,* ed. B. J. Reagan. Washington, D.C.: Smithsonian Institution press.

May, John R. 1982. *Religion in Film.* Knoxville: University of Tennessee Press.

May, Lary. 1983. *Screening Out the Past: The Birth of Mass Culture and the Motion Picture Industry.* Chicago: University of Chicago Press.

———. 2000. *The Big Tomorrow: Hollywood and the Politics of the American Way.* Chicago: University of Chicago Press.

Mayne, Judith. 1990. *The Woman at the Keyhole: Feminism and Woman's Cinema.* Bloomington: Indiana University Press.

Mays, Benjamin E., and Joseph W. Nicholson. 1999. "The Genius of the Negro Church." In *African American Religious History: A Documentary Witness,* ed. M. C. Sennett. Durham: Duke University Press.

McConachie, Bruce A. 1992. *Melodramatic Formations: American Theatre and Society, 1820–1870.* Iowa City: University of Iowa Press.

McConnell, Dan R. 1988. *A Different Gospel: Biblical and Historical Insights into the Word of Faith Movement.* Peabody, Mass.: Hendrickson.

McDonald, Paul. 2000. *The Star System: Hollywood's Production of Popular Identities.* London: Wallflower.

McNally, David, and Karl Speak. 2002. *Be Your Own Brand: A Breakthrough Formula for Standing Out from the Crowd:* San Francisco: Berrett–Koehler.

McRoberts, Omar M. 2003. *Streets of Glory: Church and Community in a Black Urban Neighborhood.* Chicago: University of Chicago.

McWilliams, Carey. 1973. *Southern California: An Island on the Land.* Santa Barbara: Peregrine Smith.

Menger, Pierre-Michel. 1999. "Artistic Labor Markets and Careers." *Annual Review of Sociology* 25:541–574.

Mezias, Stephen J., and Jerome C. Kuperman. 2000. "The Community Dynamics of Entrepreneurship: The Birth of the American Film Industry, 1895–1929." *Journal of Business Ventures* 16:209–233.

Miles, Margaret R. 1997. *Seeing and Believing: Religion and Values in the Movies.* Boston: Beacon Press.

Miller, Donald E. 1997. *Reinventing American Protestantism: Christianity and the New Millennium.* Berkeley: University of California Press.

Miller, Donald E., and Tetsunao Yamamori. 2007. *Global Pentecostalism: The New Face of Christian Social Engagement.* Berkeley: University of California Press.

Minkin, Lewis. 1997. *Exits and Entrances: Political Research as a Creative Art.* Sheffield, U.K.: Sheffield Hallam University Press.

Moley, Raymond. 1945. *The Hays Office.* New York: Bobbs-Merrill.

Monitor Company. 1999. *U.S. Runaway Film and Television Production Study Report.* Santa Monica, Calif.: Monitor.

Montgomery, Sarah S., and Michael D. Robinson. 1993. "Visual Artists in New York: What's Special about Person and Place?" *Journal of Cultural Economics* 17:17–39.

Montoya, Peter, and Tim Vandehey. 2003. *The Brand Called You: The Ultimate Brand-Building and Business Development Handbook to Transform Anyone into an Indispensable Personal Brand.* Santa Ana, Calif.: Personal Branding Press.

Montoya, Peter, Tim Vandehey, and Paul Viti. 2002. *The Personal Branding Phenomenon.* Santa Ana, Calif.: Peter Montoya.

Myrdal, Gunner. 1944. *An American Dilemma: The Negro Problem and Modern Democracy.* New York: Harper and Brothers.

Neitz, Mary Jo. 1987. *Charisma and Community: A Study of Religious Commitment within the Charismatic Renewal.* New Brunswick, N.J.: Transaction Books.

Nelson, Timothy J. 2004. *Every Time I Feel the Spirit: Religious Experience and Ritual in an African American Church.* New York: New York University Press.

Nichol, John Thomas. 1966. *Pentecostalism.* New York: Harper and Row.

Nielsen, Donald A. 2005. "The Protestant Ethic and the 'Spirit' of Capitalism as Grand Narrative: Max Weber's Philosophy of History." In *The Protestant Ethic Turns 100: Essays on the Centenary of the Weber Thesis,* ed. W. H. Swators Jr. and L. Kaelber. Boulder, Colo.: Paradigm.

Nizer, Louis. 1935. *New Courts of Industry: Self-Regulation under the Motion Picture Code.* New York: Longacre Press.

Noble, Trevor. 2000. *Social Theory and Social Change.* Basingstoke, U.K.: Macmillan.

Noll, Mark A. 1992. *A History of Christianity in the United States and Canada.* Grand Rapids, Mich.: Eerdmans.

Numrich, Paul David. 1995. *Old Wisdom in the New World: Americanization in Immigrant Theravada Buddhist Temples.* Knoxville: University of Tennessee Press.

Oberdeck, Kathryn. 1999. *The Evangelist and the Impresario: Religion, Entertainment, and Cultural Politics in America, 1884–1914.* Baltimore: Johns Hopkins University Press.

Oderman, Stuart. 1994. *Roscoe "Fatty" Arbuckle.* Jefferson, N.C.: McFarland.

Orsi, Robert A. 1996. *Thank You, St. Jude: Women's Devotion to the Patron Saint of Hopeless Causes.* New Haven: Yale University Press.

Paris, Arthur E. 1982. *Black Pentecostalism: Southern Religion in an Urban World*. Amherst: University of Massachusetts Press.

Patillo-McCoy, Mary. 1998. "Church Culture as a Strategy of Action in the Black Community." *American Sociological Review* 63:767–784.

Peck, Jaime. 1996. *Work-Place: The Social Regulation of Labor Markets*. New York: Guilford Press.

Pentecost, J. Dwight. 1997. *Your Adversary, the Devil*. Grand Rapids, Mich.: Kregel Publications.

Perriman, Andrew, ed. 2003. *Faith: Health and Prosperity*. Waynesboro, Ga.: Paternoster Press.

Peters, Tom. 1999. *The Brand You 50: Fifty Ways to Transform Yourself from an "Employee" into a Brand That Shouts Distinction, Commitment, and Passion!* New York: Borzoi Books.

Pickering, W.S.F. 2002. *Durkheim Today*. New York: Berghahn Books.

Pink, Daniel H. 2001. *Free Agent Nation: How America's New Independent Workers Are Transforming the Way We Live*. New York: Warner Books.

Pinn, Anne H., and Anthony B. Pinn. 2002. *Fortress Introduction to Black Church History*. Minneapolis: Fortress Press.

Pinn, Anthony B. 2002. *The Black Church in the Post–Civil Rights Era*. Maryknoll, N.Y.: Orbis Books.

Piore, Michael J., and Charles F. Sabel. 1984. *The Second Industrial Divide: Possibilities for Prosperity*. New York: Basic Books.

Pitt, Leonard, and Dale Pitt. 1997. *Los Angeles A to Z: An Encyclopedia of the City and County*. Berkeley: University of California Press.

Pointer, Richard W. 1988. *Protestant Pluralism and the New York Experience: A Study of Eighteenth Century Religious Diversities*. Bloomington: Indiana University Press.

Poland, Larry W. 2005. "A Message from Mastermedia's Chairman." In *The Media Leader Prayer Calendar 2005: July, August, September*. Redlands, Calif.: Mastermedia International.

Ponti, J. 1992. *Hollywood East*. Orlando, Fla.: Tribune Publishing.

Post, Charles Johnson. 1922. "Motion Picture Madness." *Christian Herald* 45(26): 465–466.

Powdermaker, Hortense. 1950. *Hollywood the Dream Factory: An Anthropologist Looks at the Movie-Makers*. Boston: Little, Brown.

Prindle, David F. 1988. *The Politics of Glamour: Ideology and Democracy in the Screen Actors Guild*. Madison: University of Wisconsin Press.

———. 1993. *Risky Business: The Political Economy of Hollywood*. Boulder: Westview Press.

Ramp, William. 1998. "Effervescence, Differentiation, and Representation in *The Elementary Forms*." In *Durkheim's Elementary Forms of Religious Life*, ed. N. J. Allen, W.S.F. Pickering, and W. Watts Miller. London: Routledge.

Reich, Robert B. 1991. *The Work of Nations: Preparing Ourselves for 21st-Century Capitalism*. New York: Knopf.

Rein, Irving J., Philip Kotler, and Martin R. Stoller. 1997. *High Visibility: The Making and Marketing of Professionals into Celebrities*. New York: McGraw-Hill.

Rodriguez, Robert. 1996. *Rebel without a Crew: Or, How a 23-Year-Old Filmmaker with $7,000 became a Hollywood Player*. New York: Penguin.

Roffer, Robin Fisher. 2002. *Make a Name for Yourself: Eight Steps Every Woman Needs to Create a Personal Brand Strategy for Success*. New York: Broadway Books.

Rogers, Everett M. 1995. *Diffusion of Innovations*. 4th ed. New York: Free Press.

Rojek, Chris. 2001. *Celebrity*. London: Reaktion Books.

Rosini, Vincent. 1998. "Sanctuary Cinema: The Rise and Fall of Protestant Churches as Film Exhibition Sites, 1910–1930." PhD diss., Regent University.

Ross, Marilyn, and Curtis Killorn. 2000. *Shameless Marketing for Brazen Hussies: 307 Awesome Money-Making Strategies for Savvy Entrepreneurs*. Buena Vista, Colo.: Communication Creativity.

Ross, Murray. [1941] 1967. *Stars and Strikes: Unionization of Hollywood*. New York: AMS Press.

Sanders, Cheryl J. 1996. *Saints in Exile: The Holiness-Pentecostal Experience in African American Religion and Culture*. New York: Oxford University Press.

Sargeant, Kimon Howland. 2000. *Seeker Churches: Promoting Traditional Religion in a Nontraditional Way*. New Brunswick, N.J.: Rutgers University Press.

Schatz, Thomas. 1983. *Old Hollywood/New Hollywood: Ritual, Art, and Industry*. Ann Arbor: UMI Research Press.

Scheler, Max. 1973. *Formalism in Ethics and Non-Formal Ethics of Values: A New Attempt toward the Foundation of an Ethical Personalism*. Translated by M. S. Frings and R. L. Funk. Evanston, Ill.: Northwestern University Press.

Schutz, Alfred. 1967. *The Phenomenology of the Social World*. Evanston, Ill.: Northwestern University Press.

Schutz, Alfred, and Thomas Luckmann. 1973. *The Structures of the Life-World*. Evanston Ill.: Northwestern University Press.

Schutz, Alfred, and Helmut R. Wagner. 1982. *Life Forms and Meaning Structure*. London: Routledge and Kegan Paul.

Scott, Allen J. 1988a. *Metropolis: From the Division of Labor to Urban Form*. Berkeley: University of California Press.

————. 1988b. *New Industrial Spaces: Flexible Production Organization and Regional Development in North America and Western Europe*. London: Pion.

————. 2005. *On Hollywood: The Place, the Industry*. Princeton: Princeton University Press.

Seligman, Adam B. 2000. *Modernity's Wager: Authority, the Self, and Transcendence*. Princeton: Princeton University Press.

Sennett, Richard. 1998. *The Corrosion of Character*. New York: W. W. Norton.

————. 2005. *The Culture of the New Capitalism*. New Haven: Yale University Press.

Shibley, Mark A. 1998. "Contemporary Evangelicals: Born-Again and World Affirming." *Annals of the American Academy of Political and Social Science* (Americans and Religions in the Twenty-First Century) 558, July: 67–87.

Shiel, Mark. 2001. "Cinema and the City in Theory and History." In *Cinema and the City: Film and Urban Societies in a Global Context*, ed. M. Shiel and T. Fitzmaurice. Malden, Mass.: Blackwell.

Shiffler, Harold C. 1953. "The Opposition of the Presbyterian Church in the United States of America to the Theatre in America, 1750–1891." Ph.D. diss., State University of Iowa.

Silber, Lee. 2001. *Self-Promotion for the Creative Person: Get the Word Out about Who You Are and What You Do*. New York: Three Rivers Press.

Simpson, Robert. 1970. "A Black Church: Ecstasy in a World of Trouble." PhD diss., Washington University.

Sklar, Robert. 1994. *Movie-Made America: A Cultural History of American Movies, Revised and Updated*. New York: Vintage.

Skokeid, Moshe. 1995. *A Gay Synagogue in New York*. New York: Columbia University Press.

Smilde, David. 2007. *Reason to Believe: Cultural Agency in Latin American Evangelicalism*. Berkeley: University of California Press.

Smith, Catherine Parsons. 1993. "Founding the Hollywood Bowl." *American Music* 11(2): 206–242.

Smith, Christian. 2003. *Moral, Believing Animals: Human Personhood and Culture*. Oxford: Oxford University Press.

Smith, Murray. 1998. "Theses on the Philosophy of Hollywood History." In *Contemporary Hollywood Cinema*, ed. S. Neale and M. Smith. New York: Routledge.

Smith, R. Drew. 2005. *Long March Ahead: African American Churches and Public Policy in Post–Civil Rights America*. Durham: Duke University Press.

Snow, David A., Jr. E. Burke Rochford, Steven K. Worden, and Robert D. Benford. 1986. "Frame Alignment Processes, Micromobilization, and Movement Participation." *American Sociological Review* 54:464–481.

Spickard, James V., J. Shawn Landres, and Meredith B. McGuire. 2002. *Personal Knowledge and Beyond: Reshaping the Ethnography of Religion*. New York: New York University Press.

Staiger, Janet. 1982. "Dividing Labor for Production Control: Thomas Ince and the Rise of the Studio System." In *American Film Industry: A Case Studies Approach*, ed. G. Kindem. Carbondale: Southern Illinois University Press.

Stark, Rodney, and Roger Finke. 2000. *Acts of Faith: Explaining the Human Side of Religion*. Berkeley: University of California Press.

Starr, Kevin. 1985. *Inventing the Dream: California through the Progressive Era*. New York: Oxford University Press.

Stone, Bryan P. 2000. *Faith and Film: Theological Themes at the Cinema*. St. Louis, Mo.: Chalice Press.

Storper, Michael. 1989. "The Transition to Flexible Specialization in the U.S. Film Industry: External Economies, the Division of Labor, and Crossing Industrial Divides." *Cambridge Journal of Economics* 13:273–305.

Storper, Michael, and Susan Christopherson. 1987. "Flexible Specialization and Regional Industrial Agglomerations: The Case of the US Motion-Picture Industry." *Annals of the Association of American Geographers* 77:260–282.

Strenski, Ivan. 2006. *The New Durkheim*. New Brunswick, N.J.: Rutgers University Press.

Swidler, Ann. 1986. "Culture in Action: Symbols and Strategies." *American Sociological Review* 51:273–288.

Synan, Vinson. 1997. *The Holiness-Pentecostal Tradition: Charismatic Movements in the Twentieth Century*. 2nd ed. Grand Rapids, Mich.: Eerdmans.

Szafran, Robert F. 1996. The Effect of Occupational Growth on Labor Force Task Characteristics. *Work and Occupations* 23:54–86.

Teele, James E., ed. 2002. *E. Franklin Frazier and* Black Bourgeoisie. Columbia: University of Missouri Press.

Thernstrom, Stephan. 1973. *The Other Bostonians: Poverty and Progress in the American Metropolis, 1880–1970*. Cambridge, Mass.: Harvard University Press.

Thomas, Linda E. 2004. *Living Stones in the Household of God: The Legacy and Future of Black Theology*. Minneapolis: Fortress Press.

Thompson, Kristin. 1985. *Exporting Entertainment: America in the World Film Market, 1907–1934*. London: British Film Institute.

Torrence, Bruce T. 1982. *Hollywood: The First Hundred Years*. New York: New York Zoetrope.

Tudor, Andrew. 2000. "Sociology and Film." In *Film Studies: Critical Approaches*, ed. J. Hill and P. C. Gibson. New York: Oxford University Press.

Tweed, Thomas A. 2006. *Crossing and Dwelling: A Theory of Religion*. Cambridge, Mass.: Harvard University Press.

Van Maanen, John. 1988. *Tales of the Field: On Writing Ethnography*. Chicago: University of Chicago Press.

Van Yoder, Steven. 2003. *Get Slightly Famous: Become a Celebrity in Your Field and Attract More Business with Less Effort*. Berkeley: Bay Tree Publishing.

Vasey, Ruth. 1997. *The World According to Hollywood, 1918–1939*. Madison: University of Wisconsin Press.

Wacker, Grant. 2001. *Heaven Below*. Cambridge, Mass.: Harvard University Press.

Warner, R. Stephen. 1988. *New Wine in Old Wineskins: Evangelicals and Liberals in a Small-Town Church*. Berkeley: University of California Press.

———. 1993. "Work in Progress toward a New Paradigm for the Sociological Study of Religion in the United States." *American Journal of Sociology* 98:1044–1093.

———. 2004. "Enlisting Smelser's Theory of Ambivalence to Maintain Progress in Sociology of Religion's New Paradigm." In *Self, Social Structure, and Beliefs: Explorations in Sociology*, ed. Jeffrey C. Alexander, Gary T. Marx and Christine. L. Williams. Berkeley: University of California Press.

———. 2005. *A Church of Our Own: Disestablishment and Diversity in American Religion*. New Brunswick, N.J.: Rutgers University Press.

Wasko, Janet. 1982. *Movies and Money*. Norwood, N.J.: Ablex.

———. 2003. *How Hollywood Works*. Thousand Oaks, Calif.: Sage Publications.

Webb, Sydney, and Beatrice Webb. 1932. *Methods of Social Study*. London: Longman Green.

Weber, Max. 1978. *Economy and Society: An Outline of Interpretive Sociology*. Berkeley: University of California Press.

Weiss, Paul R., and Robert R. Faulkner. 1983. "Credits and Craft Production: Freelance Social Organization in the Hollywood Film Industry." *Symbolic Interaction* 6:111–123.

West, Cornel. 1999. "Afro-American Music: From Bebop to Rap." In *The Cornel West Reader*, ed. Cornel West. New York: Basic Civitas Books.

Williams, Melvin D. 1974. *Community in a Black Pentecostal Church: An Anthropological Study*. Pittsburgh: University of Pittsburgh Press.

Wilmore, Gayraud S. 1998. *Black Religion and Black Radicalism: An Interpretation of the Religious History of African Americans*. 3rd ed., revised and enlarged. Maryknoll, N.Y.: Orbis Books.

Wuthnow, Robert. 2001. *I Come Away Stronger: How Small Groups Are Shaping American Religion*. Grand Rapids, Mich.: Eerdmans.

———. 2007. *After the Baby Boomers: How Twenty- and Thirty-Somethings Are Shaping the Future of American Religion*. Princeton: Princeton University Press.

Winston, Diane H. 1999. *Red-Hot and Righteous: The Urban Religion of the Salvation Army*. Cambridge, Mass.: Harvard University Press.

Wyatt, Justin. 1994. *High Concept: Moves and Marketing in Hollywood*. Austin: University of Texas Press.

Yallop, David A. 1976. *The Day the Laughter Stopped: The True Story of Fatty Arbuckle*. London: Hodder and Stoughton.

Young, Lawrence A. 1997. *Rational Choice Theory and Religion: Summary and Assessment*. New York: Routledge.

Young, Robert, Jr. 1994. *Roscoe "Fatty" Arbuckle: A Bio*. Westport, Conn.: Greenwood.

Zierer, C. M. 1947. "Hollywood—World Center of Motion–Picture Production." *Annals of the American Academy of Political and Social Science* 254:12–17.

Zollo, Paul. 2002. *Hollywood Remembered: An Oral History of Its Golden Age*. New York: Cooper Square Press.

Index

Numbers in italics refer to figures

About the Author

GERARDO MARTI is assistant professor of sociology at Davidson College and author of *A Mosaic of Believers: Diversity and Innovation in a Multiethnic Church* (2005). He received his Ph.D. at the University of Southern California and has studied racial and ethnic dynamics in churches and congregational responses to social change.